WICKED COOL PERL SCRIPTS

WICKED COOL PERL SCRIPTS

Useful Perl Scripts That Solve Difficult Problems

by Steve Oualline

NO STARCH PRESS

San Francisco

Publisher: William Pollock
Managing Editor: Elizabeth Campbell
Cover and Interior Design: Octopod Studios
Developmental Editor: Elizabeth Zinkann
Copyeditor: Judy Flynn
Compositor: Riley Hoffman
Proofreader: Nancy Riddiough

For information on book distributors or translations, please contact No Starch Press, Inc. directly:

No Starch Press, Inc.
555 De Haro Street, Suite 250, San Francisco, CA 94107
phone: 415.863.9900; fax: 415.863.9950; info@nostarch.com; www.nostarch.com

The information in this book is distributed on an "As Is" basis, without warranty. While every precaution has been taken in the preparation of this work, neither the author nor No Starch Press, Inc. shall have any liability to any person or entity with respect to any loss or damage caused or alleged to be caused directly or indirectly by the information contained in it.

Library of Congress Cataloging-in-Publication Data

```
Oualline, Steve.
  Wicked cool Perl scripts : useful Perl scripts that solve difficult problems / Steve Oualline.
-- 1st ed.
    p. cm.
  Includes index.
  ISBN 1-59327-062-3
1. Perl (Computer program language) 2. Object-oriented programming (Computer science)  I. Title.
  QA76.73.P22Q523 2006
  005.13'3--dc22
                                                      2005026999
```

BRIEF CONTENTS

CONTENTS IN DETAIL

2
WEBSITE MANAGEMENT
21

3
CGI DEBUGGING
45

4
CGI PROGRAMS

5
INTERNET DATA MINING

6
UNIX SYSTEM ADMINISTRATION 91

7
PICTURE UTILITIES

8
GAMES AND LEARNING TOOLS

9
DEVELOPMENT TOOLS

183

10
MAPPING

197

11
REGULAR EXPRESSION GRAPHER   243

INDEX   305

INTRODUCTION

If you're like most people, you've felt frustrated at one time or another because you just couldn't do what you wanted to do with your computer. That one simple and obvious utility that would make your life so much easier was missing. Whether it was a utility to get a stock quote, to show off your photograph collection, or even to display your favorite comics, it just wasn't there.

This book is all about writing those utilities quickly and easily. Perl is the ideal language for writing utilities. The language itself frees you from many of the details of programming and lets you just write something useful. The language is ideal for text manipulation, and let's face it, most utility programming is 95 percent text processing.

Because it is so useful, Perl has become the language of choice for utility programmers.

Wicked Cool Perl Programs

So what makes a "wicked cool" Perl script? First, the script must be useful. It must solve a real-world problem. Many of the scripts in this book have been used out in the field in some form or other.

Cool scripts are ones that solve a difficult problem. Actually, the more difficult, the better. And if the solution turns out to be simple and elegant, well, that makes it all the cooler.

You Are Not a Dummy

For this book, it is assumed that you are not a dummy. In other words, I'm assuming that you can think and read. You should have a working knowledge of Perl and know how to download and install modules from CPAN (http://cpan.perl.org).

Also, I expect that you know how to use the perldoc command to get documentation on the various modules mentioned in the book. For that reason, I don't waste your time and money by reproducing parts of the online documentation available to you.

It should be noted that although you are not a dummy, you may have to deal with a few, and this book helps you write utilities that make that job easier.

Plain Old Documentation (POD)

Writing a utility is one thing. Getting people to use it is another. In order for a program to become popular, people have to know how to use the thing.

All the Perl scripts in this book have a POD section. However, because the book also documents the scripts, the documentation has been omitted in the print version of the scripts. The downloadable version of the scripts do have a POD section in them.

How This Book Is Organized

Chapter 1: General Purpose Utilities

Perl is an ideal language for the small but helpful programs for everyday use. Chapter 1 includes scripts for tasks such as currency conversion, generating daily reminders, and finding duplicate files.

Chapter 2: Website Management

Perl and the Web go together. This chapter contains scripts that make web administration easier. You can use the scripts in this chapter to check your website for integrity, check for hackers, and even throw hackers off your system.

Chapter 3: CGI Debugging

This chapter includes a variety of techniques and tools for debugging CGI programs.

Chapter 4: CGI Programs

Now that you know how to debug CGI programs, you can try a few. The programs in Chapter 4 provide a Internet guest book, a visitor counter, and a random joke generator.

Chapter 5: Internet Data Mining

There is a lot of data on the Internet. This chapter shows you ways of extracting it. For example, you can get a daily stock quote or download your favorite comics.

Chapter 6: Unix System Administration

Perl is an ideal language for automating system administration tasks. This includes things like adding and deleting users as well as detecting system hogs and throwing them off the system.

Chapter 7: Picture Utilities

The digital camera revolutionized photography, but did you ever try to paste disk files into a photo album? Perl lets you create and edit an electronic photo album with ease.

Chapter 8: Games and Learning Tools

This chapter shows some simple teaching tools for kids who are two years old and older.

Chapter 9: Development Tools

Perl has the ability to analyze and report on large amounts of text. This can help you as a developer when it comes to things like figuring out the structure of large programs or eliminating dead code.

Chapter 10: Mapping

What does Perl have to do with hiking the Grand Canyon (a place so primitive that at the bottom you can't even get an Internet connection)? The answer is that Perl can be used to download, view, and print government topological maps and aerial photographs.

Chapter 11: Regular Expression Grapher

Perl's regular expression language is powerful, compact, and cryptic. Unless you present things graphically, in which case even the worst regular expressions become simple to do.

1

GENERAL-PURPOSE UTILITIES

The *P* in Perl stands for *Practical.* The language was designed by Larry Wall as a practical solution to some of the scripting problems he was having. It turns out that because his design was so good, the language he created not only solved his problems, but also helped many other people solve theirs.

Perl is ideal for creating scripts that solve the everyday problems that you encounter in the daily use of your system.

So let's take a look at some of these everyday problems and see how easy it is for Perl to solve them.

#1 Automatic Help Option

Writing a wicked cool Perl script is nice, but it's even better if you can get other people to use it. One of the things most users really want is a help function. Our first wicked cool Perl script is a module to implement a --help operation.

Most good Perl scripts use the Plain Old Documentation (POD) feature of Perl to describe themselves. This module intercepts the --help on the command line and then prints out the POD for the program being run.

NOTE *The official versions of the scripts in this book do contain POD. However, the documentation has been removed for the versions printed here to save space and eliminate redundancy. The full versions of the scripts (with POD) can be downloaded from the website www.nostarch.com/wcps.htm.*

The Code

```
1 use strict;
2 use warnings;
3
4 INIT {
5    if (($#ARGV == 0) && ($ARGV[0] eq "--help")) {
6        system("perldoc $0");
7        exit (0);
8    }
9 }
10
11 1;
```

Using the Module

To use the module, simply put the following line in your code:

```
use help;
```

Here's a small test program:

```
1 #!/usr/bin/perl
2 use strict;
3 use warnings;
4 =pod
5
6 =head1 NAME
7
8 Help test.
9
10 =head1 DESCRIPTION
11
12 If you read this the test worked.
13
14 =cut
15
```

```
16 use help;
17 print "You didn't put --help on the command line\n";
```

The Results

```
HELP_TEST(1)  User Contributed Perl Documentation    HELP_TEST(1)

NAME
       Help test.

DESCRIPTION
       If you read this the test worked.

perl v5.8.              2004-10-10              HELP_TEST(1)
```

How It Works

Perl has a number of special control blocks. In this program, the INIT block is called before the main program starts. It looks on the command line, and if it sees --help, it prints the documentation. The printing is done using the perldoc command, which is part of the Perl distribution.

The command looks for the program specified on the command line (in this case, it's the name of the program, or $0) and prints the program's documentation.

#2 Finding Duplicate Files

Duplicate files are a problem for me. I'll download pictures from my camera, forget I downloaded them, and download them again. I also get a lot of audio files from the Internet and many are duplicates of items I already have.[1] The result is that there's a lot of needless duplication on my system. So a script that locates duplicate files can be very useful when doing spring cleaning on a hard drive.

The Code

```
1 #!/usr/bin/perl
2 use strict;
3 use warnings;
4 use File::Find;
5 use Digest::MD5;
6
7 ##########################################################
```

---

[1] Note to the MPAA: These are old radio shows from the '30s and '40s and the copyrights have long expired. So don't sue me.

```
 8 # find_dups(@dir_list) -- Return an array containing a list
 9 #        of duplicate files.
10 ###########################################################
11 sub find_dups(@)
12 {
13     # The list of directories to search
14     my @dir_list = @_;
15
16     # If nothing there, return nothing
17     if ($#dir_list < 0) {
18         return (undef);
19     }
20
21     my %files;  # Files indexed by size
22
23     # Go through the file tree and find all
24     # files with a similar size
25     find( sub {
26             -f &&
27             push @{$files{(stat(_))[7]}}, $File::Find::name
28         }, @dir_list
29     );
30
31     my @result = ();    # The resulting list
32
33     # Now loop through the list of files by size and see
34     # if the md5 is the same for any of them
35     foreach my $size (keys %files) {
36         if ($#{$files{$size}} < 1) {
37             next;
38         }
39         my %md5;          # MD5 -> file name array hash
40
41         # Loop through each file of this size and
42         # compute the MD5 sum
43         foreach my $cur_file (@{$files{$size}}) {
44             # Open the file.  Skip the files we can't open
45             open(FILE, $cur_file) or next;
46             binmode(FILE);
47             push @{$md5{
48                 Digest::MD5->new->addfile(*FILE)->hexdigest}
49             }, $cur_file;
50             close (FILE);
51         }
52         # Now check for any duplicates in the MD5 hash
53         foreach my $hash (keys %md5) {
54             if ($#{$md5{$hash}} >= 1) {
55                 push(@result, [@{$md5{$hash}}]);
56             }
```

```
57          }
58      }
59      return @result
60  }
61
62  my @dups = find_dups(@ARGV);
63
64  foreach my $cur_dup (@dups) {
65      print "Duplicates\n";
66      foreach my $cur_file (@$cur_dup) {
67          print "\t$cur_file\n";
68      }
69  }
```

Running the Script

To run the script, simply put a list of directories to be scanned on the command line:

```
$ dup-files.pl /radio
```

The Results

```
Duplicates
        /radio/O_and_H_48-11-07_In_A_Rut.mp3
        /radio/O_and_H_48-11-14_The_Kids_Go_Away_Overnight.mp3
Duplicates
        /radio/Superman_-_411105_The_Silver_Arrow_4_o.mp3
        /radio/Superman_-_411107_The_Silver_Arrow_5_o.mp3
Duplicates
        /radio/3403456_Marco_Polo_-_Chapter_34_xcompletex.mp3
        /radio/Marco_Polo_-_Chapter_34_xcompletex.mp3
Duplicates
        /radio/radio.oldtime.highspeed.excluded.log
        /radio/radio.oldtime.excluded.log
        /radio/radio.oldtime.matched_extension_no_filter.log
        /radio/radio.oldtime.highspeed.matched_ext_no_filter.log
        /radio/radio.oldtime.excluded.log
        /radio/radio.oldtime.matched_extension_no_filter.log
```

How It Works

In Perl there's a module for practically everything. By looking through CPAN you can find the module File::Find::Duplicates. The module is quite clever. It first checks the size of the file (a quick operation), and if it finds two files with the same size, it does an MD5 checksum of the two files.

There's just one problem with this module—it doesn't always work. Sometimes it will miss duplicates. So you need to write your own duplicate location code.

However, studying the code gives us some ideas. The code of this module is quite clever. It first checks the size of each file (a fast operation) and then checks for duplicates only on files of the same size. (Checking for duplicates is a slow operation.) The problem is that the code fails if you have the following files:

a	size 1,000 bytes
a.dup	size 1,000 bytes
b	size 1,000 bytes
b.dup	size 1,000 bytes

The code will find the duplicate pair: a and a.dup. However, it will fail to find the other (b and b.dup). That's because, by design, the code assumes that for a given file size (in this example, 1,000 bytes), you'll have at most only one duplication. (In this example, there are two.)

So you need to create your own duplication detection logic. The first thing you do is use the File::Find module to locate all the files in the directories you are searching for. You then create a hash named %files whose key is the file size and whose value is an array containing the filenames of that size.

```
25    find( sub {
26            -f &&
27            push @{$files{(stat(_))[7]}}, $File::Find::name
28        }, @dir_list
29    );
```

This operation leaves us with a %files hash that looks like this:

```
%files = (
    485 => [ 'single.c']
    13667 => ['sample.mp3', 'alt_sample.mp3']
)
```

Going through this hash, you can see that no file would ever match single.c, but it is possible that sample.mp3 and alt_sample.mp3 match each other.

The code:

```
35    foreach my $size (keys %files) {
```

goes through the list.

Next you skip any entries where there's only one file in the name list:

```
36        if ($#{$files{$size}} < 1) {
37            next;
38        }
```

At this point you have at least two possible duplicates. In order to tell if they are really duplicates, you compute an MD5 hash of the files:

```
43        foreach my $cur_file (@{$files{$size}}) {
44            # Open the file.  Skip the files we can't open
45            open(FILE, $cur_file) or next;
46            binmode(FILE);
47            push @{$md5{
48                Digest::MD5->new->addfile(*FILE)->hexdigest}
49            }, $cur_file;
50            close (FILE);
51        }
```

The result is a hash named %md5 whose key is made up of MD5 hashes and whose value is an array of files with those hashes. And since you can assume that two files that have the same MD5 hash are duplicates, any entries in this hash with more that one value indicates a duplicate file. All you have to do is stuff the results into a @result array:

```
53        foreach my $hash (keys %md5) {
54            if ($#{$md5{$hash}} >= 1) {
55                push(@result, [@{$md5{$hash}}]);
56            }
```

This gives us a two-dimensional array containing the duplicate files. The only thing left to do is print the results:

```
64 foreach my $cur_dup (@dups) {
65     print "Duplicates\n";
66     foreach my $cur_file (@$cur_dup) {
67         print "\t$cur_file\n";
68     }
69 }
```

Hacking the Script

Any script can be enhanced and this one's no different. I frequently run this script on old-time radio shows I download from the Internet. These files contain a half hour of MP3 audio. Needless to say, they aren't small. So computing the MD5 checksum for these files takes time.

One way of speeding things up is to add a cache. Every time you compute a new MD5 checksum, it's added to the cache. When you want to get the checksum for a file, you check the cache first and only compute the real MD5 checksum if the file's not there.

A cache is not a complex object. It can be implemented as a hash using the filename as the key and the MD5 checksum as the value. And the Storable module can be used to write the hash out on disk and read it back again. Thus, with a little effort you can speed up this script greatly.

I've implemented another hack for my own site. When I download photographs from my camera, I save a backup copy of each photograph in a RAW directory. This means that there are lots of duplicates of the form . . . /photo/ p12345.jpg and . . . / photo/raw/p12345.jpg. In cases like this it's easy to hack the script to ignore such duplicates.

#3 Checking for Changed Files

Sometimes it's useful to figure what files have changed on your system. For example, you might want to know what a software upgrade actually touched. Other times you want to make sure that files on your system *don't* change. For example, system-critical configuration files or commands should remain intact. Changes in these files can indicate that your system has been hacked.

This script checks a filesystem and reports any changes made since the last time it was run.

The Code

```
 1 use strict;
 2 use warnings;
 3 use File::Find;
 4 use Digest::MD5;
 5 use Storable qw(nstore retrieve);
 6
 7 # File in which to store the change information
 8 my $info_file_name = ".change.info";
 9
10 #####################################################
11 # md5(file) -- Give a file, return the MD5 sum
12 #####################################################
13 sub md5($)
14 {
15     my $cur_file = shift;
16
17     open(FILE, $cur_file) or return ("");
18     binmode(FILE);
19     my $result = Digest::MD5->new->addfile(*FILE)->hexdigest;
20     close (FILE);
21     return ($result);
22 }
23
```

```perl
24 # Hash reference containing the existing data
25 #       key -- file name
26 #       value -- MD5 sum
27 my $file_info;
28 # Hash of the "real" data
29 my %real_info;
30
31 # The list of directories to search
32 my @dir_list = @ARGV;
33
34 #
35 # Check for an existing information file and
36 # read it if there is one.
37 if (-f $info_file_name) {
38     $file_info = retrieve($info_file_name);
39 }
40
41 # If nothing there, return nothing
42 if ($#dir_list < 0) {
43     print "Nothing to look at\n";
44     exit (0);
45 }
46
47 # Go through the file tree and store the information on the
48 # files.
49 find( sub {
50         -f && ($real_info{$File::Find::name} = md5($_));
51     }, @dir_list
52 );
53
54 #
55 # Check for changed, added files
56 # (clear any entries from the stored information for
57 # any files we found.)
58 foreach my $file (sort keys %real_info) {
59     if (not defined($file_info->{$file}))  {
60         print "New file: $file\n";
61     } else {
62         if ($real_info{$file} ne $file_info->{$file}) {
63             print "Changed: $file\n";
64         }
65         # else the same
66         delete $file_info->{$file};
67     }
68 }
69
70 #
71 # All file information for existing files has been
72 # removed from the information data.  So what's
73 # left is information on deleted files.
```

```
74 #
75 foreach my $file (sort keys %$file_info) {
76     print "Deleted: $file\n";
77 }
78
79 nstore \%real_info, $info_file_name;
```

Running the Script

The script is run with the command:

```
$ change.pl <dir> [<dir>...]
```

It scans the directories specified on the command line and prints out any changes it sees.

The file .change.info is used to store the change information.

The Results

```
$ changed.pl test
Changed: test/beta
New file: test/new-file
Deleted: test/beta
```

How It Works

The basic operation of this script is to compute an MD5 hash of the files as they exist on disk (called %real_info) and compare it to the information saved the last time the script was run (contained in the hash reference $file_info).

The first step in this process is to retrieve any old information and stuff it into $file_info. To do this, you use the Storable::retrieve function:

```
35 # Check for an existing information file and
36 # read it if there is one.
37 if (-f $info_file_name) {
38     $file_info = retrieve($info_file_name);
39 }
```

Now that you have the old state of the files, you need the current state. You use the File::Find module to search the directory tree and compute an MD5 checksum for each file:

```
47 # Go through the file tree and store the information on the
48 # files.
49 find( sub {
```

```
50        -f && ($real_info{$File::Find::name} = md5($_));
51    }, @dir_list
52 );
```

This gives two hashes, the one referenced by $file_info containing the old information and %real_info reflecting the current state of the system. Now all you have to do is compute the difference between the two.

First you go through the %real_info hash and see if any files have been added or changed:

```
58 foreach my $file (sort keys %real_info) {
59     if (not defined($file_info->{$file}))  {
60         print "New file: $file\n";
61     } else {
62         if ($real_info{$file} ne $file_info->{$file}) {
63             print "Changed: $file\n";
64         }
65         # else the same
66         delete $file_info->{$file};
67     }
68 }
```

This loop also has the side effect of deleting all the entries of $file_info that have a corresponding entry in %real_info. This means that when the loop finishes, the only files that are left in $file_info are the files that were deleted since the last time the program was run.

You print them out to tell the user what disappeared:

```
75 foreach my $file (sort keys %$file_info) {
76     print "Deleted: $file\n";
77 }
78
```

The final step is to write out the information on the existing files so that it can be used in a later run. Again, the Storable module is used; this time the nstore function is called to store the %real_info hash. (The nstore function stores the data in a portable format; the store function's data is nonportable. Since both functions do the same thing, why not be portable and use nstore?) Here is the code:

```
79 nstore \%real_info, $info_file_name;
```

Our data is safely stored, ready for the next time the script is run. This time, however, it will be loaded into the $file_info variable and the process will begin again.

Hacking the Script

The script has a problem. The file information is stored in only one location, the file .change.info in your current directory. This can easily be remedied by the addition of a command-line option to specify the location of the information file.

It should be noted that there are a number of quality, high-speed, file-scanning programs available. They are designed to detect when someone may be hacking your system. One of the most popular is a program called Tripwire, which can be obtained from http://sourceforge.net/projects/tripwire.

However, if you need a short script to detect file changes (a script that's easily modified), this one will do the job.

#4 Date Reminder

The commercial calendar programs out there, such as Microsoft Outlook, do a good job of reminding you of your wife's birthday, *on her birthday, when it's much too late to get her a present.* What's really needed is a program that reminds you when an important date is *approaching.*

It would also be nice if the program could also tell you how many days have elapsed since an important event, such as, for example, how many days since you sent out a rebate form.

The Code

```
 1 #
 2 # Usage: remind.pl [<calendar-file>]
 3 #
 4 # File format:
 5 #        date<tab>delta<tab>Event
 6 #
 7 #        Date -- a date
 8 #        delta --
 9 #                -xxx -- Remind after the event for xxx days
10 #                +xxx -- Remind before the event for xxx days
11 use strict;
12 use warnings;
13 use Time::ParseDate;
14 use Date::Calc(qw(Delta_Days));
15
16 ############################################################
17 # time_toYMD($time) -- Convert unit time into a year, month
18 #        and day.  Returns an array containing these three
19 #        values
20 ############################################################
21 sub time_to_YMD($)
22 {
23     my $time = shift;   # Time to convert
```

```perl
24
25      my @local = localtime($time);
26      return ($local[5]+1900, $local[4]+1, $local[3]);
27  }
28  #------------------------------------------------------------
29  #
30  my $in_file = $ENV{'HOME'}."/calendar";
31
32  if ($#ARGV == 0) {
33      $in_file = $ARGV[0];
34  }
35  if ($#ARGV > 0) {
36      print STDERR "Usage: $0 [calendar-file]\n";
37  }
38
39  open IN_FILE, "<$in_file" or
40      die("Unable to open $in_file for reading");
41
42  # Today's date as days since 1970
43  my @today_YMD = time_to_YMD(time());
44
45  while (<IN_FILE>) {
46      # Lines that begin with "#" are comments
47      if ($_ =~ /^\s+#/) {
48          next;
49      }
50      # Blank lines don't count
51      if ($_ =~ /^\s*$/) {
52          next;
53      }
54      # The data on the line
55      my @data = split /\t+/, $_, 3;
56      if ($#data != 2) {
57          next;   # Silently ignore bad lines
58      }
59      my $date = parsedate($data[0]);
60      if (not defined($date)) {
61          print STDERR "Can't understand date $data[0]\n";
62          next;
63      }
64      my @file_YMD= time_to_YMD($date);
65      # Difference between now and the date specified
66      my $diff = Delta_Days(@today_YMD, @file_YMD);
67      if ($data[1] > 0) {
68          if (($diff >= 0) && ($diff < $data[1])) {
69              print "$diff $data[2]";
70          }
71      } else {
72          if (($diff < 0) && ($diff < -($data[1]))) {
```

```
73              print "$diff $data[2]";
74          }
75      }
76 }
```

Running the Script

The script uses an input file containing a date, and a number of days. If the number of days is positive, you will be reminded of the event before it happens. (Wife's birthday in 30 days, get present now!) If the number is negative, you will be informed of the number of days which have passed since the event occurred. (They said the rebate would come in 6 to 8 weeks. It's been 80 days, what's going on?) Here's an example:

```
Oct 14   -100    Rebate Seagate $10
Sept 12  -100    Rebate Costco $50
Nov 1    +30     Wife's birthday
```

The Results

```
$ remind.pl events.txt
-3 Rebate Seagate $10
-5 Rebate Costco $50
14 Wife's birthday
```

This indicates that it's been only three days since I sent out my Seagate rebate form and five since the Costco rebate form was sent. Nothing to worry about there.

It's also two weeks until my wife's birthday, so I'd better start shopping as soon as I finish this chapter.

How It Works

For hours, minutes, and seconds you use a hexasegimal (base 60) system that comes from the ancient Babylonians. But then you suddenly shift to base 24 for the hours in a day (or base 12 and base 2 if you wish to use AM and PM).

But things really fall apart when it comes to the number of days in a month. You see, the Romans, specifically Julius Caesar, gave us our base for the modern calendar. This good work was negated by the fact that the Romans decided to name some of the months after politicians. Thus July is actually named in honor of Julius Caesar.

The problem is that Augustus Caesar decided that his month, August, had to be at least as grand as July and decided that his month also had to have 31 days. So he stole an extra day from February. (February was named after a feast, Februa, so it was safe to steal days from this month.) As a result of politics, we have the mess that is the modern day calendar.

And we haven't even touched on some of the other problems, such as the fact that the days from September 3 to September 13, 1752 are missing entirely. That's when the switch from the Julian to the Gregorian calendar was made. Because the Julian calendar was so far off at that time, they had to remove 11 days from it to catch up.

The good news is that as far as Perl is concerned, all this calendar insanity is mostly hidden from you by some Perl modules. The Time::ParseDate module is designed to convert time/data specifications into something usable by a program.

This script needs to know the number of days between two dates. The Date::Calc module can calculate date differences for us. There's just one problem. Time::ParseDate returns the date/time in Unix standard format (number of sections since January 1, 1970) and Date::Calc wants things in Year, Month, Day.

Fortunately, the built-in function localtime splits Unix time into its component fields. So if you combine the three fields and do a little bookkeeping, you can perform your calculations.

You start by reading in a line from a calendar file and parsing it:

```
45 while (<IN_FILE>) {
46     # Lines that begin with "#" are comments
47     if ($_ =~ /^\s+#/) {
48         next;
49     }
50     # Blank lines don't count
51     if ($_ =~ /^\s*$/) {
52         next;
53     }
54     # The data on the line
55     my @data = split /\t+/, $_, 3;
56     if ($#data != 2) {
57         next;    # Silently ignore bad lines
58     }
59     my $date = parsedate($data[0]);
60     if (not defined($date)) {
61         print STDERR "Can't understand date $data[0]\n";
62         next;
63     }
```

The parsedate function returns the date in Unix format and the date calculation module needs it as Year, Month, Day. So you convert it:

```
64     my @file_YMD= time_to_YMD($date);
```

Now you can compute the difference between the date in the file and the current date:

```
65     # Difference between now and the date specified
66     my $diff = Delta_Days(@today_YMD, @file_YMD);
```

If you want to be reminded about an upcoming event, and the event is in range, it's printed:

```
67    if ($data[1] > 0) {
68        if (($diff >= 0) && ($diff < $data[1])) {
69            print "$diff $data[2]";
70        }
```

Otherwise, you want to be reminded about a past event. So if the event is in range, it's printed:

```
71    } else {
72        if (($diff < 0) && ($diff < -($data[1]))) {
73            print "$diff $data[2]";
74        }
75    }
76 }
```

Hacking the Script

The core of this script utilizes logic that lets you count up or down days to specified dates. The script can easily be adapted for other counting tasks. For example, you may wish to count down the number of days until a deadline or display the number of days your favorite politician has left in office.

Computers are good at counting, and Perl's modules are good at hiding the complexities of time and dates. Thus it's easy to put the two together to perform any time-based calculations you require.

#5 Currency Converter

When traveling internationally, it's very easy to become confused by the differences between the various currencies out there. Knowing the exchange rate is vital for international transactions.

Converting between one currency and another is a simple calculation, providing you know the exchange rate. Since rates are continually changing, that can prove to be a bit tricky. This script actually goes to a website maintained by XE.com, downloads the exchange rate, and then performs the calculation. This means that the result will be an accurate conversion using up-to-the-minute rates.

The Code

```
1 #
2 # Convert currency from one type to another
3 #
4 # Usage: money.pl <amount><from-code> <to-code>
5 #
6 # Where:
```

```perl
 7 #         <from-code>, <to-code> -- ISO Currency codes
 8 #
 9
10 # Note: There are other currency modules out there,
11 # but this one looks like it does the most
12 #
13 # The drawback is that you must be connected to the
14 # Internet to use it.
15 use Finance::Currency::Convert::XE;
16
17 # The object for the converter
18 my $converter = new Finance::Currency::Convert::XE();
19
20 sub usage() {
21     print "Usage is $0 <amount><code> <to-code>\n";
22     exit (8);
23 }
24 if (($#ARGV == 0) && ($ARGV[0] eq "-l")) {
25     # Warning: This depends on the internals of the converter
26     my $info = $converter->{Currency};
27     foreach my $symbol (sort keys %$info) {
28         print "$symbol  $info->{$symbol}->{name}\n";
29     }
30     exit (0);
31 }
32 if ($#ARGV != 1) {
33     usage();
34 }
35
36 if ($ARGV[0] !~
37 #       +--------------------------- Begin string
38 #       | ++++----------------------- Optional sign
39 #       | ||||+++-------------------- 0 or more digits
40 #       | ||||||||                    (decimal part)
41 #       | ||||||||   ++--------------- Literal "."
42 #       | ||||||||   ||++------------- Digits
43 #       | ||||||||+++|||||+----------- Group but no $x
44 #       | |||||||||||||||||+---------- 0 or 1 times
45 #       |+|||||||||||||||||+--------- put in $1
46 #       |||||||||||||||||||| +++----- One/more non spaces
47 #       ||||||||||||||||||||+|||+---- Put in $2
48 #       ||||||||||||||||||||||||+--- End of line
49     /^([-+]?\d*(?:\.\d*)?)(\S+)$/) {
50     usage();
51 }
52 my $amount = $1;          # Amount to convert
53 my $from_code = $2;       # Code of the original currency
54 my $to_code = $ARGV[1];   # Code we converting to
55
56 # Amount must have at least one digit in it
57 if ($amount !~ /\d/) {
```

```
58    usage();
59 }
60
61 my $new_amount = $converter->convert(
62                    'source' => $from_code,
63                    'target' => $to_code,
64                    'value' => $amount,
65                    'format' => 'text'
66            );
67
68 if (not defined($new_amount)) {
69     print "Could not convert: " . $converter->error . "\n";
70     exit (8);
71 }
72
73 my @currencies = $converter->currencies;
74
75 print "$amount $from_code => $new_amount\n";
```

Running the Script

The first argument to the script is an amount to convert followed by the currency code. For example, $1.23 in US dollars is specified as 1.23USD. The second argument is the currency code for the currency you want.

If you don't know the code for your currency, you can run the program with a single -1 parameter and list the currency codes.

The Results

```
$ money.pl -l
ARS     Argentinian Pesos
AUD     Australian Dollars
BBD     Barbados Dollars
BGL     Bulgarian Leva
BMD     Bermuda Dollars
BRL     Brazilian Real
...
```

For example, A Hong Kong shop advertises three Microsoft Windows CDs for $7.00 (Hong Kong). What's that in US money?

```
$ money.pl 7.00HKD USD
7.00 HKD => 0.90 United States Dollars
```

How It Works

The first version of this script was designed around the Finance::Currency::Convert::Yahoo module. However, it quickly became apparent that Yahoo! has changed the format of its currency conversion web page and caused the module to break . . . So rather than try in fix it, I went searching for another module.

This lead me to the `Finance::Currency::Convert::XE` module. To perform a currency conversion, all you have to do is give this module four things:

1. The amount you wish to convert.
2. The code of the currency you are converting from.
3. The currency code of the result.
4. The result format. In this case, since all you are doing is printing the answer, the format is `'text'`, which makes the result look nice.

So the heart of the script is as follows:

```
61 my $new_amount = $converter->convert(
62                   'source' => $from_code,
63                   'target' => $to_code,
64                   'value' => $amount,
65                   'format' => 'text'
66          );
```

There's one other function that this script performs. If you use a -l on the command line, it lists the currency codes. It does this by using an undocumented feature of the currency converter module.

The modules stores information about each currency in an internal hash named currency. The code list comes from the contents of this hash. The keys of the hash are the currency codes and the value is a hash reference that contains information about the currency. In particular, the name entry contains the text name of the currency.

The code to go through this list and print the currency codes looks like this:

```
25    # Warning: This depends on the internals of the converter
26    my $info = $converter->{Currency};
27    foreach my $symbol (sort keys %$info) {
28        print "$symbol  $info->{$symbol}->{name}\n";
29    }
```

Hacking the Script

The script is currently limited to the currencies understood by XE.com. Unfortunately, not all currencies are supported. If you need something exotic like the Maco Pataca, you're out of luck.

One solution to this problem is to use multiple modules for conversion. However, at the time of this writing, the Yahoo! module is not working.

The nice thing about the Internet is that there are lots of sources of information. The nice thing about Perl is that it's an ideal language for grabbing information off the Internet and parsing it. By putting the two together, you should be able to create some very wicked cool Perl scripts.

2

WEBSITE MANAGEMENT

Managing a website is a demanding task. You have to keep track of hundreds of details and assure that the site runs smoothly. Part of this task involves checking the content for consistency and mistakes and analyzing log files to locate problems.

This chapter describes some Perl tools that can automate some of a webmaster's routine maintenance tasks, giving them time to combat the unexpected problems that make a webmaster's life so exciting.

#6 Website Link Checker

One of the most vexing problems facing a webmaster is making sure that all the links on their website are correct. Internal links are difficult to deal with. Every time a file is added, removed, or changed on your website, there is the possibility of generating dead links.

External links are even worse. Not only are they not under your control, but they disappear without a moment's notice.

What's needed is a way of automatically checking a site for links that just don't work. That's where Perl comes in.

The Code

```perl
1  #
2  # Usage: site-walk.pl <top-url>
3  #
4  use strict;
5  use warnings;
6
7  use HTML::SimpleLinkExtor;
8  use LWP::Simple;
9  use URI::URL;
10
11 my $top_url;    # The URL at the top of the tree
12
13 # Indexed by link name
14 # Value =
15 #       Internal -- Good internal link
16 #       External -- Good External link
17 #       Broken   -- Broken link
18 my %links;
19
20 ########################################################
21 # is_ours($url) -- Check to see if a URL is part of this
22 #       website.
23 #
24 # Returns
25 #       undef -- not us
26 #       1 -- URL part of this website
27 ########################################################
28 sub is_ours($)
29 {
30     my $url = shift;    # The URL to check
31
32     if (substr($url, 0, length($top_url)) ne $top_url) {
33         return (undef);
34     }
35     return (1);
36 }
37
38 ########################################################
39 # process_url($url)
40 #
41 # Read an html page and extract the tags.
42 #
```

```perl
43 # Set $links{$url} to Broken, Internal, External
44 # depending on the nature of the url
45 #######################################################
46 no warnings 'recursion';          # Turn off recursion warning
47
48 sub process_url($);       # Needed because this is recursive
49 sub process_url($)
50 {
51     my $url = shift;     # The file url to process
52
53     # Did we do it already
54     if (defined($links{$url})) {
55         return;
56     }
57     # It's bad unless we know it's OK
58     $links{$url} = "Broken";
59
60     my @head_info = head($url);
61     if ($#head_info == -1) {
62         return; # The link is bad
63     }
64
65     $links{$url} = "External";
66
67     # Return if it does not belong to this tree
68     if  (not is_ours($url)) {
69         return;
70     }
71     $links{$url} = "Internal";
72
73     # If the document length is not defined then it's
74     # probably a CGI script
75     if (not defined($head_info[1])) {
76         return;
77     }
78
79     # Is this an HTML page?
80     if ($head_info[0] !~ /^text\/html/) {
81         return;
82     }
83
84     # The parser object to extract the list
85     my $extractor = HTML::SimpleLinkExtor->new();
86
87     my $data = get($url);
88     if (not defined($data)) {
89         $links{$url} = "Broken";
90         return;
91     }
92
```

```
93     # Parse the file
94     $extractor->parse($data);
95
96     # The list of all the links in the file
97     my @all_links = $extractor->links();
98
99     # Check each link
100    foreach my $cur_link (@all_links) {
101        # The page as URL object
102        my $page = URI::URL->new($cur_link, $url);
103
104        # The absolute version of the URL
105        my $full = $page->abs();
106
107        # Now go through he URL types we know about
108        # and check what we can check
109        if ($full =~ /^ftp:/) {
110            next;       # Ignore ftp links
111        } elsif ($full =~ /^mailto:/) {
112            next;        # Ignore mailto links
113        } elsif ($full =~ /^http:/) {
114            process_url($full);
115        } else {
116            print "Strange URL: $full -- Skipped.\n";
117        }
118    }
119 }
120 # Turn off deep recursion warning
121 use warnings 'recursion';
122
123 if ($#ARGV != 0) {
124     print STDERR "$0 <top-url>\n";
125     exit(8);
126 }
127 $top_url = $ARGV[0];
128
129 process_url($top_url);
130
131 my @internal;   # List of internal links
132 my @external;   # List of external links
133 my @broken;     # List of broken links
134 my @strange;    # List of strange links
135 # If we get any strange links, something broke in the program
136
137 # Sort the links into categories
138 foreach my $cur_key (keys %links) {
139     if ($links{$cur_key} eq "Internal") {
140         push(@internal, $cur_key);
141     } elsif ($links{$cur_key} eq "External") {
142         push(@external, $cur_key);
```

```
143         } elsif ($links{$cur_key} eq "Broken") {
144             push(@broken, $cur_key);
145         } else {
146             push(@strange, $cur_key);
147         }
148 }
149
150 #
151 # Print the results
152 #
153 print "Internal\n";
154 foreach my $cur_url (sort @internal) {
155     print "\t$cur_url\n";
156 }
157 print "External\n";
158 foreach my $cur_url (sort @external) {
159     print "\t$cur_url\n";
160 }
161 print "Broken\n";
162 foreach my $cur_url (sort @broken) {
163     print "\t$cur_url\n";
164 }
165 if ($#strange != -1) {
166     print "Strange\n";
167     foreach my $cur_url (sort @strange) {
168         print "\t$cur_url\n";
169     }
170 }
```

Running the Script

The script takes, one argument: the top-level URL for the website:

```
$ site-check.pl http://www.oualline.com
```

The script will check the given URL and all URLs on that site, or more technically, the top URL and all URLs that begin with the same absolute URL as the given one.

The Results

```
Internal
    http://www.oualline.com
    http://www.oualline.com/10/.vimrc
    http://www.oualline.com/10/top_10.html
    http://www.oualline.com/10/vimrc.html
    http://www.oualline.com/cgi-bin/errata.pl?book=c
    http://www.oualline.com/cgi-bin/errata.pl?book=cpp
```

```
http://www.oualline.com/cgi-bin/errata.pl?book=vim
http://www.oualline.com/col/bully.html
http://www.oualline.com/col/check.html
http://www.oualline.com/col/cpm.html
http://www.oualline.com/col/excuse.html
```
. . . more links omitted . . .

External
```
http://www.exam-ta.ac.uk/practicalc.htm
http://www.nostarch.com/hownotc.htm
http://www.nostarch.com/images/hownotc_cov.gif
http://www.openoffice.org/
http://www.powaymidlandrr.org/
http://www.vim.org/
```

Broken
```
http://www.amazon.com/exec/obidos/ts/book-reviews/0764531050/
thedanubetravelg/002-3438930-8810611
http://www.newriders.com/appendix/0735710015.pdf
http://www.newriders.com/books/title.cfm?isbn=0735710015
http://www.oualline.com/hello/hello1_pl_4.html
http://www.oualline.com/hello/hello1_pl_a.html
http://www.oualline.com/ship/ins/ins.sxi
http://www.oualline.com/teach/slides/port.pdf
```

How It Works

The process is fairly simple:

1. Read a web page.
2. Check to make sure that all the links are correct.
3. If any link on the page is a link to this website, repeat the process for this link.

In practice things are not quite that simple. There are about 5,000 little details to worry about. Most of the actual checking work is done in the process_file function. Its job is to process a URL and create a hash called %links that contains the results of that processing. The key of %links is the URL itself, and the value is Broken, External, or Internal.

The first thing the function does is check to see if it already has processed this URL. After all, there's no reason to do the same work twice:

```
53    # Did we do it already
54    if (defined($links{$url})) {
55        return;
56    }
```

You start by assuming the worst: specifically, that the link is broken. If it later passes all tests, you'll change its status to something else:

```
57    # It's bad unless we know it's OK
58    $links{$url} = "Broken";
```

The next step is to actually check the link. For this, you use the head function from the LWP::Simple package. This not only checks the link but gives you some information that you use later. However, if the head function returns nothing, the link is broken and you give up at this point (leaving $links{$url} set to Broken):

```
60    my @head_info = head($url);
61    if ($#head_info == -1) {
62        return; # The link is bad
63    }
```

At this point, you know the URL is good, so you assume that it is an external link and then test your assumption by calling is_ours. If the assumption is true, you're done and no further processing is needed:

```
65    $links{$url} = "External";
66
67    # Return if it does not belong to this tree
68    if  (not is_ours($url)) {
69        return;
70    }
```

The is_ours subroutine is very simple. All it does is check to see if the beginning of the URL matches the top web page you started with:

```
28 sub is_ours($)
29 {
30    my $url = shift;     # The URL to check
31
32    if (substr($url, 0, length($top_url)) ne $top_url) {
33        return (undef);
34    }
35    return (1);
36 }
```

Back to your process_url function: You've figured out that the URL is good and now know that it's one of yours. This means that it is an internal link:

```
71    $links{$url} = "Internal";
```

Your link-checking program now needs to go through this internal URL and look for any links that it may have. But there are certain types of URLs that you don't want to check. These include dynamically generated data (i.e., CGI scripts). Because the web server does not know the length of dynamic data, the size field of the header ($head_info[1]) is zero. If you find such a header, you don't process the URL:

```
75    if (not defined($head_info[1])) {
76        return;
77    }
```

A website can contain a lot of different types of files, such as images, raw text, and binary data. Only an HTML page can contain links. So you check the header to make sure that the MIME type ($head_info[x]) is "text/html":

```
79    # Is this an HTML page?
80    if ($head_info[0] !~ /^text\/html/) {
81        return;
82    }
```

If you get this far, then you have a internal URL of an HTML page. You need to check every link on this page. First you grab the page using the get function from the LWP::Simple module (if this fails, then the link suddenly became broken between the time you called the head function and now):

```
87    my $data = get($url);
88    if (not defined($data)) {
89        $links{$url} = "Broken";
90        return;
```

You've got the page; now you need the links. Perl has a module called HTML::SimpleLinkExtor that will parse a web page, figure out what links it contains, and return them to you as an array.

```
84    # The parser object to extract the list
85    my $extractor = HTML::SimpleLinkExtor->new();
...
92
93    # Parse the file
94    $extractor->parse($data);
95
96    # The list of all the links in the file
97    my @all_links = $extractor->links();
```

Now all you have to do is go through each one and check it:

```
100   foreach my $cur_link (@all_links) {
```

Unfortunately, this is not just as simple as calling `process_url` on each link. First of all, there are two flavors of links, absolute and relative. An absolute link looks like this:

```
http://www.oualline.com/vim_cook.html
```

A relative link looks like this:

```
check.html
```

Since you started on the page:

```
http://www.oualline.com/col
```

the actual absolute URL you want to use is:

```
http://www.oualline.com/col/check.html
```

Again, there is a Perl module, `URI::URL`, that can be used to take a relative URL and turn it into an absolute one. Once you have the absolute URL, you can it back into the `process_url` function for checking:

```
100    foreach my $cur_link (@all_links) {
101        # The page as URL object
102        my $page = URI::URL->new($cur_link, $url);
103
104        # The absolute version of the URL
105        my $full = $page->abs();
```

You finally have a URL that you can check. But not all URLs are checkable. For example, there is no way to check a mailto-type URL. So as a final filter, you examine the URL and only check the protocols you know about, specifically HTTP. The FTP and mailto protocols are not checked. When we encounter a protocol we don't know about, such as telnet (i.e., telnet://www.terminalserver.com) or ed2k (i.e., ed2k://ed2k .fileshare.com/moves/5135.ed2k), we log it. That way the user is aware that something strange has been seen and we let him worry about it.

```
106
107        # Now go through the URL types we know about
108        # and check what we can check
109        if ($full =~ /^ftp:/) {
110            next;       # Ignore ftp links
111        } elsif ($full =~ /^mailto:/) {
112            next;       # Ignore mailto links
```

```
113          } elsif ($full =~ /^http:/) {
114              process_url($full);
115          } else {
116              print "Strange URL: $full -- Skipped.\n";
117          }
118      }
119 }
```

After process_url does its work, you have a hash called %links that contains the results. You need to sort out the elements of this hash into something more useful, so you go through the hash and produce the arrays @internal, @external, and @broken. If something goes wrong with your program, you stick any unknown hash entry in the @strange array:

```
137 # Sort the links into categories
138 foreach my $cur_key (keys %links) {
139      if ($links{$cur_key} eq "Internal") {
140          push(@internal, $cur_key);
141      } elsif ($links{$cur_key} eq "External") {
142          push(@external, $cur_key);
143      } elsif ($links{$cur_key} eq "Broken") {
144          push(@broken, $cur_key);
145      } else {
146          push(@strange, $cur_key);
147      }
148 }
```

What's left is to print the result. First you print the internal links:

```
153 print "Internal\n";
154 foreach my $cur_url (sort @internal) {
155      print "\t$cur_url\n";
156 }
```

The external, broken, and strange links are printed in a similar manner.

Hacking the Script

The script does a good job of checking HTTP-type links. However, no checking is done of mailto- and FTP-type links. Code could be added to verify that the mailto links point to a valid email address. Also, it's possible to check to see that the server in an FTP link exists. With a little more code, you could check the link itself.

There are other protocols that are not covered by this script, including things like RST, telnet, and HTTPS. These can easily be added.

The basic framework is there, and with a little hacking it can easily be expanded.

#7 Orphan File Checker

Aside from broken links, orphan pages are the biggest problem plaguing webmasters. An orphan page is one that exists on a web server but has no link to it. In other words, there is no way to get to it.

The previous script checks (and lists) all the links on a site. You now need a way to compare this against the list of files on your site to make sure that every page is visible to the outside world.

The Code

```
1 use strict;
2 use warnings;
3 use Getopt::Std;
4 use URI;
5
6 use File::Find ();
7 use vars qw/*name/;      # Name of the file from find
8 *name   = *File::Find::name;
9
10 use vars qw/$opt_s $opt_w/;
11
12 # List of files on the website
13 my @file_list;
14
15 # Called by find for each file
16 sub wanted
17 {
18     # Record only files
19     if (-f $_) {
20         push(@file_list, $name);
21     }
22 }
23
24 getopts("s:w:");
25 if ((not defined($opt_s)) ||
26     (not defined($opt_w)) ||
27     $#ARGV != -1) {
28     print STDERR "Usage is $0 -s<site> -w<walk-file>\n";
29 }
30 if ($opt_s !~ /^\//) {
31     die("Path for -s must be absolute");
32 }
33 if (! -d $opt_s) {
34     die("$opt_s is not a directory");
35 }
36 $opt_s =~ s/\/$//;
37
38 # Traverse the site
39 File::Find::find({wanted => \&wanted}, $opt_s);
```

```
40
41 # Now create a hash key=>file, value='o'
42 my %site = map {$_, 'o'} @file_list;
43
44 # Read the walking file
45 open IN_FILE, "<$opt_w" or die("Could not open $opt_w");
46
47 # Go through the list of linked pages and record them in
48 # the hash
49 <IN_FILE>;        # Skip "Internal" line
50 while (<IN_FILE>) {
51     if (substr($_,0,1) ne "\t") {
52         last;
53     }
54     # The URL as parts
55     my $url = URI->new($_);
56     # The path component
57     my $path = $url->path;
58
59     # Removing any trailing /
60     $path =~ s/\/$//;
61     $site{$opt_s.$url->path} = 's';
62 }
63
64 # Go through the %site list and find the orphans
65 foreach my $cur_file (sort keys %site) {
66     if ($site{$cur_file} ne 's') {
67         print "Orphan: $cur_file\n";
68     }
69 }
```

Running the Script

The command line for the script looks like this:

```
$ site-orphan.pl -w<walk-file> -s<site-url>
```

The *walk-file* is the name of the file containing the output of the site-orphan.pl script. The other parameter specifies the top URL for the site, as in this example:

```
$ site-orphan.pl -wwalk.out -shttp://www.oualline.com
```

The Results

```
Orphan: /var/www/html/addon-modules/.htaccess
Orphan: /var/www/html/addon-modules/HOWTO_get_modules.html
Orphan: /var/www/html/errata/vim.jpg
```

```
Orphan: /var/www/html/handcar.jpg
Orphan: /var/www/html/hello.pl
Orphan: /var/www/html/index.shtml
Orphan: /var/www/html/writing.long/junk/shirt.gif
Orphan: /var/www/html/writing.long/junk/shirt.html
Orphan: /var/www/html/writing.long/junk/shirt.pnm
Orphan: /var/www/html/writing.long/junk/shirt.shtml
```

How It Works

The script starts by getting a list of all the files on the web server. To do this, the `File::Find` module is used. Actually, the initial version of the script started out as the result of a `find2pl` command:

```
$ find2pl find '$opt_s' -type f
```

The results of this command were heavily edited so that the script now finds all the files and puts them in the `@file_list` array:

```
15 # Called by find for each file
16 sub wanted
17 {
18     # Record only files
19     if (-f $_) {
20         push(@file_list, $name);
21     }
22 }

38 # Traverse the site
39 File::Find::find({wanted => \&wanted}, $opt_s);
```

Next you turn the array into a hash whose key is the filename and whose value is `'o'`, indicating that this file is an orphan (assume all files are orphans until you know otherwise):

```
41 # Now create a hash key=>file, value='o'
42 my %site = map {$_, 'o'} @file_list;
```

Next you read in the file produced by site-walk.pl and change all the entries for all the files you find to `'s'`. Actually, it's a little more difficult than that. For each line, you deconstruct the URL into its components. You are interested in the path part of the URL:

```
54     # The URL as parts
55     my $url = URI->new($_);
56     # The path component
57     my $path = $url->path;
```

You first must normalize the path by removing any trailing /. Since the path is relative to the top level path given by the -s option, you must also add the missing part of the path back in when you set the value in the hash:

```
59      # Removing any trailing /
60      $path =~ s/\/$//;
61      $site{$opt_s.$url->path} = 's';
```

After you finish processing the internal section of the input file, you have a hash whose key is the filename and whose value is 's' if there is a link to it and 'o' if it's an orphan. All you have to do is print the orphans:

```
64 # Go through the %site list and find the orphans
65 foreach my $cur_file (sort keys %site) {
66      if ($site{$cur_file} ne 's') {
67          print "Orphan: $cur_file\n";
68      }
69 }
```

Hacking the Script

The script as written prints all orphaned files. It would be nice to have an exclude list that allows you to skip any files you don't care about. Also, it might be nice to integrate this functionality into the site-check.pl program and have a one-stop shop for web checking.

#8 Hacker Detection

There are a lot of dumb hackers and worms out there. Many of them try to break into my web server using old exploits that work on Microsoft systems. Many of these exploits are used to try to access the program cmd.exe in the WINNT directory.

I run Linux, so I can tell you that no matter what you send to my box, you're not going to get access to an MS-DOS command prompt.

To identify the bad guys, I created a small script that scans the Apache error log looking for obvious hacking attempts and printing out the top hackers.

The Code

```
1 #!/usr/bin/perl
2 #
3 # Print out a list of who tried to hack
4 # the system.
5 #
6 # Uses a simple technique to detect hacking
7 # entries, specifically
```

```perl
 8 #
 9 # 1) Attempts to access any URL with the word
10 #       "winnt" in it.
11 # 2) Attempts to access a cgi script which doesn't
12 #       exist.
13
14 #
15 # Usage:
16 #       who_hacked <error_log> [<error_log> ...]
17
18 use strict;
19 use warnings;
20 use Socket;      # For AF_INET
21
22 my %hackers;     # Who hacked
23
24 while (<>) {
25     $_ =~ /client ([^\]]*)\]/;
26     my $who = $1;                  # who hacked us
27
28     # Did someone try to get to the NT stuff
29     if ($_ =~ /winnt/) {
30         $hackers{$who}++;
31         next;
32     }
33
34     # Did someone try to exploit a bad URL
35     if ($_ =~ /cgi-bin/) {
36         $hackers{$who}++;
37         next;
38     }
39
40     # Did someone try the %2E trick
41     if ($_ =~ /%2E/) {
42         $hackers{$who}++;
43         next;
44     }
45 }
46
47 my @hack_array; # Hackers as an array
48
49 # Turn page hash into an array
50 foreach my $hacker (keys %hackers) {
51     push(@hack_array, {
52         hacker => $hacker,
53         count => $hackers{$hacker}
54     });
55 }
56
57 # Get the "top" hackers
```

```
58  my @hack_top =
59      sort { $b->{count} <=> $a->{count} } @hack_array;
60
61  for (my $i = 0; $i < 25; ++$i) {
62      if (not defined($hack_top[$i])) {
63          last;
64      }
65      # Turn address into binary
66      my $iaddr = inet_aton($hack_top[$i]->{hacker});
67
68      # Turn address into name (and stuff)
69      my @host_info = gethostbyaddr($iaddr, AF_INET);
70
71      # Handle bad names
72      if (not defined($host_info[0])) {
73          @host_info = "--unknown--";
74      }
75      printf "%3d %-16s %s\n", $hack_top[$i]->{count},
76          $hack_top[$i]->{hacker}, $host_info[0];
77  }
```

Running the Script

To run the script, simply point at your Apache error logs:

```
$ who-hacked.pl /var/log/httpd/error_log*
```

The Results

```
561 192.168.0.30     vcr.oualline.com
 16 69.46.195.55     --unknown--
  8 66.193.160.126   --unknown--
  7 208.34.72.10     --unknown--
  6 66.193.231.55    shiva.gameanon.net
  5 65.207.49.69     host69.aetherquest.com
  4 212.253.2.202    --unknown--
  1 67.127.197.89    adsl-67-127-197-89.dsl.lsan03.pacbell.net
  1 208.57.32.21     san-cust-208.57.32.21.mpowercom.net
  1 218.1.164.46     --unknown--
  1 207.192.252.238  cm-207-192-252-238.stjoseph.mo.npgco.com
  1 64.79.3.92       Host03.ImageSnap.Com
  1 202.107.202.14   --unknown--
  1 207.192.241.9    --unknown--
```

This printout shows that the number-one person who tried to hack my website, by far, is me. *Me???* What's going on? Why do these results show over 500 hacking attempts by one of my machines? Has the machine been compromised?

Upon closer examination of the logs, I discover that the hacking attempts all occurred during the same hour-long period. This coincides with the time I was running a security checker on my website. So it's true; I hacked myself.

The other hacks look like they came from dynamically assigned host names. It probably means that these people are either script kiddies or using Windows machines that were infected by a worm of some sort.

How It Works

A typical error_log file looks like this:

```
[Sat May 01 19:14:41 2004] [error] [client 69.46.195.55] File doe
s not exist: /var/www/html/......winnt
[Sat May 01 19:14:47 2004] [error] [client 69.46.195.55] File doe
s not exist: /var/www/html/....
[Sat May 01 19:14:48 2004] [error] [client 69.46.195.55] File doe
s not exist: /var/www/html/....
[Sat May 01 19:14:48 2004] [error] [client 69.46.195.55] Invalid
URI in request GET //%2E%2E/aaaaaa/../%2E%2E/./%2E%2E/
aaaaaaaaaaaaaaaaaaaaaaaaaaaaaaaaaaaaaaaaaaaaaaaaaaaaaaaaaaaaaaaaa
aaaaaaaaaaaaaaaaaaaaaaaaaaaaaaaaaaaaaaaaaaaaaaaaaaaaaaaaaaaaaaaaa
aaaaaaaaaaaaaaaaaaaaaaaaaaaaaaaaaaaaaaaaaaa/../%2E%2E\ HTTP/1.0
```

The script goes through the error log and first finds the address of the host that caused the error (this is called the *client* in Apache terms):

```
25      $_ =~ /client ([^\]]*)\]/;
26      my $who = $1;              # who hacked us
```

Next it looks for common hacks. This includes attempts to access anything in the WINNT directory:

```
28      # Did someone try to get to the NT stuff
29      if ($_ =~ /winnt/) {
30          $hackers{$who}++;
31          next;
32      }
```

Also, someone may want to see if I left any of the demo CGI scripts on my system. These can sometimes be used to hack:

```
34      # Did someone try to exploit a bad URL
35      if ($_ =~ /cgi-bin/) {
36          $hackers{$who}++;
37          next;
38      }
```

Finally, I check to see if the hacker is trying to reference files they shouldn't using the %2E trick. %2E is the dot character (.) encoded in hex. Hackers use the ".." directory (%2E%2E) in a URL in an attempt to access pages they shouldn't. There's no reason to encode the dot, so any time you see %2E, it's probably someone hacking:

```
40    # Did someone try the %2E trick
41    if ($_ =~ /%2E/) {
42        $hackers{$who}++;
43        next;
44    }
```

The result of all this checking is a hash named %hackers whose key is the hacker's IP address and whose value is the number of hack attempts. I now use the same technique used in the previous script to turn this hash into a sortable array:

```
47 my @hack_array; # Hackers as an array
48
49 # Turn page hash into an array
50 foreach my $hacker (keys %hackers) {
51     push(@hack_array, {
52         hacker => $hacker,
53         count => $hackers{$hacker}
54     });
55 }
56
57 # Get the "top" hackers
58 my @hack_top =
59     sort { $b->{count} <=> $a->{count} } @hack_array;
```

Next the results are printed and that's it.

Hacking the Script

The script checks for some basic hack attempts. As a result, it only checks for hacks that are blatant and common. Obviously there is room for more sophisticated hack checking. But this is a good framework in which to start analyzing your web server errors.

#9 Locking Out Hackers

Finding out who's trying to hack your system is one thing. But what do you do about it? One solution is to lock out the attacking machine from your system for 30 minutes. This should slow down attempts by worms and script kiddies to access your system.

The Code

```
1 #!/usr/bin/perl
2 # WARNING: There are many different ways to lock
```

```perl
 3 # a system out.  This script uses
 4 #       /sbin/route add <ip> reject
 5 # Adjust this command to suit your system.
 6 #
 7 #
 8 # When someone tries to hack us, lock him out
 9 # of the system for 30 minutes.
10 #
11 # Lockout is accomplished by setting the route
12 # for the bad systems to an impossible value
13 #
14 #
15 # Uses a simple technique to detect hacking
16 # entries, specifically
17 #
18 # 1) Attempts to access any URL with the word
19 #       "winnt" in it.
20 # 2) Attempts to access a cgi script which doesn't
21 #       exist.
22
23 #
24 # Note: There are better security solutions out there.
25 # You may want to check out http://www.snort.org for
26 # one.
27
28
29
30 #
31 # Usage:
32 #       lock-out.pl <error_log>
33 #       (Assumes that error_log is still being written)
34
35 use strict;
36 use warnings;
37 use File::Tail;
38 use Socket;       # For AF_INET
39
40 use constant JAIL_TIME => (30*60);      # 30 minutes
41 use constant TIMEOUT => (30);           # Check every 30 sec.
42
43 # Key -> Who hacked, value => Time left in route jail
44 my %hackers;
45
46 #
47 # Lock out a user by sending all his packets to nowhere
48 #
49 sub lock_out($) {
50     my $who = shift;    # Who to lock out
51
52     # Put the IP address in jail
```

```
53     $hackers{$who} = time() + JAIL_TIME;
54     my $now = localtime;          # The time now
55     print "$now Locking out $who\n";
56     system("/sbin/route add $who reject");
57 }
58 #
59 # Unlock a user by removing a lock
60 #
61 sub unlock_out($) {
62     my $who = shift;      # Who to not lock out
63
64     my $now = localtime;          # The time now
65     print "$now Unlocking out $who\n";
66     system("/sbin/route del $who reject");
67 }
68 #
69 # Return the name of a hacker if this is a hack entry
70 #
71 sub is_hacker($)
72 {
73     my $line = shift;    # Line from the log
74
75
76     $line =~ /client ([^\]]*)\]/;
77     my $who = $1;                  # who hacked us
78
79     # Did someone try to get to the NT stuff
80     if ($line =~ /winnt/) {
81         return ($who);
82     }
83
84     # Did someone try to exploit a bad URL
85     if ($line =~ /cgi-bin/) {
86         return ($who);
87     }
88     # Did someone try the %2E trick
89     if ($line =~ /%2E/) {
90         return ($who);
91         next;
92     }
93     return (undef);
94 }
95 #-------------------------------------------------------------
96 if ($#ARGV != 0) {
97     print "Usage is $0 <error-log>\n";
98     exit (8);
99 }
100
101 my $in_file = File::Tail->new(name => $ARGV[0]);
```

```
102
103 while (1) {
104     my $nfound;        # Number of FDs on which
105                        # select found something
106     my $timeleft;      # Time left in the timeout
107     my @pending;       # File::Tail items with input pending
108
109     # Wait for I/O from the log file, or a timeout
110     ($nfound, $timeleft, @pending) = File::Tail::select(
111         undef, undef, undef, TIMEOUT, $in_file);
112
113     if ($#pending != -1) {
114         # Read the line from the file
115         my $line = $pending[0]->read();
116
117         # Get who (if anyone) hacked us
118         my $who = is_hacker($line);
119         if (defined($who)) {
120             lock_out($who);
121         }
122     }
123     # Check to see if anyone should come back
124     foreach my $who (keys %hackers) {
125         if ($hackers{$who} < time()) {
126             unlock_out($who);
127             delete $hackers{$who};
128         }
129     }
130 }
131
```

Running the Script

To run the script, you must be root. That's because the script plays with the routing table to lock out bad people. You then point the program at the Apache error log and wait for things to happen:

```
# lock-out.pl /var/log/httpd/error_log
```

The Results

```
Wed Oct 20 19:04:16 2004 Locking out 202.107.202.14
Wed Oct 20 19:09:16 2004 Locking out 207.192.241.9
Wed Oct 20 19:14:16 2004 Locking out 207.192.252.238
Wed Oct 20 19:44:40 2004 Unlocking out 202.107.202.14
Wed Oct 20 19:49:40 2004 Unlocking out 207.192.241.9
Wed Oct 20 19:54:40 2004 Unlocking out 207.192.252.238
```

How It Works

The script makes use of the File::Tail module. This module looks at a file and tells you when lines are added to the file. It even knows when log files are rotated and resets itself if that happens.

So if you point it to your Apache error log, you'll get any errors that come as they happen.

The first step is to create the File::Tail object:

```
101 my $in_file = File::Tail->new(name => $ARGV[0]);
```

Next comes a loop where you wait for something to come in on the error log. The wait times out after 30 seconds to give you a chance to remove the lockout on anyone who's been put on ice for more than 30 minutes.

The select call gets you the next line or times out. If it times out, @pending will be empty:

```
109     # Wait for I/O from the log file, or a timeout
110     ($nfound, $timeleft, @pending) = File::Tail::select(
111         undef, undef, undef, TIMEOUT, $in_file);
```

You now check the log file to see if anyone attempted to hack your system. The hack detection code embedded in the function is_hacker has been previously discussed. The interesting part of this code is the fact that if you do find someone, you lock them out:

```
113     if ($#pending != -1) {
114         # Read the line from the file
115         my $line = $pending[0]->read();
116
117         # Get who (if anyone) hacked us
118         my $who = is_hacker($line);
119         if (defined($who)) {
120             lock_out($who);
121         }
122     }
```

Next you check to see if there is a system whose lockout time has expired. If so, you process it and remove the lock:

```
123     # Check to see if anyone should come back
124     foreach my $who (keys %hackers) {
125         if ($hackers{$who} < time()) {
126             unlock_out($who);
127             delete $hackers{$who};
128         }
129     }
```

Locking out a hacker is easy. All you do is change the route for their system to "reject." This tells the network to ignore any message to and from this system. This is accomplished using a simple route command:

```
49 sub lock_out($) {
50     my $who = shift;     # Who to lock out
51
52     # Put the IP address in jail
53     $hackers{$who} = time() + JAIL_TIME;
54     my $now = localtime;         # The time now
55     print "$now Locking out $who\n";
56     system("/sbin/route add $who reject");
57 }
```

When removing a lock, you need to delete the "reject" route. Again this is done with a simple route command:

```
61 sub unlock_out($) {
62     my $who = shift;     # Who to not lock out
63
64     my $now = localtime;         # The time now
65     print "$now Unlocking out $who\n";
66     system("/sbin/route del $who reject");
67 }
```

So what happens is that someone tries to hack, gets locked, gets discouraged, and goes somewhere else.

Hacking the Script

As an intrusion detection and prevention system, this is pretty primitive. It only detects a limited set of obvious attacks. You can add additional tests to detect additional types of attacks.

The lockout code is specific to Linux. There are probably better ways of preventing hackers from getting to your system. Changing the route is primitive, but it does work.

Also, the script locks everybody out who tries to hack. This may not be what you want, as I discovered when I ran this script and my security scanner at the same time. The result is that the lockout script detected the security scan and locked me out of my own server.

So although the script does a simple job well, there's lots of room for improvements and enhancements.

NOTE   *Intrusion detection is a science. There is no better protection for your system than to have someone who knows what they are doing set it up and monitor it for suspicious activity. A smart, experienced human being is still the best form of security protection around.*

3

CGI DEBUGGING

Perl and the Web were made for each other. The Perl language is ideal for processing text in an environment where speed does not matter. Perl can munch text and use it to produce dynamic web pages with ease.

But programming in a CGI environment is not the easiest thing in the world. There is no built-in CGI debugger. Also, error messages and other information can easily get lost or misplaced. In short, if your program is not perfect, things can get a little weird.

In this chapter, I'll show you some of the Perl hacks you can use to help debug your CGI programs.

#10 Hello World

This is the CGI version of "Hello World." In spite of it being a very simple program, it is extremely useful. Why? Because if you can run it, you know that your server is properly configured to run CGI programs. And from bitter experience I can tell you that sometimes configuring the server is half the battle.

The Code

```
 1 #!/usr/bin/perl -T
 2
 3 use strict;
 4 use warnings;
 5
 6 print <<EOF
 7 Content-type: text/html
 8
 9 <HEAD><TITLE>Hello</TITLE></HEAD>
10 <BODY>
11 <P>
12 Hello World!
13 </BODY>
14
15 EOF
```

Running the Script

To run the script, just point your web browser at the correct URL. If you are using the default Apache configuration, the script resides in ~apache/cgi-bin/hello.pl and the URL to run it is http://server/cgi-bin/hello.pl.

The Results

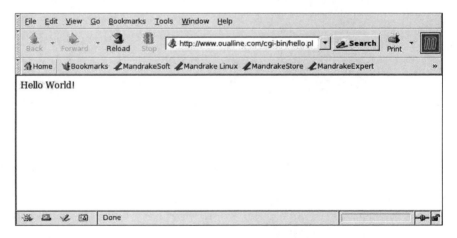

How It Works

The script just writes out its greeting, so the script itself is very simple.

The purpose of the script is to help you identify all the problems outside the script that can prevent CGI scripts from running.

Hacking the Script

In this section, I'm supposed to tell you how to enhance the script. But really, what can you do with "Hello World!"?

I suppose you could enhance it by saying "Hello Solar System," "Hello Galaxy," or "Hello Universe." You are limited only by your imagination.

#11 Displaying the Error Log

One of the problems with developing CGI scripts is that there's no error displayed when you make a syntax error or other programming mistake. All you get is a screen telling you Internal Server Error. That tells you next to nothing.

The real information gets redirected to the error_log file. The messages in this file are extremely useful when it comes to debugging a program.

However, these files are normally only accessible by a few users such as apache and root. These are privileged accounts and you don't want to give everybody access to them.

So we have a problem. Programmers need to see the log files, and the system administrators want to keep the server protected. The solution is to write a short Perl script to let a user view the last few lines of the error_log.

The Code

```
 1 #!/usr/bin/perl -T
 2 use strict;
 3
 4 use CGI::Thin;
 5 use CGI::Carp  qw(fatalsToBrowser);
 6 use HTML::Entities;
 7
 8 use constant DISPLAY_SIZE => 50;
 9
10
11 # Call the program to print out the stuff
12 print <<EOF ;
13 Content-type: text/html
14 \n
15 <HEAD><TITLE>Error Log</TITLE></HEAD>
16 <BODY BGCOLOR="#FF8080">
17 <H1>Error Log</H1>
18 EOF
19
20 if (not open IN_FILE, "</var/log/httpd/error_log") {
21     print "<P>Could not open error_log\n";
22     exit (0);
23 }
```

```
24
25
26  # Lines from the file
27  my @lines = <IN_FILE>;
28
29  my $start = $#lines - DISPLAY_SIZE + 1;
30  if ($start < 0) {
31      $start = 0;
32  }
33  for (my $i = $start; $i <= $#lines; ++$i) {
34      print encode_entities($lines[$i]), "<BR>\n";
35  }
```

Running the Script

The script must be installed in the CGI program directory and must be setuid to root (or some other user who has access to the error logs). It is accessed through a web browser.

The Results

From this display you can see that the last script run was bad.pl and it errored out because of a Premature end of script header error. (Translation: we forgot the #!/usr/bin/perl at the top of the script.)

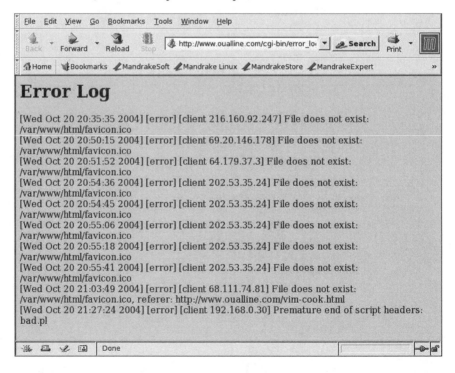

How It Works

The script starts with the magic line that runs Perl with the -T flag. The -T tells Perl to turn on *taint* checks. This helps prevent malicious user input from doing something nasty inside your program. It is a good idea to turn on taint for any CGI program. (We'll discuss taint mode in more detail in the next chapter.)

```
1 #!/usr/bin/perl -T
```

The script makes use of the CGI::Carp module. This module will catch any fatal errors and print out an error message that is readable by the browser. This means that error messages show up in the browser instead of going only to the error log.

This is especially a good idea for this script. If this script errors out, you can't use the error log script to find out what went wrong (because this is the error log script).

```
5 use CGI::Carp  qw(fatalsToBrowser);
```

Start by outputting a page header. The background color chosen for the errors is #FF8080, which is a sort of sick pink. It looks ugly, but the color screams "Errors!"

```
12 print <<EOF ;
13 Content-type: text/html
14 \n
15 <HEAD><TITLE>Error Log</TITLE></HEAD>
16 <BODY BGCOLOR="#FF8080">
17 <H1>Error Log</H1>
18 EOF
```

Next, open the log file and read all lines in it:

```
26 # Lines from the file
27 my @lines = <IN_FILE>;
```

Finally it's just a matter of printing the last 50 lines. The only trick is that you can't print them directly (they contain text and you want HTML). So the text is processed through the encode_entities function to turn nasty ASCII characters into something a browser can understand.

```
33 for (my $i = $start; $i <= $#lines; ++$i) {
34     print encode_entities($lines[$i]), "<BR>\n";
35 }
```

Hacking the Script

One problem with this script is that it exposes the entire error log to anyone who can access the page. You may want to utilize authentication to prevent unauthorized usage.

Or you can restrict the listing so that only the information for programs created by the user is displayed.

#12 Printing Debugging Information

CGI programming requires different skills. Not only do you have to know Perl programming, but also HTML and HTML forms. Sometimes what's in the form and what you think is in the form differ. As a result, the inputs to your CGI program aren't what it expects and the program fails.

To help locate errors, it's nice to know the exact inputs to a program. This shows the use of a debug function that prints out all the CGI and environment parameters, giving the programmer a lot of extremely useful debugging information.

The Code

```
1 #!/usr/bin/perl -T
2 use strict;
3
4 use CGI::Thin;
5 use CGI::Carp  qw(fatalsToBrowser);
6 use HTML::Entities;
7
8 #
9 # debug -- print debugging information to the screen
10 #
11 sub debug()
12 {
13     print "<H1>DEBUG INFORMATION</H1>\n";
14     print "<H2>Form Information</H2>\n";
15     my %form_info = Parse_CGI();
16     foreach my $cur_key (sort keys %form_info) {
17         print "<BR>";
18         if (ref $form_info{$cur_key}) {
19             foreach my $value (@{$form_info{$cur_key}}) {
20                 print encode_entities($cur_key), " = ",
21                     encode_entities($value), "\n";
22             }
23         } else {
24             print encode_entities($cur_key), " = ",
25                 encode_entities(
26                     $form_info{$cur_key}), "\n";
```

```
27        }
28    }
29    print "<H2>Environment</H2>\n";
30    foreach my $cur_key (sort keys %ENV) {
31        print "<BR>";
32        print encode_entities($cur_key), " = ",
33        encode_entities($ENV{$cur_key}), "\n";
34    }
35 }
36
37 # Call the program to print out the stuff
38 print "Content-type: text/html\n";
39 print "\n";
40 debug();
```

Using the Function

To use the function, simply put it in your CGI program and call it.

The Results

Here's the result of running the script. The form we filled in to get to this script took two parameters, a width and a height. From the debug output you can see the values we filled in.

You can also see all the environment information passed to us by the CGI system.

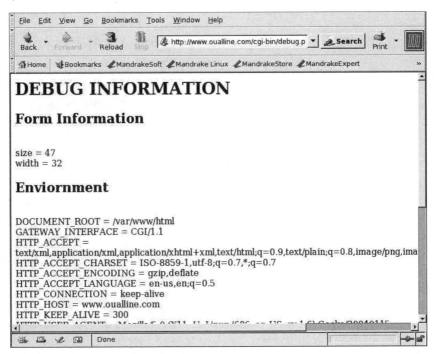

How It Works

The script uses the `Parse_CGI` function to grab all the CGI parameters. These are stored in the hash `%form_hash`:

```
15    my %form_info = Parse_CGI();
```

The hash creates a

```
form_variable => value
```

mapping. But there is a problem. Some form elements, like a multiple-selection list, can have more than one value. In that case the "value" returned is not a real value but instead a reference to an array of values.

In order to print things, your code needs to know the difference between the two. This is done using the ref function. If you have an array reference, you print the elements. If you have something else, you just print the value:

```
16    foreach my $cur_key (sort keys %form_info) {
17        print "<BR>";
18        if (ref $form_info{$cur_key}) {
19            foreach my $value (@{$form_info{$cur_key}}) {
20                print encode_entities($cur_key), " = ",
21                    encode_entities($value), "\n";
22            }
23        } else {
24            print encode_entities($cur_key), " = ",
25                encode_entities(
26                    $form_info{$cur_key}), "\n";
27        }
28    }
```

The environment is printed using a similar system. Since you don't have to worry about multiple values this time, the printing is a bit simpler:

```
30    foreach my $cur_key (sort keys %ENV) {
31        print "<BR>";
32        print encode_entities($cur_key), " = ",
33            encode_entities($ENV{$cur_key}), "\n";
34    }
```

Between the environment and the CGI parameters, you've printed every input to a CGI program.

Hacking the Script

In the field, it would be nice to be able to turn on and off the debugging output at will. One technique is use a remote shell on the server to create a file such as /tmp/cgi_debug and, if it is present, turn on the debugging.

The debug function can also be augmented to print out more information, such as the state of program variables or the contents of information files.

Printing information to the screen is one of the more useful ways of getting debugging information out of a CGI system.

#13 Debugging a CGI Program Interactively

Perl comes with a good interactive debugger. There's just one problem with it: You have to have a terminal to use it. In the CGI programming environment, there are no terminals.

Fortunately, there is another Perl debug, ptkdb. (The module name is Devel::ptkdb. If you install this module, you've installed the debugger.)

The ptkdb debugger requires a windowing system to run. In other words, if the web server can contact your X server, you can do interactive debugging of your CGI script.

The only trick is how to get things started. That's where this debugging script comes in.

The Code

```
1 #!/usr/bin/perl -T
2 #
3 # Allows you to debug a script by starting the
4 # interactive GUI debugger on your X screen.
5 #
6 use strict;
7 use warnings;
8
9 $ENV{DISPLAY} = ":0.0"; # Set the name of the display
10 $ENV{PATH}="/bin:/usr/bin:/usr/X11R6/bin:";
11
12 system("/usr/bin/perl -T -d:ptkdb hello.pl");
```

Running the Script

The first thing you need to do is edit the script and make sure that it sets the environment variable *DISPLAY* to the correct value. The name of the main screen of an X Window System is *host*:0.0, where *host* is the name of the host running the X server. If no host is specified, then the local host is assumed.

NOTE   *If you are running an X Window System with multiple displays, the display name may be different. But if you're smart enough to connect multiple monitors to your computer, you're smart enough to set the display without help.*

The other thing you'll need to do is to change the name of the program being debugged. In this example, it's hello.pl, but you should use the name of your CGI program.

Once you've made these edits and copied the start-debug.pl script into the CGI directory, point your browser at the start-debug.pl script:

```
$ mozilla http://localhost/cgi-bin/start-debug.pl
```

The Results

The script will start a debugging session on the script you specified.

You can now use the debugger to go through your code step by step in order to find problems.

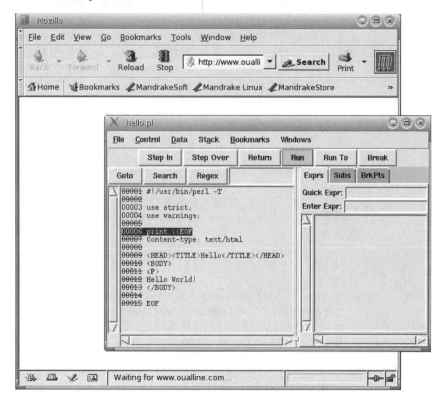

How It Works

The simple answer is that it executes the following command:

```
$ perl -d:ptkdb script
```

Unfortunately, there are a few details you have to worry about. First, the script is run with the taint option:

```
1 #!/usr/bin/perl -T
```

Taint mode turns on extra security checks which prevent a Perl program from using user-supplied data in an insecure manner.

Next you set the display so that the debugger knows where to display its window:

```
9 $ENV{DISPLAY} = ":0.0"; # Set the name of the display
```

Because taint checks are turned on, the system function will not work. That's because the system function uses the PATH environment variable to find commands. Since PATH comes from the outside, it's tainted and cannot be used for anything critical.

The solution is to reset the path in the script. Once this is done, PATH is untainted and the system function works:

```
10 $ENV{PATH}="/bin:/usr/bin:/usr/X11R6/bin:";
```

All that's left is to run the real script with debugging enabled:

```
12 system("/usr/bin/perl -T -d:ptkdb hello.pl");
```

Hacking the Script

This script is extremely limited. It can only debug programs named hello.pl. With a little work, you could create a CGI interface to the front end and make the script debug anything.

This brings us to the other problem with this script: no security. If you can get to the program, you can get to the debugger. From the debugger, you can do a lot of damage. It would be nice if the script let only good people run it.

But as a debugging tool, it's a whole lot better than the usual CGI debugging techniques of hope, pray, and print.

4

CGI PROGRAMS

Perl powers the Web. That's because it's the ideal language for writing a very simple program that can read text input, perform simple calculations on the data, and write out the results. Because it is so good at this, it's used to power most of the CGI scripts in the world.

With Perl, it's easy to quickly create small yet robust CGI form handlers and thus create a wicked cool website.

#14 Random Joke Generator

The first thing you learn in public speaking is to start off with a joke. So let's start off with a short program that throws up a random joke every time it's run.

The Code

```
1 #!/usr/bin/perl -T
2 # Random joke generator
3 use strict;
4 use warnings;
```

```
 5
 6 use CGI;
 7 use CGI::Carp qw(fatalsToBrowser);
 8 use HTML::Entities;
 9
10 # Untaint the environment
11 $ENV{PATH} = "/bin:/usr/bin";
12 delete ($ENV{qw(IFS CDPATH BASH_ENV ENV)});
13
14     print <<EOF ;
15 Content-type: text/html
16
17 <HTML>
18 <HEAD>
19     <TITLE>Random Joke</title>
20 </HEAD>
21 <BODY BGCOLOR="#FFFFFF">
22 <P>
23 EOF
24
25 my @joke = `/usr/games/fortune`;
26 foreach (@joke) {
27     print HTML::Entities::encode($_), "<BR>\n";
28 }
```

Running the Script

Install the script joke.pl in your CGI directory and point your browser at
http://*hostname*/cgi-bin/joke.pl. Replace *hostname* with the hostname of
your web server.

The Results

Your results will vary. Remember, this is a random joke generator.

How It Works

The short answer is the script takes the output of the fortune program and puts it on the script. The longer answer is that are a few details to go through.

You start off Perl with the -T switch. This turns on taint mode, which is always a good idea with CGI scripts (this will be discussed in more detail later):

```
1 #!/usr/bin/perl -T
```

The next line directs errors to the browser rather than hiding them in the error logs:

```
7 use CGI::Carp qw(fatalsToBrowser);
```

You're going to use an external command, fortune, to do the dirty work. Before you can execute the command, you need to untaint the environment. (The environment is tainted because a malicious user could set it to something bad. If you set it with a known good set of values, it's untainted.) Here's the code:

```
10 # Untaint the environment
11 $ENV{PATH} = "/bin:/usr/bin";
12 delete ($ENV{qw(IFS CDPATH BASH_ENV ENV)});
```

Next comes a little bookkeeping to print out the start of the page:

```
14    print <<EOF ;
15 Content-type: text/html
16
17 <HTML>
18 <HEAD>
19    <TITLE>Random Joke</title>
20 </HEAD>
21 <BODY BGCOLOR="#FFFFFF">
22 <P>
23 EOF
```

Use the fortune command to generate a random joke:[1]

```
25 my @joke = `/usr/games/fortune`;
```

---

[1] The fortune program is a semi-standard Unix and Linux command that was designed to simulate a fortune cookie but has turned into general silliness.

Each line in the joke is encoded (to turn nasty characters such as < into something printable) and printed:

```
26 foreach (@joke) {
27     print HTML::Entities::encode($_), "<BR>\n";
28 }
```

That's it.

Hacking the Script

This script illustrates how you can connect a simple text-generating program to the Web. In this example, I used a joke generator, but it can be anything, and perhaps something more useful. But on the other hand, don't discount the value of a good laugh.

#15 Visitor Counter

This program lets someone know how many times a web page has been visited.

The Code

```
 1 #!/usr/bin/perl -T
 2 use strict;
 3 use warnings;
 4 use GD;
 5
 6 # The file containing the visitor number
 7 my $num_file = "/var/visit/vcount.num";
 8
 9 # Number to use for counter
10 my $num = 0;
11 if (-f $num_file) {
12     if (open IN_FILE, "<$num_file") {
13         $num = <IN_FILE>;
14         chomp($num);
15         close(IN_FILE);
16     }
17 }
18
19 print "Content-type: image/png\n\n";
20
21 my $font = gdGiantFont;
22 my $char_x = $font->width;
23 my $char_y = $font->height;
24
25 my $picture_x = (1 + $char_x) * length($num) + 1;
26 my $picture_y = (1 + $char_y);
```

```
27
28 my $image = new GD::Image($picture_x, $picture_y);
29 my $background = $image->colorAllocate(0,0,0);
30 $image->transparent($background);
31 my $red = $image->colorAllocate(255,0,0);
32
33 $image->string($font, 0, 0, $num ,$red);
34
35 print $image->png;
36 ++$num;
37 if (open OUT_FILE, ">$num_file") {
38     print OUT_FILE $num;
39 }
40 close OUT_FILE;
```

Running the Script

You'll need a web page that references this CGI program as an image. Here's an example:

```
<HEAD><TITLE>Visitor Counter</TITLE></HEAD>
<BODY BGCOLOR="#FFFFFF">
    <P>
    You are visitor number:<br>
    <IMG SRC="http://www.oualline.com/cgi-bin/vcount.pl"
    ALT="(visitor)">
```

The Results

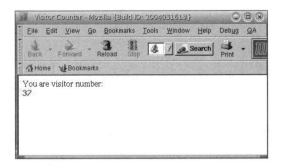

How It Works

It's very difficult to create a web page that includes a directive that tells the server to "run a CGI program and display the result here." Also, there's no way of embedding a web page within another web page. (Frames split the page up, but they don't embed anything.)

However, HTML does have a directive that allows you to embed images. And it's that directive you'll use to create your visitor counter.

All you have to do is to draw your counter instead of printing it. For the graphics, you are going to use the GD module:

```
4 use GD;
```

You are going to produce a PNG image. You need to tell the web browser what's about to appear:

```
19 print "Content-type: image/png\n\n";
```

The GD package comes with a number of different fonts. You're going to use the biggest one, so let's get a reference to it:

```
21 my $font = gdGiantFont;
```

The size of the character will affect how big your image is, so you extract these metrics from the font:

```
22 my $char_x = $font->width;
23 my $char_y = $font->height;
```

Next you compute the size of the picture you are about to generate:

```
25 my $picture_x = (1 + $char_x) * length($num) + 1;
26 my $picture_y = (1 + $char_y);
```

The next step is to create a blank canvas on which you can paint your number. You'll also set the background color to white (in RGB color space terms this is 0,0,0):

```
28 my $image = new GD::Image($picture_x, $picture_y);
29 my $background = $image->colorAllocate(0,0,0);
30 $image->transparent($background);
```

Next, allocate a color for the digits. For this script, a nice red has been selected:

```
31 my $red = $image->colorAllocate(255,0,0);
```

Now the number is drawn on the image:

```
33 $image->string($font, 0, 0, $num ,$red);
```

The only thing left is to print the image, thus sending it to the browser:

```
35 print $image->png;
```

And of course, there a little bookkeeping to do, but that's it:

```
36 ++$num;
37 if (open OUT_FILE, ">$num_file") {
38     print OUT_FILE $num;
39 }
40 close OUT_FILE;
```

Hacking the Script

The visitor counter tells you how many times your web page has been viewed, not how many people viewed it. There are ways you can attempt to detect different visitors. The simplest is to track IP addresses and not count multiple views from the same IP address.

Or you could send the browser a cookie and refuse to increment the counter for anyone who already has a cookie.

None of these systems is perfect, but all give you some idea of how many times your web page has been looked at.

Another image manipulation package can be found in the Image::Magick module. This module provides many more drawing functions, but it's harder to use.

#16 Guest Book

The visitor counter keeps track of people automatically. Another way to handle this is to ask them to voluntarily record their name for you. The guest book script lets people record their name and email address so you can contact them later.

The Code

```
 1 #!/usr/bin/perl -T
 2 use strict;
 3 use warnings;
 4
 5 use CGI;
 6 use CGI::Carp qw(fatalsToBrowser);
 7 use HTML::Entities;
 8
 9 #
10 # Configure this for your system
11 #
12 # Where the information is collected
13 my $visit_file = "/tmp/visit.list";
14
15 my $query = new CGI;      # The cgi query
16
17 # The name of the user
```

```
18  my $user = $query->param("user");
19
20  # The email of the user
21  my $email = $query->param("email");
22
23  if (not defined($user)) {
24      $user = "";
25  }
26  if (not defined($email)) {
27      $email = "";
28  }
29
30  # Untaint the environment
31  $ENV{PATH} = "/bin:/usr/bin";
32  delete ($ENV{qw(IFS CDPATH BASH_ENV ENV)});
33
34  # If there is a user defined, record it
35  if ($user ne "")
36  {
37      open OUT_FILE, ">>$visit_file" or
38          die("Could write the visitor file");
39
40      print OUT_FILE "$user\t$email\n";
41
42      close OUT_FILE;
43
44      # Turn the user into HTML
45      $user = HTML::Entities::encode($user);
46
47      # Get the visitor number from the file
48      my $visitor = `wc -l $visit_file`;
49
50      # Remove leading spaces
51      $visitor =~ s/^\s+//;
52
53      # Get the number of lines in the file
54      my @number = split /\s+/, $visitor;
55
56      print <<EOF ;
57  Content-type: text/html
58
59  <HTML>
60  <HEAD>
61      <TITLE>Guest Book</title>
62  </HEAD>
```

```
63 <BODY BGCOLOR="#FFFFFF">
64 <P>
65 Thank you $user.  Your name has been recorded.
66 <P>
67 You are visitor number $number[0]
68 EOF
69     exit (0);
70 }
71
72
73 print <<EOF;
74 Content-type: text/html
75
76 <HTML>
77 <HEAD>
78     <TITLE>Guest Book</title>
79 </HEAD>
80
81 <BODY BGCOLOR="#FFFFFF">
82     <P>
83     Please sign my guest book:
84     <FORM METHOD="post" ACTION="guest.pl" NAME="guest">
85         <P>Your name:
86             <INPUT TYPE="text" NAME="user">
87         .</P>
88
89         <P>Your E-Mail address:
90             <INPUT TYPE="text" NAME="email">
91         (optional).</P>
92
93         <P>
94             <INPUT TYPE="submit"
95             NAME="Submit" VALUE="Submit">
96         </P>
97     </FORM>
98 </BODY>
99 </HTML>
100 EOF
```

Running the Script

To run the script, you must point your web browser at it. The script will automatically sense that you are running it for the first time and ask you for your name. After you enter your name, the script runs again and displays a short thank-you message.

The Results

Initial run:

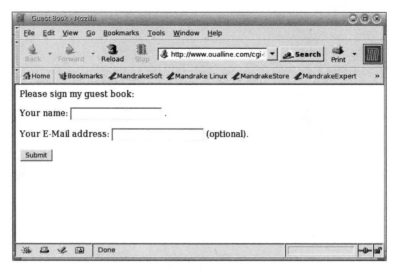

Thank-you screen:

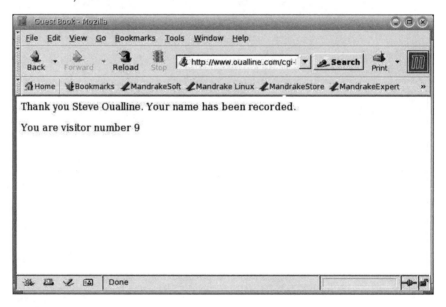

How It Works

You start by doing some initialization:

```
12 # Where the information is collected
13 my $visit_file = "/tmp/visit.list";
```

Next, you get the CGI parameters:

```
15 my $query = new CGI;     # The cgi query
16
17 # The name of the user
18 my $user = $query->param("user");
19
20 # The email of the user
21 my $email = $query->param("email");
```

If this is the first run, these values will not be defined. Let's give them default values:

```
23 if (not defined($user)) {
24     $user = "";
25 }
26 if (not defined($email)) {
27     $email = "";
28 }
```

If there is a user defined, record the information:

```
34 # If there is a user defined, record it
35 if ($user ne "")
36 {
37     open OUT_FILE, ">>$visit_file" or
38         die("Could write the visitor file");
39
40     print OUT_FILE "$user\t$email\n";
41
42     close OUT_FILE;
```

The username is encoded for printing:

```
44     # Turn the user into HTML
45     $user = HTML::Entities::encode($user);
```

You get the visitor number by counting the number of lines in the file that holds your name list:

```
47     # Get the visitor number from the file
48     my $visitor = `wc -l $visit_file`;
49
50     # Remove leading spaces
51     $visitor =~ s/^\s+//;
52
53     # Get the number of lines in the file
54     my @number = split /\s+/, $visitor;
```

Now you print a thank-you page:

```
56      print <<EOF ;
57 Content-type: text/html
58
59 <HTML>
60 <HEAD>
61      <TITLE>Guest Book</title>
62 </HEAD>
63 <BODY BGCOLOR="#FFFFFF">
64 <P>
65 Thank you $user.  Your name has been recorded.
66 <P>
67 You are visitor number $number[0]
68 EOF
69      exit (0);
70 }
```

The script has two modes of operation. You have just completed the part that handles the second mode, which is the "Thank You" mode.

If the username is not defined, you'll fall into the following code to handle the "Welcome" mode. All you do at this point is print out a welcoming page asking the user to record their name:

```
73 print <<EOF;
74 Content-type: text/html
75
76 <HTML>
77 <HEAD>
78      <TITLE>Guest Book</title>
79 </HEAD>
80
81 <BODY BGCOLOR="#FFFFFF">
82      <P>
83      Please sign my guest book:
84      <FORM METHOD="post" ACTION="guest.pl" NAME="guest">
85          <P>Your name:
86              <INPUT TYPE="text" NAME="user">
87          .</P>
88
89          <P>Your E-Mail address:
90              <INPUT TYPE="text" NAME="email">
91          (optional).</P>
92
93          <P>
94              <INPUT TYPE="submit"
95                NAME="Submit" VALUE="Submit">
96          </P>
97      </FORM>
```

```
98 </BODY>
99 </HTML>
100 EOF
```

Hacking the Script

This is a simple program that reads data from the user and writes it to a file. In this case, the data is guest information. But the program can easily be adapted to record all sorts of other information. In other words, this script can serve as the design pattern for almost any CGI input program.

#17 Errata Submission Form

I'm sure that this happens to every author. You write a book, submit the final manuscript to your publisher, and then wait. Finally, after a long time, you get a package in the mail containing your author's copies.

You pull out a copy of your brand-new book and just can't wait to show it to someone. Your wife, your friend, an innocent bystander—it doesn't matter. You just want someone to see it. So you hand them the book, they open it to a random page, and then they say, "I found a mistake . . . ."

One of the worst moments in my life occurred just after I wrote the book *Perl for C Programmers*. I handed my first book to my wife, who opened it up and said testily, "Who's Karen?"

She was looking at the dedication, which began:

> I dedicate this book to Karen, my wonderful wife, who has
> endured eight months of watching television over the sound
> of my typing...

My wife's name is not Karen; it's Chi. I had a lot of explaining to do. Turns out the publisher put someone else's dedication in my book.

After a book is published, people will find mistakes in it and send in corrections. This script provides a way for them to do it using the Web.

The Code

```
1 #!/usr/bin/perl -T
2 use strict;
3 use warnings;
4
5 use CGI;
6 use CGI::Carp qw(fatalsToBrowser);
7 use HTML::Entities;
8
9 my $collector = "oualline\@www.oualline.com";
10
11 # Message to the user (will get overridden)
12 my $msg = "Internal error";
```

```
13
14 my $query = new CGI;      # The cgi query
15
16 # The name of the user
17 my $user = $query->param("user");
18
19 # The book information from the form
20 my $book = $query->param("book");
21
22 my $where = $query->param("where");
23 my $what = $query->param("what");
24 if (defined($query->param("SUBMIT"))) {
25     if (not defined($user)) {
26         die("Required parameter \$user missing");
27     }
28     if (not defined($book)) {
29         die("Required parameter \$book missing");
30     }
31     if (not defined($where)) {
32         die("Required parameter \$where missing");
33     }
34     if (not defined($what)) {
35         die("Required parameter \$what missing");
36     }
37 }
38 if (not defined($user)) {
39     $user = "";
40 }
41 if (not defined($book)) {
42     $book = "";
43 }
44 if (not defined($where)) {
45     $where = "";
46 }
47 if (not defined($what)) {
48     $what = "";
49 }
50
51 $ENV{PATH} = "/bin:/usr/bin";
52 delete ($ENV{qw(IFS CDPATH BASH_ENV ENV)});
53
54 if (($where ne "") or ($what ne ""))
55 {
56     $book =~ /([a-z]*)/;
57     $book = $1;
58     if (not $book) {
59         $book = "Strange";
60     }
61
62     open OUT_FILE,
```

```perl
63        "|mail -s 'Errata for $book' $collector" or
64           die("Could not start the mail program");
65
66     print OUT_FILE "Book: $book\n";
67     print OUT_FILE "User: $user\n";
68     print OUT_FILE "Location: $where\n";
69     print OUT_FILE "Problem:\n";
70     print OUT_FILE "$what\n";
71     close OUT_FILE;
72
73     $msg = <<EOF;
74 <P>
75 Thank you for your submission.    If you have another
76 error, fill in the form below.
77 EOF
78 }
79
80
81 # Encode the values we are going to print
82 $user = HTML::Entities::encode($user);
83 $book = HTML::Entities::encode($book);
84
85 print <<EOF;
86 Content-type: text/html
87
88 <HTML>
89 <HEAD>
90     <TITLE>Submit an Errata</title>
91 </HEAD>
92
93 <BODY BGCOLOR="#FFFFFF">
94     $msg
95     <FORM METHOD="post" ACTION="sub_errata.pl" NAME="errata">
96        Book:
97        <SELECT NAME="book">
98           <OPTION VALUE="vim">
99              Vim (Vi Improved)
100           </OPTION>
101           <OPTION VALUE="not">
102              How not to Program in C++
103           </OPTION>
104           <OPTION VALUE="perlc">
105              Perl for C Programmer
106           </OPTION>
107           <OPTION VALUE="wcp" SELECTED>
108              Wicked Cool Perl Scripts
109           </OPTION>
110        </SELECT>
111
112        <P>Your E-Mail address:
```

```
113              <INPUT TYPE="text" NAME="user" VALUE=$user>
114          (optional).</P>
115
116          <P>Location of the error:
117              <INPUT TYPE="text" NAME="where">
118          </P>
119
120          <P>Description of the problem:<BR>
121              <TEXTAREA NAME="what" COLS="75" ROWS="10">
122              </TEXTAREA>
123          </P>
124          <P>
125              <INPUT TYPE="submit"
126               NAME="Submit" VALUE="Submit">
127          </P>
128      </FORM>
129 </BODY>
130 </HTML>
131 EOF
```

Running the Script

As with any CGI program, you run the script by pointing a web browser at it.

The Results

When the script runs for the first time, the user gets a blank form to fill in.

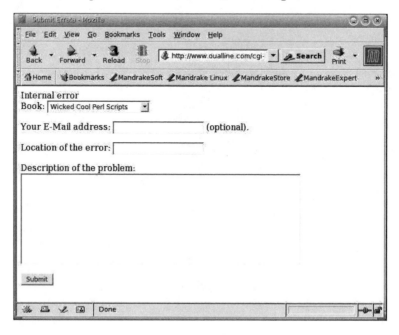

After the mistake is submitted, a confirmation message appears and the user is invited to submit another.

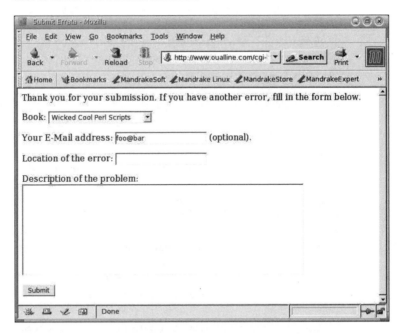

The author will receive an email for each mistake submitted.

```
Date: Tue, 26 Oct 2004 23:20:42 -0700 (PDT)
From: system user for apache-conf <apache@www.oualline.com>
To: oualline@www.oualline.com
Subject: Errata for wcp

Book: wcp
User: jruser@someplace.com
Location: Errata script
Problem:

The script does not let you pick which edition
of the book has the problem.
```

How It Works

The script is not that much different than the guest book script, except that it sends email when an input is made.

Now, sending email is normally a fairly simple operation. All you do is open a pipe to the mailer and send the data to it. That simple statement glosses over a host of security concerns.

Problem #1 is the location of the mail program. It is possible for a malicious user to screw up the environment, particularly the PATH environment variable, in an effort to trick the script into running their own program.

But how can a user convince the Apache web server to change the environment? Who said the CGI script was run from Apache? A bad guy with access to an account on your system could run the script manually after playing with the environment.

Fortunately, we are running with the taint check turned on (the -T in the top line), and any attempt to run a command without making the script secure will result in an error such as this:

```
Insecure $ENV{PATH} while running with -T switch at
script.pl line 1.
```

Before Perl will let you run a command, you must reset all environment variables that could affect the running of the program:[2]

```
51 $ENV{PATH} = "/bin:/usr/bin";
52 delete ($ENV{qw(IFS CDPATH BASH_ENV ENV)});
```

Now you come to the line that sends the mail. Here's what you would like to write:

```
open OUT_FILE, "|mail -s 'Errata for $book' $collector"
```

The problem is that $book is a parameter from the web page. A clever user can manipulate that variable and change it to anything they want. What sort of thing would a hacker put in this variable? How about changing $book to this:

```
' ; rm -rf /; '
```

This looks funny until you plug it in the mail statement:

```
mail -s 'Errata for ' ; rm -rf /; '' oualline@www.oualline.com
```

So now the shell executes a malformed mail command followed by a perfectly good and nasty hacking command with some other junk tacked onto the end.[3]

---

[2] You can define and use your own environment variables without having to worry about Perl's security logic, such as DEBUG or ENABLE_LOGGING. Only the ones that may affect security must be changed. For more information, see the Perl document: perlsec.

[3] There are some problems with this example, which would cause it to fail. But don't try this on your system unless you have lots of time on your hands and good backups. And don't try this on someone else's system unless you have a good lawyer and are willing to spend three to five years away from your computer.

Taint mode is smart enough to detect that $book came from the user and will not let it be used in a command until it is untainted. If you attempt to use user input in a command, Perl will abort your program with an error like this:

```
Insecure dependency in system while running with -T switch at
script.pl line 3.
```

For the errata script, the only legal $book parameters contain just lower-case letters. So for security, compare the variable against a regular expression to make sure that the input is legal. Anything illegal will get discarded. After this check $book will be untainted:

```
56    $book =~ /([a-z]*)/;
57    $book = $1;
```

Just because strange things can happen in CGI programs, we check to make sure that $book is set. If it's not, we give it a default value so as not to confuse the rest of the system.

```
58    if (not $book) {
59        $book = "Strange";
60    }
```

Checks like these are extremely important because Perl assumes that if you use a regular expression to extract data from a user parameter, you know what you are doing and the result is secure.

Hacking the Script

This program is a good example of a simple two-stage CGI data-collection script. In the first stage, the user fills out the form, and in the second, the form is validated and the data recorded.

Although simple, this script can easily serve as a template for you to produce your own simple (and perhaps not so simple) data-collection scripts.

5

INTERNET DATA MINING

The Internet is one of the greatest information sources in the world. There are a couple of ways of getting information from the Internet. One way is to visit web pages. You'll need a very large program called a browser to do this.[1] You'll have to get the entire web page, including information you probably don't want or need (advertisements, for example). And it's difficult to do anything with the data once you get it.

On the other hand, Perl is ideal for grabbing web pages, munching them up, and spitting out what you want. So with a little Perl magic, you can actually extract useful information from the Web.

---

[1] If you're using Windows, you'll need a very large, very bloated, and very buggy program called a browser unless you'll willing to go to the trouble of replacing the default Windows browser.

#18 Getting Stock Quotes

Anyone who's invested in stocks wants to know how their portfolio is doing. This script goes to the Internet and fetches the latest quotes for any given company.

The Code

```
1 #!/usr/bin/perl
2 use strict;
3 use warnings;
4
5 use Finance::Quote;
6
7 if ($#ARGV == -1) {
8     print STDERR "Usage is $0 <stock> [<stock> ...]\n";
9     exit (8);
10 }
11
12 # Get the quote engine
13 my $quote = Finance::Quote->new;
14
15 # Get the data
16 my %data = $quote->fetch('usa', @ARGV);
17
18 # Print the data
19 foreach my $stock (@ARGV) {
20     my $price = $data{$stock, "price"};
21     if (not defined($price)) {
22         print "No information on $stock\n";
23         next;
24     }
25     my $day   = $data{$stock, "day_range"};
26     my $year  = $data{$stock, "year_range"};
27     if (not defined($day)) {
28         $day = "????";
29     }
30     if (not defined($year)) {
31         $year = "????";
32     }
33
34     print "$stock Last: $price Day range: $day\n";
35     print "Year range: $year\n";
36 }
```

Running the Script

To run the script, simply specify the stock symbols on the command line. For example, the symbol for Google is GOOG:

```
$ quote.pl GOOG
```

The Results

```
GOOG Last: 185.97 Day range: 181.77 - 189.52
Year range: 95.96 - 194.43
```

How It Works

The program uses the `Finance::Quote` module to get the quotes. You first initialize the module:

```
12 # Get the quote engine
13 my $quote = Finance::Quote->new;
```

Next you ask the module to go to the Internet and the get the data:

```
15 # Get the data
16 my %data = $quote->fetch('usa', @ARGV);
```

The result is a hash with a two-dimensional key structure. The first key is the stock symbol (e.g., GOOG); the second is a label for the value of the hash entry. There are a lot of labels for each stock. The ones we're interested in are as follows:

price   The price of the stock

day_range   The price range for the current day (or the last day traded)

year_range   The price range for the previous year

You now go through the list of stocks and print the information.

```
18 # Print the data
19 foreach my $stock (@ARGV) {
```

First you get the price, if any. If there's no price, you fuss and stop printing:

```
20     my $price = $data{$stock, "price"};
21     if (not defined($price)) {
22         print "No information on $stock\n";
23         next;
24     }
```

Next you get the price range for the day and year:

```
25      my $day  = $data{$stock, "day_range"};
26      my $year = $data{$stock, "year_range"};
```

Just in case something goes wrong, you set default values for printing:

```
27      if (not defined($day)) {
28          $day = "????";
29      }
30      if (not defined($year)) {
31          $year = "????";
32      }
```

Finally, you print the data:

```
33
34      print "$stock Last: $price Day range: $day Year range: $y ear\n";
35 }
```

Hacking the Script

This script is designed for stocks traded in the United States only. You'll have to change line 16 if you want to use a different stock exchange.

Also, the script just fetches the stock price. If you want historical data, technical analysis, moving averages, or any of the other numbers that the experts use, you'll have to add them to the script.

I pick a stock because I think the company is doing a good job. So far this system has served me moderately well with only a few nasty surprises. As far as all those numbers go, I always thought that they were there to disguise the fact that most of the experts were really just guessing.

(I was listening to a business program today on the radio, and the financial expert told the host that the stock market was going to go up or down unless it remained stagnant. The host thought that was a very insightful and wise statement.)

#19 Comics Download

Every morning I get up, go to the computer, and read the morning paper. Actually the "paper" is a set of bookmarks in Mozilla. I happen to love editorial cartoons. Unfortunately, editorial cartoonists don't create new works daily, so I'm forced to view a large number of pictures I've seen before.

So I decided to see if Perl could help me and designed a program to download new cartoons from the Web. Old cartoons get skipped.

So now I get up, run the script, and view just the new stuff. It's amazing how a little technology can dejunk your life.

The Code

```perl
1 #!/usr/bin/perl
2 use strict;
3 use warnings;
4
5 use LWP::Simple;
6 use HTML::SimpleLinkExtor;
7 use URI;
8 use POSIX;
9
10 # Information on the comics
11 my $in_file = "comics.txt";
12
13 # File with last download info
14 my $info_file = "comics.info";
15
16 my %file_info;  # Information on the last download
17
18 ##############################################################
19 # do_file($name, $page, $link, $index)
20 #
21 # Download the given link and store it in a file.
22 #       If multiple file are present,
23 #                 $index should be different
24 #       for each file.
25 ##############################################################
26 sub do_file($$$$)
27 {
28     my $name = shift;   # Name of the file
29     my $page = shift;   # The base page
30     my $link = shift;   # Link to grab
31     my $index = shift;  # Index (if multiple files)
32
33     # Try and get the extension of the file from the link
34     $link =~ /(\.[^\$\.]*)$/;
35
36     # Define the extension of the file
37     my $ext;
38     if (defined($1)) {
39         $ext = $1;
40     } else {
41         $ext = ".jpg";
42     }
43
44     my $uri = URI->new($link);
45     my $abs_link = $uri->abs($page);
46
47     # Get the heading information of the link
48     # (and the modification time goes into $2);
```

```perl
49      my @head = head($abs_link->as_string());
50      if ($#head == -1) {
51          print "$name Broken link: ",
52              $abs_link->as_string(), "\n";
53          return;
54      }
55      if (defined($file_info{$name})) {
56          # If we've downloaded this one before
57          if ($head[2] == $file_info{$name}) {
58              print "Skipping $name\n";
59              return;
60          }
61      }
62      # Set the file information
63      $file_info{$name} = $head[2];
64
65      # Time of the last modification
66      my $time = asctime(localtime($head[2]));
67      chomp($time);         # Stupid POSIX hack
68
69      print "Downloading $name (Last modified $time)\n";
70      # The raw data from the page
71      my $raw_data = get($abs_link->as_string());
72      if (not defined($raw_data)) {
73          print "Unable to download link $link\n";
74          return;
75      }
76      my $out_name;          # Name of the output file
77
78      if (defined($index)) {
79          $out_name = "comics/$name.$index$ext";
80      } else {
81          $out_name = "comics/$name$ext";
82      }
83      if (not open(OUT_FILE, ">$out_name")) {
84          print "Unable to create $out_name\n";
85          return;
86      }
87      binmode OUT_FILE;
88      print OUT_FILE $raw_data;
89      close OUT_FILE;
90  }
91
92  #------------------------------------------------------------
93  open INFO_FILE, "<$info_file";
94  while (1) {
95      my $line = <INFO_FILE>;     # Get line from info file
96
97      if (not defined($line)) {
98          last;
99      }
```

```
100     chomp($line);
101     # Get the name and time of the last download
102     my ($name, $time) = split /\t/, $line;
103     $file_info{$name} = $time;
104 }
105 close INFO_FILE;
106
107 open IN_FILE, "<$in_file"
108     or die("Could not open $in_file");
109
110
111 while (1) {
112     my $line = <IN_FILE>;          # Get line from the input
113     if (not defined($line)) {
114         last;
115     }
116     chomp($line);
117
118     # Parse the information from the config file
119     my ($name, $page, $pattern) = split /\t/, $line;
120
121     # If the input is bad, fuss and skip
122     if (not defined($pattern)) {
123         print "Illegal input $line\n";
124         next;
125     }
126
127     # Get the text page which points to the image page
128     my $text_page = get($page);
129
130     if (not defined($text_page)) {
131         print "Could not download $page\n";
132         next;
133     }
134
135     # Create a decoder for this page
136     my $decoder = HTML::SimpleLinkExtor->new();
137     $decoder->parse($text_page);
138
139     # Get the image links
140     my @links = $decoder->img();
141     my @matches = grep /$pattern/, @links;
142
143     if ($#matches == -1) {
144         print "Nothing matched pattern for $name\n";
145         print " Pattern: $pattern\n";
146         foreach my $cur_link (@links) {
147             print "      $cur_link\n";
148         }
149         next;
150     }
```

```
151     if ($#matches != 0) {
152         print "Multiple matches\n";
153         my $index = 1;
154         foreach my $cur_link (@matches) {
155             print "    $cur_link\n";
156             do_file($name, $page, $cur_link, $index);
157             ++$index;
158         }
159         next;
160     }
161     # One match
162     do_file($name, $page, $matches[0], undef);
163 }
164
165 open INFO_FILE, ">$info_file" or
166     die("Could not create $info_file");
167
168 foreach my $cur_name (sort keys %file_info) {
169     print INFO_FILE "$cur_name  $file_info{$cur_name}\n";
170 }
171 close (INFO_FILE);
```

Running the Script

First, create a directory called comics. This is where the images will be stored.

The next thing you'll need to do is to create a comics.txt file. Each line in the file has the following format:

---

name--->url--->pattern

The parts of the format have the following meanings:

> **--->** The tab character.
>
> **name** The name of the entry. This name will be used when it comes time to store the result. It should be something simple like dilbert.
>
> **url** The URL of the web page that contains the comic. This is not the URL of the comic image itself since these URLs change from day to day. For the *Dilbert* comic strip, this would be http://www.dilbert.com.
>
> **pattern** A regular expression that will be matched to all the links within the web page, as in this example:

---

^/comics/dilbert/archive/images/dilbert\d+\.gif$

That's a lot of information, so how do you get the information filled in for each of the fields? The first field is simple: make up a name, a single word describing the comic.

For the next one, visit the website of your favorite comic. Copy the URL from the address box and put it in your code.

Now right-click on the comic and select **View Image**. You should see a screen with just the image on it. Copy the URL from this image and put it in your file. Now turn it into a regular expression by escaping all the bad characters, such as dots (.), as well as putting a caret (^) at the beginning and a dollar sign ($) at the end. If you see something that looks a date or serial number, replace the series of digits with the matching regular expression syntax. Thus dilbert2004183061028.gif becomes dilbert\d+\.gif (note the escaped dot (.) in the string).

So the line in your comics.txt file looks like this:

```
dilbert     http://www.dilbert.com/    ^http://www.dilbert.com/ comics/
dilbert/archive/images/dilbert\d+\.gif$
```

(It's all on one line with tabs separating the three pieces.)

You're not done yet. When you run the script, you'll get an error message:

```
Nothing matched pattern for dilbert
    Pattern: ^http://www\.dilbert\.com/archive/comics/dilbert/archive/images/
dilbert\d+\.gif$

/comics/dilbert/images/small_ad.gif
    /images/clear_dot.gif
    /images/ffffff_dot.gif
/comics/dilbert/archive/images/dilbert2004183061028.gif
/images/000000_dot.gif
```

(This error output has greatly been shortened.)

What's happened is that you put in a pattern that matches an absolute link and the web page contains a relative link. You now need to go through the list of image links (which the script so thoughtfully spewed out) and find one that look something like your pattern.

The entry

```
    /comics/dilbert/archive/images/dilbert2004183061028.gif
```

looks promising. So you go back to your original file and edit it so that the URL matcher now starts at /comics. The result is this:

```
^/comics/dilbert/archive/images/dilbert\d+\.gif$
```

This is now the entry you'll use when you run the script.

The Results

Here's the output of a typical run:

```
Downloading dilbert (Last modified Mon Oct  4 15:58:59 2004)
Downloading shoe (Last modified Fri Oct  1 21:11:32 2004)
Skipping userfriendly
```

```
Skipping ed_ann
Skipping ed_luck
Downloading ed_matt (Last modified Mon Oct 25 16:01:04 2004)
Downloading ed_mccoy (Last modified Wed Oct 27 21:01:09 2004)
Skipping ed_ohman
```

A set of new images is stored in the comics directory. Unfortunately, copyright laws prevent me from including them in this book.

How It Works

The script needs two pieces of information to work: (1) what to download and (2) when was it last downloaded.

The first is stored in the hand-generated configuration file comics.txt. The second is stored in the file comics.info. This file is automatically generated and updated by the script. The format of this file is as follows:

```
name date
```

The name component is the name of the comics as defined by the comics.txt file. The date component is the modification date from the image URL.

The first step is to read in the comics.info file and store it in the %file_info hash. The keys to this hash are names of the comics and the values are the last modified date.

```
 13 # File with last download info
 14 my $info_file = "comics.info";
...
 92 #-----------------------------------------------------------
 93 open INFO_FILE, "<$info_file";
 94 while (1) {
 95     my $line = <INFO_FILE>;      # Get line from info file
 96
 97     if (not defined($line)) {
 98         last;
 99     }
100     chomp($line);
101     # Get the name and time of the last download
102     my ($name, $time) = split /\t/, $line;
103     $file_info{$name} = $time;
104 }
105 close INFO_FILE;
```

Next you start on the configuration file comics.txt:

```
 10 # Information on the comics
 11 my $in_file = "comics.txt";
...
```

```
106
107 open IN_FILE, "<$in_file"
108     or die("Could not open $in_file");
```

Each line is read in and parsed:

```
111 while (1) {
112     my $line = <IN_FILE>;        # Get line from the input
113     if (not defined($line)) {
114         last;
115     }
116     chomp($line);
117
118     # Parse the information from the config file
119     my ($name, $page, $pattern) = split /\t/, $line;
```

Just in case something went wrong, you check to make sure that there are three tab-separated fields on the line. If there's no field #3, you are most likely very upset:

```
121     # If the input is bad, fuss and skip
122     if (not defined($pattern)) {
123         print "Illegal input $line\n";
124         next;
125     }
```

The script now grabs the main web page for the entry (i.e., http://www.dilbert.com). This page contains a link to the image, which is what you really want:

```
127     # Get the text page which points to the image page
128     my $text_page = get($page);
129
130     if (not defined($text_page)) {
131         print "Could not download $page\n";
132         next;
133     }
```

You have the page; now you need to extract the links so you can attempt to find one that matches your pattern. Fortunately, there is a Perl module that chews up web pages and spits out links. It's called HTML::SimpleLinkExtor. Using this module, you get a set of image links:

```
135     # Create a decoder for this page
136     my $decoder = HTML::SimpleLinkExtor->new();
137     $decoder->parse($text_page);
138
```

```
139     # Get the image links
140     my @links = $decoder->img();
```

Now all you have to do is check each link against your regular expression to see if it matches. Perl performs this amazing feat with one statement:

```
141     my @matches = grep /$pattern/, @links;
```

At this point, you may have zero, one, or more matches. Zero matches means that your regular expression is bad. Here's how to tell the user about it and list all the URLs you did find so they can correct the problem:

```
143     if ($#matches == -1) {
144         print "Nothing matched pattern for $name\n";
145         print " Pattern: $pattern\n";
146         foreach my $cur_link (@links) {
147             print "      $cur_link\n";
148         }
149         next;
150     }
```

This produces the very verbose error message you saw earlier. (Incidentally, that error message was cut to 15 percent of its real length.)

The next thing you look for is multiple matches. If you have multiple image links that match your expression, you download them all. The do_file function handles the downloading (see the following code), and all you have to do is call it. You use an index for each call to tell do_file to use different names for each image:

```
151     if ($#matches != 0) {
152         print "Multiple matches\n";
153         my $index = 1;
154         foreach my $cur_link (@matches) {
155             print "      $cur_link\n";
156             do_file($name, $page, $cur_link, $index);
157             ++$index;
158         }
159         next;
160     }
```

The only case you haven't handled yet is the one in which only one URL matches. For that, the processing is very simple; it is just a call to do_file:

```
161     # One match
162     do_file($name, $page, $matches[0], undef);
```

The do_file function does the actual work of getting the image. The first thing it does is compute the extension of the file you are going to write. The extension will be the same as the URL; if the URL has no extension, you default to .jpg:

```
33    # Try and get the extension of the file from the link
34    $link =~ /(\.[^\$\.]*)$/;
35
36    # Define the extension of the file
37    my $ext;
38    if (defined($1)) {
39        $ext = $1;
40    } else {
41        $ext = ".jpg";
42    }
```

Now comes the only tricky part of your code. You have a relative link and you need to turn it into an absolute one. Perl has a package for just about everything, but you have to know what to ask for. The language used for specifying web pages is HTML and the protocol used for web communication is called HTTP. Turns out that the package to transform relative links into absolute ones is under neither of the two names.

Instead, it's filed under URI, for Uniform Resource Indicator. This is the name of the format used to specify links. So you use the URI package to turn your relative link into an absolute one:

```
44    my $uri = URI->new($link);
45    my $abs_link = $uri->abs($page);
```

Next you get the header of the image. This first thing this tells you is whether or not the link is broken. (On my favorite editorial cartoon site, there is frequently trouble keeping the servers up.) Here's the code:

```
47    # Get the heading information of the link
48    # (and the modification time goes into $2);
49    my @head = head($abs_link->as_string());
50    if ($#head == -1) {
51        print "$name Broken link: ",
52            $abs_link->as_string(), "\n";
53        return;
54    }
```

The head function of the LWP::Simple module returns the document type, length, modification time, and other information. The modification time is in field number 2. This is checked against the modification time of the last page you downloaded.

If they are the same, you skip this page:

```
55    if (defined($file_info{$name})) {
56        # If we've downloaded this one before
57        if ($head[2] == $file_info{$name}) {
58            print "Skipping $name\n";
59            return;
60        }
61    }
```

A new comic has arrived. Store its modification time for future reference:

```
62    # Set the file information
63    $file_info{$name} = $head[2];
```

Now download the comic and write it out:

```
71    my $raw_data = get($abs_link->as_string());
...
83    if (not open(OUT_FILE, ">$out_name")) {
84        print "Unable to create $out_name\n";
85        return;
86    }
87    binmode OUT_FILE;
88    print OUT_FILE $raw_data;
89    close OUT_FILE;
```

After all the files are closed, the only thing left is a little post-download cleanup. All you need to do is write out the file information (filename, modification date pairs) so you will download only the new stuff on the next run:

```
165 open INFO_FILE, ">$info_file" or
166     die("Could not create $info_file");
167
168 foreach my $cur_name (sort keys %file_info) {
169     print INFO_FILE "$cur_name  $file_info{$cur_name}\n";
170 }
171 close (INFO_FILE);
```

Hacking the Script

Although the script is designed for comics, it can be used any time you need to grab a web page, locate a link, and get content.

Another neat trick would be to not only download the data but also create a web page that displays all your new comics. That way, you create your own morning paper that consists of nothing but comics. After all, comics are the only useful part of the paper. With a little Perl, you can create the perfect web paper: all comics and no news.

6

UNIX SYSTEM ADMINISTRATION

Perl was designed to be a simple language to let a system administrator perform everyday tasks easily. It is ideal for creating simple scripts to automate the drudgery that is system administration.

#20 Fixing Bad Filenames

In the beginning there was the command line—and the filename had form and consistency. Then came the GUI-based file manager. And people could put just about anything they wanted to in a filename. This may look nice in the GUI, but it creates real problems for those of us who still use the command line.

For example, I've had to deal with files with names that looked like this:

```
Fibber&Molly [10-1-47] "Fibber's lost $" (v\g snd!).mp3
```

Now I count no fewer than 17 nasty characters in that string that require special handling. So if I want to play from the command line I must type this:

```
$ mpg123 Fibber\&Molly\ \[10-1-47\]\ "Fibber\'s\ lost\ \$"\ \(v\\g snd\!\).mp3
```

It would be nice if there was a program that would take mean filenames and get rid of all the mean characters. That is what this script does.

The Code

```perl
 1 #!/usr/bin/perl
 2 foreach my $file_name (@ARGV)
 3 {
 4     # Compute the new name
 5     my $new_name = $file_name;
 6
 7     $new_name =~ s/[ \t]/_/g;
 8     $new_name =~ s/[\(\)\[\]<>\\]/x/g;
 9     $new_name =~ s/[\'\`]/=/g;
10     $new_name =~ s/\&/_and_/g;
11     $new_name =~ s/\$/_dol_/g;
12     $new_name =~ s/;/:/g;
13
14     # Make sure the names are different
15     if ($file_name ne $new_name)
16     {
17         # If a file already exists by that name
18         # compute a new name.
19         if (-f $new_name)
20         {
21             my $ext = 0;
22
23             while (-f $new_name.".".$ext)
24             {
25                 $ext++;
26             }
27             $new_name = $new_name.".".$ext;
28         }
29         print "$file_name -> $new_name\n";
30         rename($file_name, $new_name);
31     }
32 }
33
```

Running the Script

To run the script, just specify the bad filenames on the command line:

```
$ fix-names.pl Fibb*
```

(Wildcards work very nicely when it comes to dealing with rotten filenames. This wildcard matches the bad filename used as an example.)

The Results

```
Fibber&Molly [10-1-47] "Fibber's lost $" (v\g snd!).mp3 ->
Fibber_and_Molly_x10-1-47x_"Fibber=s_lost__dol_"_xvxg_snd!x.mp3
```

How It Works

The script loops through each file on the command line:

```
2 foreach my $file_name (@ARGV)
```

It then computes a new filename by replacing all the bad stuff in the name with something typeable. For example, the first substitution changes all spaces and tabs to _. An underscore may not be a space, but it looks like one:

```
7     $new_name =~ s/[ \t]/_/g;
```

A similar edit is applied for all the other bad things you see in filenames:

```
8     $new_name =~ s/[\(\)\[\]<>]/x/g;
9     $new_name =~ s/[\'\`]/=/g;
10    $new_name =~ s/\&/_and_/g;
11    $new_name =~ s/\$/_dol_/g;
12    $new_name =~ s/;/:/g;
```

Next, make sure that the name actually changed. If it didn't, there's no work to be done since the filename is already sane.

```
14    # Make sure the names are different
15    if ($file_name ne $new_name)
16    {
```

Renaming will fail if a file with the new name already exists. To avoid this problem, check to see if you are about to have a name collision, and if one is eminent, change your filename. This is done by adding a numerical extension to the name.

In other words, if you are renaming the file to the_file and the_file exists, try the_file.0, the_file.1, the_file.2 until you find a name that won't cause trouble:

```
17        # If a file already exists by that name
18        # compute a new name.
19        if (-f $new_name)
20        {
```

```
21          my $ext = 0;
22
23          while (-f $new_name.".".$ext)
24          {
25              $ext++;
26          }
27          $new_name = $new_name.".".$ext;
28      }
```

You've gone through all the transformations; now you're ready to do the renaming:

```
29          print "$file_name -> $new_name\n";
30          rename($file_name, $new_name);
```

The filename is fixed and you're ready for the next one.

Hacking the Script

This script doesn't get rid of all the bad characters. It just eliminates the ones I've seen in the files I've downloaded. You can easily add to the script to take care of any bad stuff you find. I've also tried to leave as much of the original filename as intact as possible—for example, mapping $ to _dol_. If you want a different mapping, feel free to change the script.

> During my college days, I got into a contest with one of my fellow computer science students. My goal was to create a file in his directory that he could not delete. And I created some files with some mean names, such as "delete.me " (note the trailing space), "-f", and others with special characters in them. Eventually he learned how to delete them all.
>
> In the end, I exploited a system bug that allowed me to stick the file seven levels deep on a system in which the directory nesting was limited to six. The operating system refused to let him even look at the file, much less delete it. (The OS was the DecSystem-10, if you're interested.)

#21 Mass File Renaming

The standard Unix/Linux rename command allows you to change the name of only one file at a time. (You can move multiple files from one directory to another but only really rename one.) If you want to rename multiple files at one time, you'll need a Perl script.

The Code

```
1 #!/usr/bin/perl
2 use strict;
3 use warnings;
```

```
 4
 5 use Getopt::Std;
 6 use vars qw/$opt_n $opt_v $opt_e/;
 7
 8 if (not getopts("nve:")) {
 9     die("Bad options");
10 }
11 if (not defined($opt_e)) {
12     die("Required option -e missing");
13 }
14
15 foreach my $file_name (@ARGV)
16 {
17     # Compute the new name
18     my $new_name = $file_name;
19
20     # Perform the substitution
21     eval "\$new_name =~ s$opt_e";
22
23     # Make sure the names are different
24     if ($file_name ne $new_name)
25     {
26         # If a file already exists by that name
27         # compute a new name.
28         if (-f $new_name)
29         {
30             my $ext = 0;
31
32             while (-f $new_name.".".$ext)
33             {
34                 $ext++;
35             }
36             $new_name = $new_name.".".$ext;
37         }
38         if ($opt_v) {
39             print "$file_name -> $new_name\n";
40         }
41         if (not defined($opt_n)) {
42             rename($file_name, $new_name);
43         }
44     }
45 }
46
```

Running the Script

The script takes the following parameters:

>   -e '*/old/new/flags*'   Editing pattern (as used in the Perl "=~ s..."
>   command).

-n Don't rename, just pretend to.

-v Print out information on what's going on.

Any other parameters are files that need renaming.
Example:

```
$ mass-rename.pl -e '/\.3/\.MP3/' test/D*.3
```

The Results

```
test/Dragnet_50_1_14.3 -> test/Dragnet_50_1_14.mp3
test/Dragnet_50_1_21.3 -> test/Dragnet_50_1_21.mp3
test/Dragnet_50_1_7.3 -> test/Dragnet_50_1_7.mp3
```

How It Works

The script begins by parsing the command line. For this, the module
Getopt::Std is used:

```
 8 if (not getopts("nve:")) {
 9     die("Bad options");
10 }
```

The -e option is required, so you check for it:

```
11 if (not defined($opt_e)) {
12     die("Required option -e missing");
13 }
```

Now you process each file:

```
15 foreach my $file_name (@ARGV)
16 {
17     # Compute the new name
18     my $new_name = $file_name;
```

The old name is turned into the new name with an eval operator. This
function treats its argument as a Perl statement and executes it. The function
is a little tricky to work with.

In this program, the editing pattern (the -e parameter) is placed in the
string. You want the results to be assigned to $new_name. If you just put this
variable inside the string without quoting, you'd get a syntax error. That's
because if you don't escape the $, eval will use the value of $new_name as part of
the command. Since you want the variable itself, literally $new_name, the dollar
sign must be escaped:

```
20     # Perform the substitution
21     eval "\$new_name =~ s$opt_e";
```

After you have the new name, you handle name collisions using the same method used in the previous script.

Finally, you print out what you are going to do (if -v is specified) and do it (if -n is not specified):

```
38          if ($opt_v) {
39              print "$file_name -> $new_name\n";
40          }
41          if (not defined($opt_n)) {
42              rename($file_name, $new_name);
43          }
```

Hacking the Script

This script is designed for people who know what they are doing. As such, it lacks many safety checks that would normally be found in an end-user script. For example, the substitute expression is not validated and there is no interactive mode to confirm each change before it takes effect.

Also, the script was designed to rename files. With a little work, it can be adapted to perform a mass relinking of symbolic links. Such a script might be useful when a disk is replaced and you need to modify all the symbolic links that referenced the old one.

This script does show how a good Perl script can eliminate a lot of repetitive drudgery from administering your system.

#22 Checking Symbolic Links

Symbolic links are nice, but they can be a real pain when they get broken. This script checks a directory tree for symbolic links and makes sure they are good.

The Code

```
1 #!/usr/bin/perl
2 use strict;
3 use warnings;
4
5 use File::Find ();
6
7 use vars qw/*name *dir *prune/;
8 *name   = *File::Find::name;
9 *dir    = *File::Find::dir;
10 *prune  = *File::Find::prune;
11
12 # Traverse desired filesystems
13 File::Find::find({wanted => \&wanted}, @ARGV);
14 exit;
15
```

```
16
17 sub wanted {
18     if (-l $_) {
19         my @stat = stat($_);
20         if ($#stat == -1) {
21             print "Bad link: $name\n";
22         }
23     }
24 }
25
```

Running the Script

The script takes a directory or set of directories as arguments. It then scans each directory tree and reports any bad links, as in this example:

```
$ sym-check.pl the_dir
```

The Results

```
Bad link: the_dir/link_to_nowhere
```

How It Works

The File::Find module is used to search the directory trees. The find function traverses each file in the directory tree and calls the wanted subroutine for each of them:

```
12 # Traverse desired filesystems
13 File::Find::find({wanted => \&wanted}, @ARGV);
```

The wanted function first checks to see if the file is a symbolic link (-l) then does a stat of the file. The stat function returns information on the actual file, not the symbolic link. (If you want link information, use the lstat function.)

If the symbolic link is broken, the stat function will return an empty list. When that occurs, you print an error message:

```
17 sub wanted {
18     if (-l $_) {
19         my @stat = stat($_);
20         if ($#stat == -1) {
21             print "Bad link: $name\n";
22         }
23     }
```

```
24 }
25
```

One more thing: The variable $_ is the name of the file relative to the current directory. The find function changes the directory, so although $_ works for things like the -l operator and the stat function, it won't do when it comes to printing the error for the user. For that you need the full name of the file, which is contained in $name.

Hacking the Script

The script was originally written by the find2perl command. The wanted function was then edited to make it work the way I wanted it to. The File::Find module can be used to locate lots of things. All you need to do is figure out what you are looking for and hack the script to find it.

Another hack would be to change the script to interactively fix the broken links or remove them. The script is good at finding problems. What you do with them is up to you.

#23 Disk Space Alarm

I ran out of disk space today. I was working on a program that produced a number of huge core dumps and filled up my disk. Of course I didn't notice it until I started to do a compile and found that my object files were getting truncated. It would have been nice to learn of the problem sooner. As it turned out, because the build broke, I was forced to clean out the core files and restart the build from scratch.

This script tells everyone when disk space is low.

The Code

```
 1 #!/usr/bin/perl
 2 use strict;
 3 use warnings;
 4
 5 use Filesys::DiskSpace;
 6
 7 my $space_limit = 5;    # Less than 5%, scream
 8
 9 if ($#ARGV == -1) {
10     print "Usage is $0 <fs> [<fs>....]\n";
11     exit (8);
12 }
13
14 # Loop through each directory in the
15 # list.
16 foreach my $dir (@ARGV) {
17     # Get the file system information
```

```
18    my ($fs_type, $fs_desc, $used,
19        $avail, $fused, $favail) = df $dir;
20
21    # The amount of free space
22    my $per_free = (($avail) / ($avail+$used)) * 100.0;
23    if ($per_free < $space_limit) {
24        # Tailor this command to meet your needs
25        my $msg = sprintf(
26          "WARNING: Free space on $dir ".
27              "has dropped to %0.2f%%",
28          $per_free);
29        system("wall '$msg'");
30    }
31 }
32
```

Running the Script

You'll probably want to set up some sort of cron job to run the script according to a schedule. But to run it manually, just put the name of one or more directories to check on the command line:

```
$ disk.pl /home
```

The Results

If there is space on the drive, nothing will happen. But if you are out of space, everyone on the system will get a message that looks something like this:

```
Broadcast message from root(pts/6) (Thu Oct 28 20:19:13 2004):

WARNING: Free space on /home has dropped to 4.00%
```

How It Works

The script loops through each directory on the command line checking for space:

```
16 foreach my $dir (@ARGV) {
```

The Filesys::DiskSpace module tells you how much space is being used on the disk. From this, you can easily compute the percentage that is free:

```
17    # Get the file system information
18    my ($fs_type, $fs_desc, $used,
19        $avail, $fused, $favail) = df $dir;
20
```

```
21    # The amount of free space
22    my $per_free = (($avail) / ($avail+$used)) * 100.0;
```

Now you check to see if the free space falls below the specified limit:

```
23    if ($per_free < $space_limit) {
24        # Tailor this command to meet your needs
```

You have a space emergency. Use the system wall command to send out a panic message to everyone.

```
25        my $msg = sprintf(
26            "WARNING: Free space on $dir ".
27                "has dropped to %0.2f%%",
28            $per_free);
29        system("wall '$msg'");
30    }
31 }
```

Hacking the Script

The free space limit is hard-coded to 5 percent. If the space falls below that, you get the message. This number can easily be changed to fit your situation.

As written, the script just warns everybody. But you can do more than just yell when you're in trouble. For example, the script could clean up the temporary directories, remove outdated log files, or remove old core files.

The script is good at discovering when a problem occurs and giving you a chance to handle it any way you want to.

#24 Adding a User

There are lots of programs out there to add a user to a Unix or Linux system. Just fill in the blanks, click the Add button, and you're done. Why write a script to do it?

If you're adding one user, this script is useless. But if you have to add several thousand, it can be very useful as the back end to a much larger batch system. (For example, if you were working at a university, you could connect this script to one that reads a list of incoming students and creates accounts for them automatically.)

The Code

```
1 #!/usr/bin/perl
2 use strict;
3 use warnings;
4 use Fcntl ':flock'; # import LOCK_* constants
5
```

```
 6 # The file we are going to change
 7 my $pw_file = "/etc/passwd";
 8 my $group_file = "/etc/group";
 9 my $shadow_file = "/etc/shadow";
10
11 # Get the login name for the user
12 my $login;        # Login name
13 print "Login: ";
14 $login = <STDIN>;
15 chomp($login);
16
17 if ($login !~ /[A-Z_a-z0-9]+/) {
18     die("No login specified");
19 }
20
21 open PW_FILE, "<$pw_file" or die("Could not read $pw_file");
22 # Lock the file for the duration of the program
23 flock PW_FILE, LOCK_EX;
24
25 # Check login information
26 my $check_uid = getpwnam($login);
27 if (defined($check_uid)) {
28     print "$login already exists\n";
29     exit (8);
30 }
31
32 # Find the highest UID.  We'll insert a new one at "highest+1".
33 my @pw_info = <PW_FILE>;
34
35 my $uid = 0;     # UID for the user
36
37 # Find biggest user
38 foreach my $cur_pw (@pw_info) {
39     my @fields = split /:/, $cur_pw;
40     if ($fields[2] > 60000) {
41         next;
42     }
43     if ($fields[2] > $uid) {
44         $uid = $fields[2];
45     }
46 }
47 $uid++;
48
49 # Each user gets his own group.
50 my $gid = $uid;
51
52 # Default home directory
53 my $home_dir = "/home/$login";
54
55 print "Full Name: ";
```

```
56 my $full_name = <STDIN>;
57 chomp($full_name);
58
59 my $shell = ""; # The shell to use
60 while (! -f $shell) {
61     print "Shell: ";
62     $shell = <STDIN>;
63     chomp($shell);
64 }
65
66 print "Setting up account for: $login [$full_name]\n";
67
68 open PW_FILE, ">>$pw_file" or
69     die("Could not append to $pw_file");
70 print PW_FILE
71 "${login}:x:${uid}:${gid}:${full_name}:${home_dir}:$shell\n";
72
73 open GROUP_FILE, ">>$group_file" or
74     die("Could not append to $group_file");
75 print GROUP_FILE "${login}:x:${gid}:$login\n";
76 close GROUP_FILE;
77
78 open SHADOW, ">>$shadow_file" or
79     die("Could not append to $shadow_file");
80 print SHADOW "${login}:*:11647:0:99999:7:::\n";
81 close SHADOW;
82
83 # Create the home directory and populate it
84 mkdir($home_dir);
85 chmod(0755, $home_dir);
86 system("cp -R /etc/skel/.[a-zA-Z]* $home_dir");
87 system("find $home_dir -print ".
88       "-exec chown ${login}:${login} {} \\;");
89
90 # Set the password for the user
91 print "Setting password\n";
92 system("passwd $login");
93
94 flock(PW_FILE,LOCK_UN);
95 close(PW_FILE);
```

Running the Script

The script is interactive. It runs with no parameters and prompts you for all input.

NOTE   *This script is system specific and can potentially damage your system. You should take the usual precautions such as backing up critical files, checking the code to make sure it does the correct thing on your system, and testing it out on an experimental computer first.*

The Results

```
# add_user.pl
Login: jruser
Full Name: J  . R. User
Shell: /bin/bash
Setting up account for: jruser [J. R. User]
/home/jruser
/home/jruser/.bash_logout
/home/jruser/.bash_profile
/home/jruser/.bashrc
/home/jruser/.mailcap
/home/jruser/.screenrc
Setting password
Changing password for user jruser.
New UNIX password:
Retype new UNIX password:
passwd: all authentication tokens updated successfully.
```

How It Works

Actually setting up a user is a fairly simple process. All you do is edit a few files. That being said, get the editing wrong and you can badly screw up your system and possibly prevent anyone from logging in.

The script performs the following steps:

1. Get the username from the operator.
2. Lock the password file.
3. Make sure the user doesn't exist.
4. Generate a user ID (UID) for the user.
5. Create an entry in /etc/passwd.
6. Create an entry in /etc/groups.
7. Create an entry in /etc/shadow.
8. Create the user's home directory.
9. Copy all of the files in the skeleton directory (/etc/skel) into the new home directory.
10. Change ownership of all these files so that they are owned by the user.
11. Call the passwd program to set the initial password for the user.
12. Unlock the /etc/passwd file.

Each one of these steps is simple. Remembering them all is not.

Let's see how the script accomplishes these steps:

1. Get the username from the operator. Also validate it to make sure that it's legal:

```
11 # Get the login name for the user
12 my $login;        # Login name
13 print "Login: ";
14 $login = <STDIN>;
15 chomp($login);
16
17 if ($login !~ /[A-Z_a-z0-9]+/) {
18     die("No login specified");
19 }
```

2. Lock the password file. This prevents anyone else from adding the user while you work on the file:

```
21 open PW_FILE, "<$pw_file" or die("Could not read $pw_file");
22 # Lock the file for the duration of the program
23 flock PW_FILE, LOCK_EX;
```

3. Make sure that the user doesn't exist. This is accomplished by getting the UID of the new user. Since the new user doesn't exist, this should fail and return an undefined value:

```
25 # Check login information
26 my $check_uid = getpwnam($login);
27 if (defined($check_uid)) {
28     print "$login already exists\n";
29     exit (8);
30 }
```

4. Generate a UID for the user. The program goes through the password file and finds the highest UID that's less than 60000. The 60000 limit is there because there are some special UIDs that have a high number. For example, the account nobody has a UID of 65534.

    The UID for the new user will come after the highest one you find (line 47):

```
32 # Find the highest UID.  We'll use "highest+1" for our new user.
33 my @pw_info = <PW_FILE>;
34
35 my $uid = 0;     # UID for the user
36
37 # Find biggest user
38 foreach my $cur_pw (@pw_info) {
39     my @fields = split /:/, $cur_pw;
```

```
40    if ($fields[2] > 60000) {
41        next;
42    }
43    if ($fields[2] > $uid) {
44        $uid = $fields[2];
45    }
46 }
47 $uid++;
```

5. The script gets some additional information needed for the password entry. It also assumes that GUI = UID. In other words, each user has their own group. Once this information is obtained, you can create an entry in /etc/passwd:

```
68 open PW_FILE, ">>$pw_file" or
69    die("Could not append to $pw_file");
70 print PW_FILE
71 "${login}:x:${uid}:${gid}:${full_name}:${home_dir}:$shell\n";
```

6. Create an entry in /etc/groups:

```
73 open GROUP_FILE, ">>$group_file" or
74    die("Could not append to $group_file");
75 print GROUP_FILE "${login}:x:${gid}:$login\n";
76 close GROUP_FILE;
```

7. Create an entry in /etc/shadow:

```
78 open SHADOW, ">>$shadow_file" or
79    die("Could not append to $shadow_file");
80 print SHADOW "${login}:*:11647:0:99999:7:::\n";
81 close SHADOW;
```

8. Create the user's home directory:

```
83 # Create the home directory and populate it
84 mkdir($home_dir);
85 chmod(0755, $home_dir);
```

9. Copy all the files in the skeleton directory (/etc/skel) into the new home directory:

```
86 system("cp -R /etc/skel/.[a-zA-Z]* $home_dir");
```

10. Change the ownership of all these files so that they are owned by the user:

```
87 system("find $home_dir -print ".
88        "-exec chown ${login}:${login} {} \\;");
```

11. Call the `passwd` program to set the initial password for the user:

```
90 # Set the password for the user
91 print "Setting password\n";
92 system("passwd $login");
```

12. Unlock the /etc/passwd file:

```
94 flock(PW_FILE,LOCK_UN);
```

Hacking the Script

The script gets the username and other information through interactive prompts. But there's nothing to prevent it from getting that information from a configuration file or even a list of incoming students. The script does the job; how you feed the beast is up to you.

#25 Disabling a User

One of your students has violated the no hacking policy repeatedly. So you're going to give him a time-out for a few weeks and turn off his account.

NOTE *This script is system dependent. Don't run it on your system until you've inspected it and know it fits your operation.*

The Code

```
1 #!/usr/bin/perl
2 use strict;
3 use warnings;
4
5 if ($#ARGV != 0) {
6     print STDERR "Usage is $0 <account>\n";
7 }
8
9 my $user = $ARGV[0];
10
11 # Get login information
12 my $uid = getpwnam($user);
13 if (not defined($uid)) {
14     print "$user does not exist.\n";
15     exit (8);
16 }
17
18 system("passwd -l $user");
19 my @who = `who`;
20 @who = grep /^$user\s/,@who;
21 foreach my $cur_who (@who) {
```

```
22     my @words = split /\s+/, $cur_who;
23     my $tty = $words[1];
24
25     if (not open(YELL, ">>/dev/$tty")) {
26         next;
27     }
28     print YELL <<EOF ;
29 *********************************************************
30 URGENT NOTICE FROM THE SYSTEM ADMINISTRATOR
31
32 This account is being suspended.  You are going to be
33 logged out in 10 seconds.  Please exit immediately.
34 *********************************************************
35 EOF
36     close YELL;
37 }
38 sleep(10);
39 my @procs = `ps -u $user`;
40 shift @procs;
41 foreach my $cur_proc (@procs) {
42     $cur_proc =~ /(\d+)/;
43     if (defined($1)) {
44         print "Killing $1\n";
45         kill 9, $1;
46     }
47 }
```

Running the Script

The script takes one parameter, the username:

```
# dis_user.pl jruser
```

The Results

```
Locking password for user jruser
passwd: Success
```

If the user is logged in, he's about to get a shock. A message appears on his terminal:

```
*********************************************************
URGENT NOTICE FROM THE SYSTEM ADMINISTRATOR

This account is being suspended.  You are going to be
logged out in 10 seconds.  Please exit immediately.
*********************************************************
```

Ten seconds later he is logged out whether he wants to be or not.

How It Works

The script first checks to see if the user exists using the same getpwnam method we used in add_user.pl.

It then calls the passwd program to lock the user out:

```
18 system("passwd -l $user");
```

Next it uses the who command to see if the user is logged in. If you find the user, you determine which terminal he's on:

```
19 my @who = `who`;
20 @who = grep /^$user\s/,@who;
21 foreach my $cur_who (@who) {
22     my @words = split /\s+/, $cur_who;
23     my $tty = $words[1];
```

Now you open that terminal and yell at the user. Actually, you just write out a message to him:

```
25     if (not open(YELL, ">>/dev/$tty")) {
26         next;
27     }
28     print YELL <<EOF ;
29 ********************************************************
30 URGENT NOTICE FROM THE SYSTEM ADMINISTRATOR
31
32 This account is being suspended.  You are going to be
33 logged out in 10 seconds.  Please exit immediately.
34 ********************************************************
35 EOF
36     close YELL;
37 }
```

You told the user you'd give him 10 seconds. Now do so:

```
38 sleep(10);
```

Next the ps is used to get all the processes that belong to the user. The first line of the ps output is removed because it is a heading. You process the rest:

```
39 my @procs = `ps -u $user`;
40 shift @procs;
```

The ps output is parsed and you determine the process ID of each process owned by the user. This information is used to send a kill to each process, thus throwing the user off the system with extreme force.

```
41 foreach my $cur_proc (@procs) {
42     $cur_proc =~ /(\d+)/;
43     if (defined($1)) {
44         print "Killing $1\n";
45         kill 9, $1;
46     }
47 }
```

At this point, the user is gone and the account disabled.

Hacking the Script

This script depends on a number of outside commands such as ps and who. The output of these commands varies from system to system, so it may take a little hacking to get this script to work on your system.

#26 Deleting a User

Your user has been disabled. Now get rid of him.

WARNING   *This script can destroy data and depends not only on the operating system you are using, but also on your system administration policies. Please inspect it before use.*

The Code

```
1 #!/usr/bin/perl
2 use strict;
3 use warnings;
4 use Fcntl ':flock'; # import LOCK_* constants
5
6 if ($#ARGV != 0) {
7     print STDERR "Usage is $0 <user>\n";
8     exit (8);
9 }
10
11 my $user = $ARGV[0];
12
13 sub edit_file($)
14 {
15     my $file = shift;
16
17     open IN_FILE, "<$file" or
18         die("Could not open $file for input");
```

```perl
19
20     open OUT_FILE, ">$file.new" or
21         die("Could not open $file.new for output");
22
23     while (1) {
24         my $line = <IN_FILE>;
25         if (not defined($line)) {
26             last;
27         }
28         if ($line =~ /^$user/) {
29             next;
30         }
31         print OUT_FILE $line;
32     }
33     close (IN_FILE);
34     close (OUT_FILE);
35     unlink("$file.bak");
36     rename("$file", "$file.bak");
37     rename("$file.new", $file);
38 }
39
40 my @info = getpwnam($user);
41 if (@info == -1) {
42     die("No such user $user");
43 }
44
45 open PW_FILE, "</etc/passwd" or
46     die("Could not read /etc/passwd");
47
48 # Lock the file for the duration of the program
49 flock PW_FILE, LOCK_EX;
50
51 edit_file("/etc/group");
52 edit_file("/etc/shadow");
53
54 if ($info[7] eq "/home/$user") {
55     system("rm -rf /home/$user");
56 } else {
57     print "User has a non-standard home directory.\n";
58     print "Please remove manually.\n";
59     print "Directory = $info[7]\n";
60 }
61 print "User $user -- Deleted\n";
62
63 edit_file("/etc/passwd");
64
65 flock(PW_FILE,LOCK_UN);
66 close(PW_FILE);
```

Running the Script

The user to be deleted is specified on the command line:

```
# del_user.pl jruser
```

The Results

```
# del_user.pl jruser
User jruser -- Deleted
```

How It Works

The script edits the files /etc/group, /etc/shadow, and /etc/passwd to remove any reference to the user. This is done by reading the files one at a time and looking for lines beginning with the username and a colon (:). Such lines are discarded.

The edit_file function reads from the file (e.g., /etc/group) and writes a file with the same name and a .new extension (e.g., /etc/group.new). After it completes, it performs the following renames:

```
/etc/group -> /etc/group.bak
/etc/group.new -> /etc/group
```

The script also deletes the user's home directory using the following code:

```
54 if ($info[7] eq "/home/$user") {
55     system("rm -rf /home/$user");
56 } else {
57     print "User has a non-standard home directory.\n";
58     print "Please remove manually.\n";
59     print "Directory = $info[7]\n";
```

This code performs a very important check. If the user has a nonstandard home directory, the script won't remove it. This is to avoid the "sccs" problem. The original problem occurred when an administrator discovered that there was a user "sccs" who had never logged in. So he decided to remove the account.

The first thing he did was remove the home directory of the user using this command:

```
# rm -rf ~sccs
(Don't do this!!!)
```

Turns out that "sccs" was a system account created for system use. The home directory was set to /. In other words, removing the home directory of "sccs" was the equivalent to this:

```
# rm -rf /
```

If that command doesn't scare you, then you don't know Unix. The command wipes out your entire disk. Fortunately, the administrator had recent backups and an understanding wife who didn't get angry when he didn't come home till 3:00 the next morning (restores take time)!

To avoid the "sccs" problem, only delete directories if they are in a safe place. If there is anything funny, skip this step and let the administrator do it manually.

One final note: The last file edited is /etc/passwd. That's because this is the file you lock when adding or removing users. When the file is renamed as part of the editing process, the lock is effectively nullified. So editing this file must be the last step.

Hacking the Script

Again, there are other programs out there that can delete a single user better than this one. But if you have to delete lots of users, this script can serve as the prototype for a mass deletion program.

#27 Killing a Stuck Process

I used to work for a large company that used one of the worst build systems I've ever seen. One of the biggest problems was that if you logged out without properly shutting down your development environment, one of the background programs would get stuck in the run state, trying continuously to connect to a front end that wasn't there.

As a result, you'd find several high-performance build machines slowed down by useless stuck processes. This meant that you had to spend time and effort tracking down the user or a system administrator to kill the rogue process.

Perl lets you do automatically what used to be done manually; in this case, identify and kill stuck programs.

The Code

```
 1 #!/usr/bin/perl
 2 use strict;
 3 use warnings;
 4 #
 5 # Kill stuck processes
 6 #
 7 # A stuck process is one that accumulates over an
 8 # hour of CPU time
 9 #
10 # NOTE: This program is designed to be nice.
11 #       It will send a "nice" kill (SIGTERM) to the process
12 #       which asks the process to terminate.  If you change
13 #       this to 'KILL' (SIGKILL) the process will be FORCED
14 #       to terminate.
15 #
```

```
16 #       Also no killing is done without operator interaction.
17 #
18 #       If you find that some "user" routinely gets a process
19 #       stuck, then you may wish to change this and always
20 #       kill his long running processes automatically.
21 #
22 my $max_time = 60*60;   # Max time a process can have
23                         # in seconds
24
25 # Process names which are allowed to last a long time
26 my %exclude_cmds = (
27     # Avoid KDE stuff, they really take time
28     'kdeinit:' => 1,
29     '/usr/bin/krozat.kss' => 1
30 );
31 # Users to avoid killing
32 my %exclude_users = (
33     root => 1,
34     postfix => 1
35 );
36 # Use the PS command to get bad people
37 #WARNING: Linux specific ps command
38 my @ps = `ps -A -eo cputime,pcpu,pid,user,cmd`;
39 shift @ps;       # Get rid of the title line
40 chomp(@ps);
41
42 # Loop through each process
43 foreach my $cur_proc (@ps) {
44
45     # The fields of the process (as names)
46     my ($cputime,$pcpu,$pid,$user,$cmd) =
47         split /\s+/, $cur_proc;
48
49     $cputime =~ /(\d+):(\d+):(\d+)/;
50     # CPU time in seconds instead of formatted
51     my $cpu_seconds = $1*60*60 + $2*60 + $3;
52
53     if ($cpu_seconds < $max_time) {
54         next;
55     }
56
57     if (defined($exclude_users{$user})) {
58         print "User excluded: $cur_proc\n";
59         next;
60     }
61
62     if (defined($exclude_cmds{$cmd})) {
63         print "User excluded: $cur_proc\n";
64         next;
65     }
```

```
66
67    # Someone's stuck.  Ask for the kill
68    print "STUCK: $cur_proc\n";
69    print "Kill? ";
70    my $answer = <STDIN>;
71
72    if ($answer =~ /^[Yy]/) {
73        # We kill nicely.
74        kill 'TERM', $pid;
75        print "Sent a TERM signal to the process\n";
76    }
77 }
```

Running the Script

The script should be run by root every so often to kill bad processes.

The Results

```
STUCK: mpg123
Kill? y
Sent a TERM signal to the process
```

How It Works

The program starts by running the ps command to get a list of processes:

```
36 # Use the PS command to get bad people
37 #WARNING: Linux specific ps command
38 my @ps = `ps -A -eo cputime,pcpu,pid,user,cmd`;
39 shift @ps;        # Get rid of the title line
40 chomp(@ps);
```

Now you loop through each process to see if you need to do something about it:

```
42 # Loop through each process
43 foreach my $cur_proc (@ps) {
```

You break apart the fields for easy reference:

```
45    # The fields of the process (as names)
46    my ($cputime,$pcpu,$pid,$user,$cmd) =
47        split /\s+/, $cur_proc;
```

The CPU time is formatted as HH:MM:SS. You need to turn this into something more useful.

```
49    $cputime =~ /(\d+):(\d+):(\d+)/;
50    # CPU time in seconds instead of formatted
51    my $cpu_seconds = $1*60*60 + $2*60 + $3;
```

Now you check to see if the process has exceeded your limit:

```
53    if ($cpu_seconds < $max_time) {
54        next;
55    }
```

There are some users you don't want to touch (for example, root). If you find one, you skip this process:

```
57    if (defined($exclude_users{$user})) {
58        print "User excluded: $cur_proc\n";
59        next;
60    }
```

There are also some commands that are expected to take up time. Skip these as well:

```
62    if (defined($exclude_cmds{$cmd})) {
63        print "User excluded: $cur_proc\n";
64        next;
65    }
```

If the process passes all these checks, you interactively kill it:

```
67    # Someone's stuck.  Ask for the kill
68    print "STUCK: $cur_proc\n";
69    print "Kill? ";
70    my $answer = <STDIN>;
71
72    if ($answer =~ /^[Yy]/) {
73        # We kill nicely.
74        kill 'TERM', $pid;
75        print "Sent a TERM signal to the process\n";
76    }
77 }
```

Hacking the Script

The script depends on the output of the ps command. The output of this command varies from system to system. You'll need to customize the script for your computer.

Also, killing processes is not only a technical procedure but also a political one. In other words, what constitutes a runaway, killable process is not a technical procedure, but one of policy. Once policy is decided, you can incorporate it into this script.

7

PICTURE UTILITIES

Digital photography is replacing film. Photographs can be stored, copied, printed, and shared with very little effort and without expensive equipment.

If you take a lot of photographs, you may grow tired of the repetitive chores required to process them. A good scripting language like Perl can automate your work, giving you more time to take photographs.

#28 Image Information

Digital cameras store a lot of information about a photograph in a hidden encoding in the image. Perl can make this information visible.

The Code

```
1 #!/usr/bin/perl
2 use strict;
3 use warnings;
```

```perl
4
5 my %good = (
6     'ColorSpace' => 1,
7     'ComponentsConfiguration' => 1,
8     'DateTime' => 1,
9     'DateTimeDigitized' => 1,
10     'DateTimeOriginal' => 1,
11     'ExifImageLength' => 1,
12     'ExifImageWidth' => 1,
13     'ExifVersion' => 1,
14     'FileSource' => 1,
15     'Flash' => 1,
16     'FlashPixVersion' => 1,
17     'ISOSpeedRatings' => 1,
18     'ImageDescription' => 1,
19     'InteroperabilityIndex' => 1,
20     'InteroperabilityVersion' => 1,
21     'JPEG_Type' => 1,
22     'LightSource' => 1,
23     'Make' => 1,
24     'MeteringMode' => 1,
25     'Model' => 1,
26     'Orientation' => 1,
27     'SamplesPerPixel' => 1,
28     'Software' => 1,
29     'YCbCrPositioning' => 1,
30     'color_type' => 1,
31     'file_ext' => 1,
32     'file_media_type' => 1,
33     'height' => 1,
34     'resolution' => 1,
35     'width' => 1
36 );
37
38 use Image::Info qw(image_info);
39
40
41 foreach my $cur_file (@ARGV) {
42     my $info = image_info($cur_file);
43
44     print "$cur_file --------------------------------\n";
45     foreach my $key (sort keys %$info) {
46         if ($good{$key}) {
47             print "    $key -> $info->{$key}\n";
48         }
49     }
50 }
```

Running the Script

To run the script, just type the names of the files you're interested in on the command line.

The Results

The result is a lot of information from the photograph.

```
p2230148.jpg --------------------------------
    ColorSpace -> 1
    ComponentsConfiguration -> YCbCr
    DateTime -> 2001:02:23 18:07:45
    DateTimeDigitized -> 2001:02:23 18:07:45
    DateTimeOriginal -> 2001:02:23 18:07:45
    ExifImageLength -> 960
    ExifImageWidth -> 1280
    ExifVersion -> 0210
    FileSource -> (DSC) Digital Still Camera
    Flash -> Flash fired
    FlashPixVersion -> 0100
    ISOSpeedRatings -> 125
    ImageDescription -> OLYMPUS DIGITAL CAMERA
    InteroperabilityIndex -> R98
    InteroperabilityVersion -> 0100
    JPEG_Type -> Baseline
    LightSource -> unknown
    Make -> OLYMPUS OPTICAL CO.,LTD
    MeteringMode -> Pattern
    Model -> C960Z,D460Z
    Orientation -> top_left
    SamplesPerPixel -> 3
    Software -> v874u-74
    YCbCrPositioning -> 2
    color_type -> YCbCr
    file_ext -> jpg
    file_media_type -> image/jpeg
    height -> 960
    resolution -> 72 dpi
    width -> 1280
```

How It Works

JPEG and some other image file formats store information inside the files. Because JPEG was designed for digital cameras, a lot of this information has to do with the camera and how the photograph was taken. The Perl module Image::Info knows all about the JPEG standard for embedded information and how to extract that information.

So to get the data you want, all you do is call the `Image::Info` function `image_info` and print the results (sort of):

```
41 foreach my $cur_file (@ARGV) {
42     my $info = image_info($cur_file);
```

You need to print the results, but there is a small problem. Not all the information is scalar. Sometimes references to arrays or hash references are returned. Also, some results are binary and don't print well.

So in this program, you limit the values you print to the "good" stuff, stuff you know will print nicely:

```
45     foreach my $key (sort keys %$info) {
46         if ($good{$key}) {
47             print "    $key -> $info->{$key}\n";
48         }
49     }
50 }
```

Hacking the Script

A clever programmer could print everything. For example, the program can be hacked to detect whether or not the data is binary and transform it into something useful. You could also detect complex data values (arrays, hashes, arrays of hashes, etc.) and print them as well.

It all depends on what you want to get out of your camera. This script gets everything, but once you decide what's useful, it shouldn't be too hard to cut it down so only the good stuff is printed.

#29 Creating a Thumbnail

It's not nice to put full-size images on a web page. A small gallery of 15 pictures can take up to 40MB of space (and that's using a low-resolution camera). So most people use thumbnails that you can click to get the full picture. Almost all image manipulation programs will let you scale an image interactively. But what if you want to do it for a series of snapshots? The interactive approach is long and boring. Perl lets you automate it.

The Code

NOTE   *The code uses the `Image::Magick` module. If your operating system contains the Perl module for ImageMagick (RedHat calls it perl-ImageMagick) you'll probably want to install it from the package. Because of all the support libraries required, you might not want to download this module from CPAN. It's easier to get it from the ImageMagick website (www.imagemagick.org) and install the entire package (command-line tools, libraries, and Perl module) at once.*

```perl
1  #!/usr/bin/perl
2  use strict;
3  use warnings;
4
5  use Image::Magick;
6  use constant X_SIZE => 100;
7  use constant Y_SIZE => 150;
8
9  sub do_file($)
10 {
11     my $file = shift;   # The file to create
12                         # thumbnail of
13
14     my $image = Image::Magick->new();
15     my $status = $image->Read($file);
16     if ($status) {
17         print "Error $status\n";
18         return;
19     }
20     print "Size ", $image->Get('width'), " x ",
21         $image->Get('height'), "\n";
22
23     my $x_scale = X_SIZE / $image->Get('width');
24     my $y_scale = Y_SIZE / $image->Get('height');
25     my $scale = $x_scale;
26     if ($y_scale < $scale) {
27         $scale = $y_scale;
28     }
29     print "Scale $scale (x=$x_scale, y=$y_scale)\n";
30     my $new_x = int($image->Get('width') * $scale + 0.5);
31     my $new_y = int($image->Get('height') * $scale + 0.5);
32     print "New $new_x, $new_y\n";
33
34     $status = $image->Scale(
35         width => $new_x, height => $new_y);
36
37     if ($status) {
38         print "$status\n";
39     }
40     $status = $image->Write("_thumb/$file");
41     if ($status) {
42         print "Error $status\n";
43     }
44 }
45
46 if (! -d "_thumb") {
47     mkdir("_thumb");
```

```
48 }
49 foreach my $cur_file (@ARGV) {
50     do_file($cur_file);
51 }
```

Running the Script

To run the script, put the name of the file you want to process on the command line, as in this example:

```
$ thumb.pl p1010017.jpg
```

The Results

A scaled image of the file will be put in the directory _thumb.[1]

How It Works

The Image::Magick module lets you do all sorts of things to images:

```
5 use Image::Magick;
```

First, you create the image object and read in the file data from the full-size file:

```
14     my $image = Image::Magick->new();
15     my $status = $image->Read($file);
```

ImageMagick function calls return undef if no error occurred and an error message if one did. The following code aborts if the Read failed:

```
16     if ($status) {
17         print "Error $status\n";
18         return;
19     }
```

The Get function returns information about the image. In this case, you want to know the size of the image so you can compute the scale factor:

```
23     my $x_scale = X_SIZE / $image->Get('width');
24     my $y_scale = Y_SIZE / $image->Get('height');
```

You now have two scale factors. We need to decide which one we are going to use for our picture. If the picture is tall and skinny, we'll need to use the $y_scale. If the picture is short and fat, we'll need to use $x_scale. The smaller

---

[1] The directory used to be <dot>thumb until I tried to burn it into a CD-ROM and found that the ISO9660 standard considers the name illegal.

the scale number, the more the picture is reduced. So in order to make sure our picture fits in the thumbnail size we selected, we need to use the smaller of the two scale numbers.

```
25    my $scale = $x_scale;
26    if ($y_scale < $scale) {
27        $scale = $y_scale;
28    }
```

This scale factor computes the actual size of the scaled image:

```
30    my $new_x = int($image->Get('width') * $scale + 0.5);
31    my $new_y = int($image->Get('height') * $scale + 0.5);
```

Now the ImageMagick scale function is called to resize the image:

```
34    $status = $image->Scale(
35        width => $new_x, height => $new_y);
36
```

The resulting thumbnail is written to a new file:

```
40    $status = $image->Write("_thumb/$file");
```

Hacking the Script

The ImageMagick module contains a tremendous number of functions you can use to manipulate images. This script uses only one of them. The enhancements and effects you choose to use depend on what you want your thumbnails to look like.

#30 Photo Gallery

Taking pictures is only half the fun. The other half is sharing them with your friends and family. This script makes it easy to turn your photograph collection into a web gallery.

The Code

```
1 #!/usr/bin/perl -I/usr/local/lib
2 use strict;
3 use warnings;
4
5 # CONFIGURATION SECTION
6 use constant ACROSS => 6;        # Number of photos across
7 use constant X_SIZE => 100;
8 use constant Y_SIZE => 150;
```

```
 9
10 use POSIX;
11
12 use Image::Magick;
13 use Image::Info qw(image_info);
14
15 #
16 # File format:
17 #       =title heading/title    -- Head/title of the page
18 #       =head[1234]             -- Heading
19 #       =text                   -- Start text section
20 #       =photo                  -- Start photo section
21 #       xxxxxxx.jpg             -- Picture
22 #       text                    -- Text
23
24
25 my @photo_list = ();     # List of queued photos
26
27 #################################################
28 # do_thumb($file) -- Create a thumbnail of a file
29 #################################################
30 sub do_thumb($)
31 {
32     my $file = shift;   # The file to create
33                         # thumbnail of
34
35     my $image = Image::Magick->new();
36     my $status = $image->Read($file);
37     if ($status) {
38         print "Error $status\n";
39         return;
40     }
41
42     my $x_scale = X_SIZE / $image->Get('width');
43     my $y_scale = Y_SIZE / $image->Get('height');
44     my $scale = $x_scale;
45     if ($y_scale < $scale) {
46         $scale = $y_scale;
47     }
48     my $new_x = int($image->Get('width') * $scale + 0.5);
49     my $new_y = int($image->Get('height') * $scale + 0.5);
50
51     $status = $image->Scale(
52         width => $new_x, height => $new_y);
53
54     if ($status) {
55         print "$status\n";
56     }
57     $status = $image->Write("_thumb/$file");
58     if ($status) {
```

```perl
59          print "Error $status\n";
60      }
61 }
62 ##########################################################
63 # info_date($file) -- Return the data (from the info section)
64 #
65 # Returns the date from the jpeg info or undef if none.
66 ##########################################################
67 sub info_date($)
68 {
69     my $file = shift;
70
71     my $info = image_info($file);
72     if (not defined($info)) {
73         return (undef);
74     }
75     if (not defined($info->{DateTime})) {
76         return (undef);
77     }
78     if ($info->{DateTime} eq "0000:00:00 00:00:00") {
79         return (undef);
80     }
81     # This can be formatted better
82     return ($info->{DateTime});
83 }
84 ##########################################################
85 # file_date($file) -- Compute the date from the
86 #        file modification date.
87 #
88 # Returns date as a string
89 ##########################################################
90 sub file_date($)
91 {
92     my $file = shift;    # The file name
93
94     # File information
95     my @stat = stat("$file");
96
97     # Date as a string (f) is the code for file
98     my $date = strftime(
99         "%a %B %d, %C%y <BR>%r(f)", localtime($stat[9]));
100
101     return ($date);
102 }
103 ##########################################################
104 # get_date($file) -- Get a date from the file
105 #
106 # Returns date as a string
107 ##########################################################
108 sub get_date($)
```

```
109 {
110     my $file = shift;   # The file to get the information on
111     my $date;    # The date we've seen
112
113     $date = info_date($file);
114     if (defined($date)) {
115         return ($date);
116     }
117
118     return (file_date($file));
119 }
120
121 ################################################
122 # do_file -- Print the cell for a single file
123 ################################################
124 sub do_file($)
125 {
126     # The name of the file we are writing
127     # (Can be undef for the end of the table)
128     my $cur_file = shift;
129
130     if (defined($cur_file)) {
131         if (! -f "_thumb/$cur_file") {
132             do_thumb($cur_file);
133         }
134         print <<EOF;
135         <A HREF="$cur_file">
136         <IMG SRC=_thumb/$cur_file>
137         </A><BR>
138 EOF
139         my $date = get_date($cur_file);
140         print "$date<BR>\n";
141     } else {
142         print "            \n";
143     }
144 }
145 ################################################
146 # dump_photo -- Dump the list of photos we've
147 #        accumulated
148 ################################################
149 sub dump_photos() {
150     my $i;      # Photo index
151
152     if ($#photo_list < 0) {
153         return;
154     }
155     print "<TABLE>\n";
156     while ($#photo_list >= 0) {
157         print "    <TR>\n";
158         for ($i = 0; $i < ACROSS; $i++) {
```

```
159             # The photo we are processing
160             print "        <TD>\n";
161             do_file(shift @photo_list);
162             print "        </TD>\n";
163         }
164         print "    </TR>\n";
165     }
166     print "</TABLE>\n";
167 }
168
169 #########################################################
170 if (! -d "_thumb") {
171     mkdir("_thumb");
172 }
173
174 # Current mode for non = lines
175 my $mode = "Photo";       # The current mode (Photo/Text)
176
177 # Loop over each line of the input
178 while (<>) {
179     chomp();
180
181     if (/^=title\s+(.*)/) {
182         dump_photos();
183         print <<EOF;
184 <HEAD><TITLE>$1</TITLE></HEAD>
185 <BODY BGCOLOR="#FFFFFF">
186 <H1 ALIGN="center">$1</H1>
187 <P>
188 EOF
189         next;
190     }
191     if (/^=head([1-4])\s+(.*$)/) {
192         dump_photos();
193         print "<H$1>$2</H$1>\n";
194         next;
195     }
196
197     if (/^=text/) {
198         dump_photos();
199         $mode = "Text";
200         next;
201     }
202
203     if (/^=photo/) {
204         $mode = "Photo";
205         next;
206     }
207
208     if ($mode eq "Photo") {
```

```
209        if (length($_) == 0) {
210            next;
211        }
212        if (! -f $_) {
213            die("No such file $_");
214        }
215        push(@photo_list, $_);
216        next;
217    }
218    if ($mode eq "Text") {
219        print "$_\n";
220        next;
221    }
222    die("Impossible mode $mode\n");
223 }
224 dump_photos();
```

Running the Script

This program takes a page description file as input. The format is similar to the
POD format used for Perl documentation.

The script recognizes the following keywords:

=title   Defines the title of the page.

=head1   Adds a level 1 heading.

=head2, =head3, =head4   Adds other headings.

=text   Text follows. Just copy it to the page.

=photo   A list of photographs follows.

Here's a typical input file for a small gallery:

```
=title My Snapshots
=head1 Baby
=text
Ingesting a Cheerio nasally
=photo
p4240093.jpg
p4240102.jpg
pc200088.jpg
pc200090.jpg
=head1 Dog
=photo
p2230148.jpg
p2250157.jpg
p2250159.jpg
p8040360.jpg
p8040361.jpg
p8040364.jpg
```

To run the script, put the name of the configuration file on the command line and redirect the standard out to the web page file:

```
$ make_page.pl photo.txt >index.html
```

The Results

The left side of the following graphic shows a web page generated by the script. If we click on one of the thumbnails, we get the full picture as shown on the right.

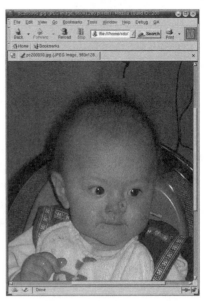

How It Works

The main body of the program is a big while loop that reads in each line and processes it.

First you check for an =title line. If that's present, you print the <TITLE> section of the HTML page. Actually, before printing any HTML, the script always calls dump_photos (this function will be explained later):

```
181     if (/^=title\s+(.*)/) {
182         dump_photos();
183         print <<EOF;
184 <HEAD><TITLE>$1</TITLE></HEAD>
185 <BODY BGCOLOR="#FFFFFF">
186 <H1 ALIGN="center">$1</H1>
187 <P>
```

```
188  EOF
189          next;
190      }
```

Next you check to see if you have any =head*n* lines. When one is found, you print an <H*n*> line:

```
191      if (/^=head([1-4])\s+(.*$)/) {
192          dump_photos();
193          print "<H$1>$2</H$1>\n";
194          next;
195      }
```

So the line

```
=head3 Dog Washing
```

turns into the HTML line

```
<H3>Dog Washing</H3>
```

An =text line indicates that the following lines are text. All you do is record the mode change and continue:

```
197      if (/^=text/) {
198          dump_photos();
199          $mode = "Text";
200          next;
201      }
```

The same thing is done for =photo:

```
203      if (/^=photo/) {
204          $mode = "Photo";
205          next;
206      }
```

If you get to this point, you have normal text. If you are in "Photo" mode, the line contains the name of an image file and you store it for later processing:

```
208      if ($mode eq "Photo") {
209          if (length($_) == 0) {
210              next;
211          }
212          if (! -f $_) {
213              die("No such file $_");
```

```
214        }
215        push(@photo_list, $_);
216        next;
217    }
```

A text line goes straight to the output as is:

```
218    if ($mode eq "Text") {
219        print "$_\n";
220        next;
221    }
```

As the program goes through your input file, it builds up a list of photographs in the array @photo_list. When it encounters text, it calls dump_photo to write out an HTML table containing the images.

Each cell of the table contains a thumbnail picture that serves as a link to the full-size image and the date the picture was taken. A typical cell entry looks like this:

```
<TD>
    <A HREF="p8040360.jpg">
        <IMG SRC=_thumb/p8040360.jpg>
    </A><BR>
    2001:08:04 11:30:40<BR>
</TD>
```

The table has six columns and as many rows as needed. The dump_photos function contains the actual code to produce the table:

```
149 sub dump_photos() {
150     my $i;        # Photo index
151
152     if ($#photo_list < 0) {
153         return;
154     }
155     print "<TABLE>\n";
156     while ($#photo_list >= 0) {
157         print "    <TR>\n";
158         for ($i = 0; $i < ACROSS; $i++) {
159             # The photo we are processing
160             print "        <TD>\n";
161             do_file(shift @photo_list);
162             print "        </TD>\n";
163         }
164         print "    </TR>\n";
165     }
166     print "</TABLE>\n";
167 }
```

Every time a photo cell is printed, @photo_list is reduced by one (shift @photo_list). If there are not enough photos to complete a row, then do_file will be called with an undefined value. That's OK, though, because it's smart enough to handle it.

Here's what the do_file function does for files:

1. Creates a thumbnail if needed.

2. Writes out the HTML link to the original file.

3. Gets the date of the picture and prints it.

If there is no picture defined, the cell is filled with the HTML version of the empty string: .

```
124 sub do_file($)
125 {
126     # The name of the file we are writing
127     # (Can be undef for the end of the table)
128     my $cur_file = shift;
129
130     if (defined($cur_file)) {
131         if (! -f "_thumb/$cur_file") {
132             do_thumb($cur_file);
133         }
134         print <<EOF;
135         <A HREF="$cur_file">
136         <IMG SRC=_thumb/$cur_file>
137         </A><BR>
138 EOF
139         my $date = get_date($cur_file);
140         print "$date<BR>\n";
141     } else {
142         print "                 \n";
143     }
144 }
```

The do_thumb function uses the subroutine described in the previous script to create a thumbnail.

The get_date function gets the date for the file. It first tries to get the data from the hidden fields in the image using info_date and then tries to get it from the creation time of the file using the function file_date:

```
108 sub get_date($)
109 {
110     my $file = shift;    # The file to get the information on
111     my $date;     # The date we've seen
112
113     $date = info_date($file);
114     if (defined($date)) {
```

```
115        return ($date);
116    }
117
118    return (file_date($file));
119 }
```

The info_date function uses the Image::Info module to extract the date from the image itself. If there is a problem, it returns undef. (The date information is part of the JPEG image standard used by almost all digital cameras. Every one I've seen will fill in the date fields in the image.)

The function has undergone one modification since I first wrote it. After I found out about the Image::Info module, I went out and shot a bunch of pictures and downloaded them to my computer. Using the make_page.pl script, I created a web page with the dates and discovered that all my pictures were taken on 0000:00:00 00:00:00. (Guess who forget to set the date on his new digital camera.)

So the info_date function also checks for stupid operator tricks and returns undef if the date is present but meaningless:

```
67 sub info_date($)
68 {
69    my $file = shift;
70
71    my $info = image_info($file);
72    if (not defined($info)) {
73        return (undef);
74    }
75    if (not defined($info->{DateTime})) {
76        return (undef);
77    }
78    if ($info->{DateTime} eq "0000:00:00 00:00:00") {
79        return (undef);
80    }
81    # This can be formatted better
82    return ($info->{DateTime});
83 }
```

If a date is not available from the image itself, you get it from the creation time of the file. The file_date function uses stat to get the creation date and strftime to turn it into something readable:

```
90 sub file_date($)
91 {
92    my $file = shift;    # The file name
93
94    # File information
95    my @stat = stat("$file");
96
97    # Date as a string (f) is the code for file
98    my $date = strftime(
```

```
 99            "%a %B %d, %C%y <BR>%r(f)", localtime($stat[9]));
100
101        return ($date);
102 }
```

Hacking the Script

This script creates a simple but useful photo gallery. There are fancier ways of displaying pictures. For example, you could split the page up into frames with the thumbnails on one side and full-size photographs on the other. Clicking on a thumbnail would change the image displayed in the main frame.

You could also use a slide show to present your pictures. Each photograph appears at full size on a page with buttons to navigate to the next and previous picture. It's even possible to hack the script to sort your photographs by date and put each day's result on a different web page. It's also possible to create a greeting card using the photo or photos. Web designs can become quite elaborate, and this script can be hacked to keep up with them.

#31 Card Maker

Here's a fun project: If you have a digital camera and a laser printer, you can create your own greeting cards. A single 8.5×11 sheet of paper folded twice makes a wonderful birthday invitation or Christmas card. However, creating the card can be a little tricky.

The folded greeting card looks like this:

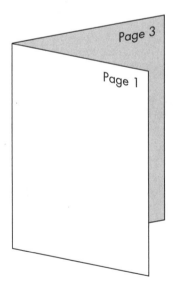

Here's the unfolded sheet:

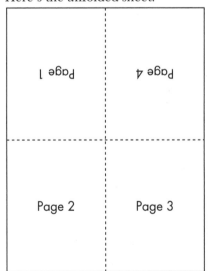

Printing a page in four pieces can be tricky, especially when the contents of half of the pieces are upside down, but Perl is up to the task.

The Code

```
 1 use strict;
 2 use warnings;
 3 use Image::Magick;
 4 use Getopt::Std;
 5
 6 # The four images (one for each quad)
 7 use vars qw/$opt_1 $opt_2 $opt_3 $opt_4
 8             $opt_o $opt_O $opt_C $opt_E/;
 9
10 # Size of an image in X and Y
11 my $xi_size;
12 my $yi_size;
13
14 # Font for text.  Must exist on the system.
15 # Use xlsfonts to find your font
16 my $font =
17 '-adobe-helvetica-medium-r-normal--25-180-100-100-p-130-iso8729-1';
18
19 # If you installed the ImageMagick Generic font
20 # let's use that.  It works better.
21 if (-f 'Generic.ttf') {
22     $font = 'Generic.ttf';
23 }
24
25 my @text;        # Text for the display
26 #######################################
27 # status_check($result)
28 #
29 # Check an ImageMagick return status
30 # and if it indicates an error -- die.
31 #######################################
32 sub status_check($)
33 {
34     my $result = shift;
35     if (not($result)) {
36         return;
37     }
38     die("ImageMagick Error $result");
39 }
40
41 #######################################
42 # read_text -- Read the text file
43 #######################################
44 sub read_text($)
```

```perl
45 {
46     my $file = shift;      # File to read
47
48     open IN_FILE, "<$file" or
49         die("Could not open $file");
50
51     my $index;              # Index into the text array
52     while (<IN_FILE>) {
53         if (/^=text\s*(\d+)/) {
54             if (($1 < 1) or ($1 > 4)) {
55                 die("Illegal text page $1");
56             }
57             $index = $1-1;
58             next;
59         }
60         if (/^=size\s*(\d+)/) {
61             if (not defined($index)) {
62                 die("=size before =text");
63             }
64             $text[$index]->{size} = $1;
65             next;
66         }
67         if (not defined($index)) {
68             die("Text data before =text");
69         }
70         # ImageMagick has problems with empty lines
71         if ($_ eq "\n") {
72             $_ = " \n";
73         }
74         $text[$index]->{text} .= $_;
75     }
76     close (IN_FILE);
77 }
78
79 #######################################
80 # do_image($number, $name) -- Read an image
81 #       file and scale it fit into a
82 #       quad
83 #######################################
84 sub do_image($$)
85 {
86     my $number = shift; # Image number
87     my $name = shift;    # Name of the image
88
89     # The image
90     my $image = Image::Magick->new;
91     status_check($image->Read($name));
92
93     if (index($opt_E, $number) >= 0) {
94         status_check($image->Emboss(
```

```
 95            radius => 3, sigma => 1));
 96      }
 97      if (index($opt_C, $number) >= 0) {
 98          status_check($image->Charcoal(
 99              radius => 3, sigma => 1));
100      }
101      if (index($opt_O, $number) >= 0) {
102          status_check($image->OilPaint(radius => 3));
103      }
104
105      status_check($image->Scale(
106              geometry => "${xi_size}x${yi_size}"
107      ));
108      return ($image);
109 }
110 #######################################
111 #
112 #    +-----------+-----------+ ^   ^
113 #    |           |           | |   |
114 #    |           |           | |   | yq_size
115 #    |           |           | |   |
116 #    |           |           | |   |
117 #    |           |           | |   v
118 #    +-----------+-----------+ |
119 #    |           |           | |
120 #    |           |           | |
121 #    |           |           | |
122 #    |           |           | | y_size
123 #    |           |           | |
124 #    |           |           | |
125 #    +-----------+-----------+ v
126 #    <-------- x_size ------->
127 #    <- xq_size ->
128 #######################################
129
130 getopts("1:2:3:4:o:O:C:E:");
131 if ($#ARGV > 0) {
132      print <<EOF ;
133 Usage $0 [options] [images] <text-template>
134
135 Options:
136      -o <out-file> -- Specify output file
137      -O<numbers>   -- Oil Paint the given images
138      -C<numbers>   -- Charcoal the given images
139      -E<numbers>   -- Emboss the given images
140
141 Images
142      -1<image>     -- Image for page 1
143      -2<image>     -- Image for page 2
144      -3<image>     -- Image for page 3
```

```
145    -4<image>     -- Image for page 4
146 EOF
147     exit(8);
148 }
149 if ($#ARGV == 0) {
150     read_text($ARGV[0]);
151 }
152 if (not defined($opt_E)) {
153     $opt_E = "";
154 }
155 if (not defined($opt_C)) {
156     $opt_C = "";
157 }
158 if (not defined($opt_O)) {
159     $opt_O = "";
160 }
161
162 # Our sizes are set for an 8.5x11 sheet
163 #       of paper at 75 dpi
164 #
165 #TODO: Set the DPI / paper size
166 my $x_size = int(8.5*75);
167 my $y_size = int(11*75);
168
169 my $xq_size = int($x_size / 2);
170 my $yq_size = int($y_size / 2);
171
172 # Allow 10% margin on each side
173 my $x_margin = int($xq_size * 0.10);
174 my $y_margin = int($yq_size * 0.10);
175
176 $xi_size = $xq_size - $x_margin;
177 $yi_size = $yq_size - $y_margin;
178
179 # The card we are making
180 my $card = Image::Magick->new;
181
182 $card->Set(size => "${x_size}x${y_size}");
183 status_check($card->ReadImage("xc:white"));
184
185 # Draw a line across the middle
186 my $x1 = 0;
187 my $x2 = $x_size;
188 my $y1 = int($y_size/2) - 1;
189 my $y2 = int($y_size/2) + 1;
190
191 status_check($card->Draw(
192         fill => "Black",
193         stroke=>"Black",
194         primitive => "rectangle",
```

```
195          points=>"$x1,$y1 $x2,$y2")
196 );
197
198 $x1 = int($x_size/2) - 1;
199 $x2 = int($x_size/2) + 1;
200 $y1 = 0;
201 $y2 = $y_size;
202
203 status_check($card->Draw(
204          fill => "black",
205          stroke=>"black",
206          primitive => "rectangle",
207          points=>"$x1,$y1 $x2,$y2")
208 );
209
210
211
212 if (defined($opt_1)) {
213     # The image we are depositing on the screen
214     my $image_1 = do_image(1, $opt_1);
215
216     # Pages 1,4 are upside down
217     status_check($image_1->Rotate(degrees => 180));
218
219     # The corner of the centered image
220     my $center_x =
221         int(($xq_size - $image_1->Get('width'))/2);
222     my $center_y =
223         int(($yq_size - $image_1->Get('height'))/2);
224
225     status_check($card->Composite(image=>$image_1,
226             x => $center_x, y => $center_y));
227 }
228
229 if (defined($opt_2)) {
230     # The image we are depositing on the screen
231     my $image_2 = do_image(2, $opt_2);
232
233     # The corner of the centered image
234     my $center_x =
235         int(($xq_size - $image_2->Get('width'))/2);
236     my $center_y =
237         int(($yq_size - $image_2->Get('height'))/2);
238
239     status_check($card->Composite(image=>$image_2,
240         x => $center_x, y => $center_y + $yq_size));
241 }
242
243 if (defined($opt_3)) {
244     # The image we are depositing on the screen
```

```perl
245    my $image_3 = do_image(3, $opt_3);
246
247    # The corner of the centered image
248    my $center_x =
249        int(($xq_size - $image_3->Get('width'))/2);
250    my $center_y =
251        int(($yq_size - $image_3->Get('height'))/2);
252
253    status_check($card->Composite(image=>$image_3,
254        x => $center_x + $xq_size,
255        y => $center_y + $yq_size));
256 }
257
258 if (defined($opt_4)) {
259    # The image we are depositing on the screen
260    my $image_4 = do_image(4, $opt_4);
261
262    # Pages 1,4 are upside down
263    status_check($image_4->Rotate(degrees => 180));
264
265    # The corner of the centered image
266    my $center_x =
267        int(($xq_size - $image_4->Get('width'))/2);
268    my $center_y =
269        int(($yq_size - $image_4->Get('height'))/2);
270
271    status_check($card->Composite(image=>$image_4,
272        x => $center_x + $xq_size, y => $center_y));
273 }
274
275 if (defined($text[0])) {
276    if (not defined($text[0]->{size})) {
277        $text[0]->{size} = 10;
278    }
279    status_check($card->Annotate(
280            text => $text[0]->{text},
281            pointsize => $text[0]->{size},
282            font => $font,
283            x => $xq_size - $x_margin,
284            y => $yq_size - $y_margin,
285            align => 'left',
286            rotate => 180));
287 }
288
289 if (defined($text[1])) {
290    if (not defined($text[1]->{size})) {
291        $text[1]->{size} = 10;
292    }
293    status_check($card->Annotate(
294            text => $text[1]->{text},
295            pointsize => $text[1]->{size},
```

```
296              font => $font,
297              x => $x_margin,
298              y => $yq_size + $y_margin)
299          );
300 }
301
302 if (defined($text[2])) {
303     if (not defined($text[2]->{size})) {
304         $text[2]->{size} = 10;
305     }
306     status_check($card->Annotate(
307              text => $text[2]->{text},
308              pointsize => $text[2]->{size},
309              font => $font,
310              x => $xq_size + $x_margin,
311              y => $yq_size + $y_margin)
312          );
313 }
314
315 if (defined($text[3])) {
316     if (not defined($text[3]->{size})) {
317         $text[3]->{size} = 10;
318     }
319     status_check($card->Annotate(
320              text => $text[3]->{text},
321              pointsize => $text[3]->{size},
322              font => $font,
323              x => $x_size - $x_margin,
324              y => $yq_size - $y_margin,
325              align => 'left',
326              rotate => 180)
327          );
328 }
329
330
331 if (not defined($opt_o)) {
332     $opt_o = "card_out.ps";
333 }
334 print "Writing $opt_o\n";
335 $card->Write($opt_o);
```

Running the Script

The command line for the program is as follows:

```
card.pl [-1image-file] [-2image-file]
    [-3image-file] [-4image-file]
    [-oout-file] [-Oimages] [-Cimages]
    [-Eimages] [text-file]
```

There are four pages to the card. The options -1*image-file*, -2*image-file*, -3*image-file*, and -4*image-file* specify the images to use for each of the pages. Each image is optional.

The output file is selected by the -o*output-file*. The default output file is card.ps. Although the default output file format is PostScript, you can specify any type of graphic file that ImageMagick understands. For example, you could create a PNG image of the page by specifying the output file my_card.png.

If you want any of the images to be processed through an oil-painting filter (simulates an oil painting), use the option -O followed by the image numbers. For example, -O34 turns the images on pages 3 and 4 into oil paintings.

The -E option uses an embossing filter, and -C uses a charcoal drawing filter.

Finally there is *text-file*, which specifies the text for the card. Each entry in the text file looks like this:

```
=text page
=size point

Multiple lines of text for the page
```

Let's now take a look at an example of a birthday invitation. On the first page is a little bit of art produced by someone who's a better programmer than an artist:

The second page contains a picture of the little girl giving the party:

The other input file specifies the text to be put on each page:

```
=text 3
=size 24
Where:  Grace's House

When: April 24

Time: 10:30 - 2:30

Food -- Games -- Fun

=text 4
=size 16
Please RSVP
(858)-555-1212
```

The script is invoked with the following command:

```
card.pl -1birthday.png -2grace.jpg \
    -ocard.png birthday.txt
```

The Results

The result is a birthday invitation.

Effects

With the card.pl program, you can process your images through several different effects filters, including oil painting, embossing, and charcoal drawing. Here is a typical image before any filtering has been done.

What happens when you apply the oil painting filter to the image.

The results of the embossing filter.

Finally, the effects of the charcoal drawing filter.

It should be noted that the filters can turn some ordinary pictures into something special. The picture of my daughter is not one of those pictures. In particular, the charcoal drawing filter has turned my beautiful daughter into something that looks like a snarling fiend. But if you find the right image, the proper effects filter can work wonders.

How It Works

The basic functions of this script can be summarized as follows:

1. Create a blank page.
2. Draw the lines across the middle for folding.
3. Read in the first image, apply the effects filters, and scale it to the proper size.
4. Use the ImageMagick Compose function to put it on the page.
5. Repeat this process for the other three images.
6. Use the ImageMagick Annotate function to put the text on the page.
7. Write out the result.

Let's take a look at these steps in detail.

You start by computing some numbers. The output image is going to be 8.5×11 at 75 dpi. You need to determine the size of the image in pixels:

```
166 my $x_size = int(8.5*75);
167 my $y_size = int(11*75);
```

Next you need to know the location of the middle in the X and Y directions:

```
169 my $xq_size = int($x_size / 2);
170 my $yq_size = int($y_size / 2);
```

You want a 10 percent margin around each image:

```
172 # Allow 10% margin on each side
173 my $x_margin = int($xq_size * 0.10);
174 my $y_margin = int($yq_size * 0.10);
```

From these numbers, you can compute the size of the images for each of the four panels:

```
176 $xi_size = $xq_size - $x_margin;
177 $yi_size = $yq_size - $y_margin;
```

Next you need to create a blank image. First, create an image object and set its size. Then "read" in a magic built-in image file containing a blank white image:

```
179 # The card we are making
180 my $card = Image::Magick->new;
181
182 $card->Set(size => "${x_size}x${y_size}");
183 status_check($card->ReadImage("xc:white"));
```

All ImageMagick functions return undef if they work and an error message if they don't. The error-checking code has been consolidated into a single status_check function, which prints a message and aborts if it sees an error:

```
32 sub status_check($)
33 {
34     my $result = shift;
35     if (not($result)) {
36         return;
37     }
38     die("ImageMagick Error $result");
39 }
```

To divide the paper into four panels, you draw horizontal and vertical lines through the middle of the page:

```
185 # Draw a line across the middle
186 my $x1 = 0;
187 my $x2 = $x_size;
188 my $y1 = int($y_size/2) - 1;
189 my $y2 = int($y_size/2) + 1;
190
191 status_check($card->Draw(
192         fill => "Black",
193         stroke=>"Black",
194         primitive => "rectangle",
195         points=>"$x1,$y1 $x2,$y2")
196 );
197
198 $x1 = int($x_size/2) - 1;
199 $x2 = int($x_size/2) + 1;
200 $y1 = 0;
201 $y2 = $y_size;
202
203 status_check($card->Draw(
204         fill => "black",
205         stroke=>"black",
```

```
206            primitive => "rectangle",
207            points=>"$x1,$y1 $x2,$y2")
208 );
```

Now you process each image. The do_image function reads in an image, processes it through the effects filters, and resizes it. The result is an Image-Magick image object that can be composited onto the card itself.

Let's look at this function in detail. The first thing to do is create the image and read it in:

```
89      # The image
90      my $image = Image::Magick->new;
91      status_check($image->Read($name));
```

Check to see if the -E option contains your image number. If it does, you process the image through the Emboss filter:

```
93      if (index($opt_E, $number) >= 0) {
94          status_check($image->Emboss(
95              radius => 3, sigma => 1));
96      }
```

The same thing is done for the Charcoal and OilPaint filters:

```
97      if (index($opt_C, $number) >= 0) {
98          status_check($image->Charcoal(
99              radius => 3, sigma => 1));
100     }
101     if (index($opt_O, $number) >= 0) {
102         status_check($image->OilPaint(radius => 3));
103     }
```

Finally, the image is resized so that it exactly fits in one panel on your card:

```
105     status_check($image->Scale(
106             geometry => "${xi_size}x${yi_size}"
107     ));
```

The processed image is returned to the caller:

```
108     return ($image);
```

The do_image function is used in the main program to read the image for each panel. For example, the following code checks to see if you have an image for panel 1 and reads it if you do:

```
212 if (defined($opt_1)) {
213     # The image we are depositing on the screen
214     my $image_1 = do_image(1, $opt_1);
```

Since the image for panel 1 is upside down, the image is rotated 180 degrees:

```
216     # Pages 1,4 are upside down
217     status_check($image_1->Rotate(degrees => 180));
```

Next you compute the coordinates needed to center the image on the panel:

```
219     # The corner of the centered image
220     my $center_x =
221         int(($xq_size - $image_1->Get('width'))/2);
222     my $center_y =
223         int(($yq_size - $image_1->Get('height'))/2);
```

Finally, the image is placed on the card using the Composite function:

```
225     status_check($card->Composite(image=>$image_1,
226         x => $center_x, y => $center_y));
```

A similar process is used for the other three images. Only the location and rotation of the image change from panel to panel.

Now that the images are placed, it is time to add the text. The function read_text reads the file containing the text information and stores it in the array @text. This is a simple matter of text processing, so I won't go into the details. The result is that @text[0]->{text} contains the text to display for the first panel and @text[0]->{size} contains the point size for this text. The other elements of the array specify the text for the other three panels.

The text is drawn on the page using the ImageMagick Annotate function. For example, the following code draws the text for the first panel:

```
279     status_check($card->Annotate(
280         text => $text[0]->{text},
281         pointsize => $text[0]->{size},
282         font => $font,
283         x => $xq_size - $x_margin,
284         y => $yq_size - $y_margin,
285         align => 'left',
286         rotate => 180));
```

The Case of the Disappearing Text

There's one final detail to worry about: the font. When this program was first created, there was no font specification in the Annotate call. Then the program was moved to a new machine with a slightly different version of Linux and suddenly all the text disappeared.

There was no error message coming out of the Annotate call. It would report success and then not draw the text. This was extremely annoying and confusing.

After a great deal of debugging, cursing, and experimentation, I located the problem. Whatever font ImageMagick uses as the default was present on the original system and absent on the new one. As a result, I added a font specification to the program. The program starts out with a default Adobe font found in almost all Linux distributions:

```
16 my $font =
17 '-adobe-helvetica-medium-r-normal--25-180-100-100-p-130-iso8729-1';
```

The problem with using this font is that it does not scale. In other words, you can't change the point size of the font. The ImageMagick distribution contains a TrueType font format that not only looks nice but is scalable. If this font is installed on your system, the program will use it:

```
19 # If you installed the ImageMagick Generic font
20 # let's use that.  It works better.
21 if (-f 'Generic.ttf') {
22      $font = 'Generic.ttf';
23 }
```

Hacking the Script

The user interface to this program is awkward. There should be a simple and easy way of specifying everything that goes into the card, and when I figure out what it is, I'll probably rewrite the script. Also, the paper size (8.5×11) is hard-coded. This parameter should be configurable.

As it stands, the script contains the major pieces of code needed to produce greeting cards. There are lots of details you can play with, making this program a hacker's dream.

8

GAMES AND LEARNING TOOLS

I have a one-and-a-half-year-old daughter, Grace, who's just beginning to learn things. She's at an age when everyday things are new and fascinating. Turning on and off a light switch can hold her attention for quite some time.

One of the things she's learned is that the computer is very important to Daddy. She loves to come over and type on the keyboard, especially when I'm trying to write this book.

So I wrote a few programs for her, one for now (see "Teaching a Toddler" later in this chapter) and many for later as she grows up and learns more.

Learning should not be boring, so a good teaching tool should be fun. Playing games is one way of learning. For example, the solitaire game that comes with Microsoft Windows teaches people the concept of clicking and dragging the mouse.

As for myself, I find the process of writing Perl scripts both fun and educational. So let's get started with the fun part.

#32 Guessing Game

This is one of the simpler computer games. The program generates a random number in the interval 1 to 1,000 and asks you to guess it.

Guess right and you win. Guess wrong and the system adjusts the interval based on your guess and let's you try again.

This is a good game for first graders. It teaches them the basics of computer usage and how to follow instructions and even gives them an idea of how to create a binary search.

The Code

```perl
 1 use strict;
 2 use warnings;
 3
 4 my $low = 1;            # Current low limit
 5 my $high = 1000;        # Current high limit
 6
 7 # The number the user needs to guess
 8 my $goal = int(rand($high))+1;
 9
10 while (1) {
11     print "Enter a number between $low and $high: ";
12
13     # The answer from the user
14     my $answer = <STDIN>;
15     chomp($answer);
16
17     if ($answer !~ /\d+/) {
18         print "Please enter a number only\n";
19         next;
20     }
21     if ($answer == $goal) {
22         print "You guessed it.\n";
23         exit;
24     }
25     if (($answer < $low) || ($answer > $high)) {
26         print "Please stay between $low and $high.\n";
27         next;
28     }
29     if ($answer < $goal) {
30         $low = $answer;
31     } else {
32         $high = $answer;
33     }
34 }
```

Running the Script

The script is entirely interactive. Just run it.

The Results

```
$ perl guess.pl
Enter a number between 1 and 1000: 500
Enter a number between 1 and 500: 250
Enter a number between 1 and 250: 125
Enter a number between 1 and 125: 60
Enter a number between 1 and 60: 30
Enter a number between 30 and 60: 35
Enter a number between 30 and 35: 32
You guessed it.
```

How It Works

The script uses two variables, $low and $high, to hold the current limits. The hidden number is called $goal.

If the player guesses the goal, the game is over. Otherwise, the guess is used to adjust either $low or $high and the game continues.

Hacking the Script

As it stands, the script is pretty basic. But then again, it was designed for first graders, to teach some very basic math.

However, it would be nice to have a feature that records the scores of each run so that the youngster could get an idea of how well their current guessing strategy is working. Also, a high score module could be created to encourage competition between players.

Although simple, there's a lot that can be learned from this little game.

#33 Flash Cards

Unfortunately, there's still a lot of learning that requires memorization and drill. I still remember the hours I spent typing up 3×5-inch cards with my weekly French vocabulary on them.

The system I used was to go through each word one at a time. If I got the word right, the flash card was set aside. Get it wrong and the card went to the back of the stack so I could try again later.

I got pretty good at learning my French vocabulary. Unfortunately, after I passed the weekly quiz, I got good at forgetting things as well.

This script automates the process I went through with my 3×5-inch cards and gives the user a vocabulary drill.

The Code

```
1 use strict;
2 use warnings;
3
4 #
5 # perl lang.pl <flash file>
6 #
7 # File format:
8 #       question<tab>answer
9 #
10 if ($#ARGV != 0) {
11     print "Usage: is $0 <flash-file>\n";
12     exit (8);
13 }
14 open IN_FILE, "<$ARGV[0]" or
15     die("Could not open $ARGV[0] for reading");
16
17 my @list;        # List of questions and answers
18
19 #
20 # Read the stuff in
21 #
22 while (<IN_FILE>) {
23     chomp;
24     my @words = split /\t/;
25     if ($#words != 1) {
26         die("Malformed input $_");
27     }
28     push(@list,
29         {
30             question => $words[0],
31             answer => $words[1]
32         });
33 }
34
35 #
36 # Ask the questions until there are no more
37 #
38 while ($#list > -1) {
39     print "Question: $list[0]->{question}: ";
40     my $answer = <STDIN>;
41     chomp($answer);
42     if ($answer eq $list[0]->{answer}) {
43         print "Right: ",
44             "The answer is $list[0]->{answer}\n";
45         shift(@list);
46         next;
47     }
```

```
48      print "Wrong: ",
49        "The correct answer is $list[0]->{answer}\n";
50      # Push the question to the end of the list
51      push(@list, shift(@list));
52 }
53 print "All done\n";
```

Running the Script

To run the script, you'll first need to create a quiz file. Each line of this file contains the question and answer separated by a tab.

For example, a small English-to-French quiz file follows.

address	adresse
again	de nouveau
against	contre
airplane	avion
almost	presque
alongside	le long de
also	aussi
although	bien que
always	toujours
among	entre
amuse	amuser
arrive	arriver
aunt	tante
author	auteur
bacon	lard
baggage	bagage
bake	cuire
between	entre
blind	aveugle
blue	bleu
boring	ennuyeux
by chance	par accident
by heart	par coeur

This file (french.quiz) is then passed to the script on the command line:

```
$ perl lang.pl french.quiz
```

The Results

```
$ perl lang.pl french.quiz
Question: address: adresse
Right: The answer is adresse
Question: again: de noveau
Wrong: The correct answer is de nouveau
```

```
Question: against: contre
Right: The answer is contre
Question: airplane: avion
Right: The answer is avion
Question: all: trout
Wrong: The correct answer is tout
...
Question: both: tous les deux
Right: The answer is tous les deux
Question: by chance: par accident
Right: The answer is par accident
Question: by heart: par coeur
Right: The answer is par coeur
Question: again: de nouveau
Right: The answer is de nouveau
Question: all: tout
Right: The answer is tout
All done
```

How It Works

The script starts by reading in the file a line at a time:

```
22 while (<IN_FILE>) {
```

Each line is trimmed and then split into the question and answer part:

```
23     chomp;
24     my @words = split /\t/;
```

Next you add an entry from the question list. Each item in the list consists of a hash with a question and answer part:

```
28     push(@list,
29         {
30             question => $words[0],
31             answer => $words[1]
32         });
```

Once the quiz has been read into the @list array, it's time to start asking the questions.

The basic algorithm is as follows:

1. Take the top entry off the @list array and ask the question.

2. If the user supplies the right answer, throw the question away.

3. If the answer is wrong, take the top entry off of @list and put it on the bottom so the question will be re-asked later.

This process is illustrated in the following graphic.

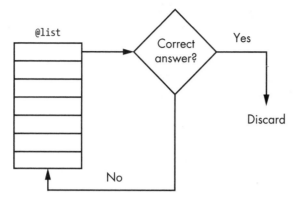

The first step is to ask the first question on the list:

```
39    print "Question: $list[0]->{question}: ";
```

The next step is to get the answer and check it:

```
40    my $answer = <STDIN>;
41    chomp($answer);
42    if ($answer eq $list[0]->{answer}) {
```

If the answer is correct, you remove the top entry from the list and the user never sees it again:

```
42    if ($answer eq $list[0]->{answer}) {
43        print "Right: ",
44            "The answer is $list[0]->{answer}\n";
45        shift(@list);
46        next;
47    }
```

If the answer is wrong, you take the question off the top of the list and put it on the bottom. You'll ask the user the question again later:

```
48    print "Wrong: ",
49     "The correct answer is $list[0]->{answer}\n";
50    # Push the question to the end of the list
51    push(@list, shift(@list));
```

When you run out of questions, the loop exits and the quiz is finished.

```
53 print "All done\n";
```

Hacking the Script

This script works fine as a simple test. It would be nice if the program kept track of some statistics to give students some idea of how much they are progressing. Ideally, each time they take a quiz, they should answer more questions correctly than they did the first time.

Also, the questions are given out in the same sequence each time. It might be better to randomize them.

But the system does a good job of giving you a basic quiz. How you customize it is up to you.

#34 Web-Based Quiz

The flash card script is a good text-based quiz. But what if you want something more graphical? That's where this script comes in.

The original requirements called for the script to be a stand-alone program. That meant using the Perl/Tk graphics module to draw the questions in a window. The script would also have to provide answer buttons as well as a few more GUI elements.

It's a lot of work to create a GUI, even a simple one, because each screen element must be specified and drawn. In the end you wind up with hundreds of simple little pieces, and the result is something large.

Ideally, it would be nice if you could get someone else to write the GUI. Turns out there's a pre-built GUI system that handles text, graphics, and user input already. It's called the web browser. So if you eliminate the custom-made GUI from your design and make the program a CGI script, you are able get rid of a tremendous amount of code.

The result is a CGI program that quizzes the user. As you will see, you use HTML to define the questions and answers and Perl to do all the asking. The finished product is a simple yet powerful quiz program.

The Code

```
 1 #!/usr/bin/perl -T
 2 #
 3 # File format
 4 #        =question
 5 #        <question page>
 6 #        =answer value
 7 #        <answer page>
 8 #        =answer value
 9 #        <answer page>
10 #        =right value
11 #        <answer page for the right answer>
12 #
13 use strict;
14 use warnings;
15
```

```
16 use CGI::Thin;
17 use CGI::Thin::Cookies;
18 use CGI::Carp;
19 use POSIX;
20 use HTML::Entities;
21 use Scalar::Util qw(tainted);
22 use Storable qw(retrieve nstore);
23
24 # Place the questions and session files are
25 # stored in
26 my $quiz_dir = "/var/quiz";
27
28 # The data from the form
29 my %cgi_data = Parse_CGI();
30
31 # Cookie information
32 my %cookies = Parse_Cookies();
33
34 # The session from the cookie
35 my $session_cookie = $cookies{QUIZ};
36
37 my $session = undef;     # The session name
38
39 # Taint checking and cleaning
40 if (defined($session_cookie) &&
41     ($session_cookie =~
            /^$quiz_dir\/session\/.session.(\d+)$/)) {
42     $session_cookie =~ /(\d+)$/;
43     $session = "$quiz_dir/session/session.$1";
44 } else {
45     $session = undef;
46 }
47
48 if (! -f $session) {
49     $session = undef;
50 }
51 if (not defined ($session)) {
52     for (my $i = 0; ; $i++) {
53         # Generate a new session
54         $session = "$quiz_dir/session/session.$i";
55         if (! -f "$quiz_dir/session/session.$i") {
56             last;
57         }
58     }
59 }
60
61 # The cookie to send to the user
62 my $cookie;
63 $cookie = Set_Cookie(
64     NAME => "QUIZ",       # Cookie's name
```

```perl
65       VALUE => $session,    # Value for the cookie
66       EXPIRE => "+3h",      # Keep cookie for 3 hours
67 );
68 print "$cookie";
69 print "Content-type: text/html\n";
70 print "\n";
71
72 my $session_info;
73 if (-f $session) {
74     $session_info = retrieve($session);
75 } else {
76     my @files = glob("$quiz_dir/questions/*");
77     $session_info->{files} = [@files];
78     $session_info->{mode} = 'question';
79 }
80
81 #################################################
82 # parse_file($file_name) -- Read / parse a file
83 #
84 # Returns a hash containing the file information
85 #################################################
86 sub parse_file($)
87 {
88     my $file_name = shift;
89
90     open IN_FILE, "<$file_name" or
91         die("Unable to open $file_name");
92
93     my %file_info;    # Information about the file
94
95     my $field;  # Field we are defining
96     my $item = undef;# Item for current field
97
98     while (my $line = <IN_FILE>) {
99         if ($line =~ /^=question/) {
100            $field = 'question';
101            $item = undef;
102        } elsif ($line =~ /=answer\s+(\S+)/) {
103            $field = 'answer';
104            $item = $1;
105        } elsif ($line =~ /=right\s+(\S+)/) {
106            $field = 'answer';
107            $item = $1;
108            $file_info{right} = $1;
109        } else {
110            if (defined($item)) {
111                $file_info{$field}->{$item} .= $line;
112            } else {
113                $file_info{$field} .= $line;
114            }
```

```
115          }
116      }
117      close (IN_FILE);
118      return (%file_info);
119 }
120
121 ##################################################
122 # display_done -- Tell the user he's done.
123 ##################################################
124 sub display_done()
125 {
126      $session_info->{mode} = 'done';
127      print <<EOF
128
129 <H1>Test Complete</H1>
130 <P>
131 Congratulations, you have finished the quiz.
132
133 EOF
134      #TODO: Need something here to go somewhere
135 }
136 ##################################################
137 # display_question -- Display the current question
138 ##################################################
139 sub display_question()
140 {
141      if ($#{$session_info->{files}} == -1) {
142          display_done();
143          return;
144      }
145
146      # Information about the file
147      my %file_info = parse_file($session_info->{files}->[0]);
148
149      print $file_info{question};
150      $session_info->{mode} = 'answer';
151 }
152
153
154 ##################################################
155 # display_answer -- Display the answer
156 ##################################################
157 sub display_answer()
158 {
159      # The information from the question file
160      my %file_info = parse_file($session_info->{files}->[0]);
161
162      # The answer the user submitted
163      my $answer = $cgi_data{answer};
164
```

```
165     # Display the answer
166     if (defined($file_info{answer}->{$answer})) {
167         print $file_info{answer}->{$answer};
168     } else {
169         print "<H1>Internal error: Undefined answer $answer</H1>\n";
170         $answer = "";
171     }
172     if ($answer eq $file_info{right}) {
173         shift @{$session_info->{files}};
174     } else {
175         my $last = @{$session_info->{files}};
176         push(@{$session_info->{files}}, $last);
177     }
178     $session_info->{mode} = 'question';
179     print <<EOF ;
180     <FORM ACTION="quiz.pl">
181     <INPUT TYPE="submit" NAME="next" VALUE="next">
182     </FORM>
183 EOF
184 }
185
186
187 if ($session_info->{mode} eq 'answer') {
188     display_answer();
189 } elsif ($session_info->{mode} eq 'question') {
190     display_question();
191 } else {
192     display_done();
193 }
194
195 # Store the data for later use
196 nstore($session_info, $session);
```

Running the Script

Before you run the script, you need to create a series of question files. These are text files consisting of a series of HTML pages separated by special tags. The format of the file looks like this:

```
=question
HTML page containing the question
=answer value
HTML page to be displayed when the user selects the given answer "value".
=answer value
Additional answer sections
=right value
Like answer, but this answer is the right one.  (=answer and =right may be in
any order.)
```

Let's look at a sample question. Here's what the raw input file looks like:

```
=question
<HEAD><TITLE>Question 1</TITLE></HEAD>
<H1>Question 1:</H1>
<P>
What does the following regular expression mean:
<pre>
/\S+/
</pre>
<P>
 
<FORM ACTION="quiz.pl">
<P>
<INPUT TYPE="submit" NAME="answer" VALUE="1">
One or more spaces.<BR>
<INPUT TYPE="submit" NAME="answer" VALUE="2">
Zero or more spaces.<BR>
<INPUT TYPE="submit" NAME="answer" VALUE="3">
One or more non-space characters.<BR>
</FORM>

=answer 1

<HEAD><TITLE>Wrong</TITLE></HEAD>
<H1>Wrong</H1>
<P>
Lower case 's' (<code>\s</code>) is used to specify
spaces.  The regular expression given uses an uppercase 'S'.  (See <i>perldoc
perlre</i> for a reference.)

=answer 2

<HEAD><TITLE>Wrong</TITLE></HEAD>
<H1>Wrong</H1>
<P>
The star character (<code>*</code>) denotes zero
or more characters.  This expression uses the
plus (<code>+</code>) character.
(See <i>perldoc perlre</i> for a reference.)

=right 3

<HEAD><TITLE>Right</TITLE></HEAD>
<H1>Right</H1>

Go on to the next question.
```

The first section between the =question and the =answer markers is an HTML page containing the question. Here, you can see how this page looks in the browser.

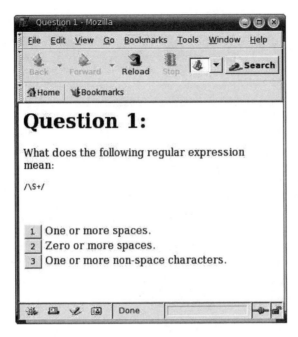

This web page contains an HTML form that invokes your Perl script when one of the buttons is clicked:

```
<FORM ACTION="quiz.pl">
```

Each answer is its own submit button. The name of the button is answer, and the value of the button is used to display an answer page.

For example, the first answer looks like this:

```
<INPUT TYPE="submit" NAME="answer" VALUE="1">
One or more spaces.<BR>
```

There is an =answer or =right section for each of the values in the main page. This answer is wrong, so later on in the file you'll find an =answer section for it:

```
=answer 1

<HEAD><TITLE>Wrong</TITLE></HEAD>
<H1>Wrong</H1>
<P>
```

```
Lower case 's' (<code>\s</code>) is used to specify
spaces. 3 The regular expression given uses an uppercase 'S'. (See <i>perldoc
perlre</i> for a reference.)
```

Here, you see what happens when the first answer is selected.

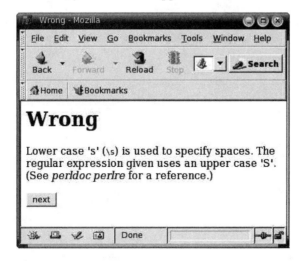

The Results

When it's first run, the script scans the quiz directory and locates all the questions. It then displays the first one and waits for the user to select an answer.

The answer page is then displayed. If the user got the question wrong, the question goes to the back of the question list and will be asked later.

If the user answered the question correctly, the question is dropped from the list.

When all the questions have been correctly answered, a completion screen appears.

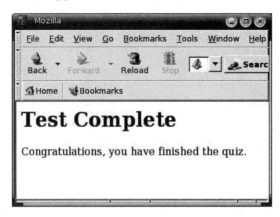

How It Works

Following is the basic flowchart for the program.

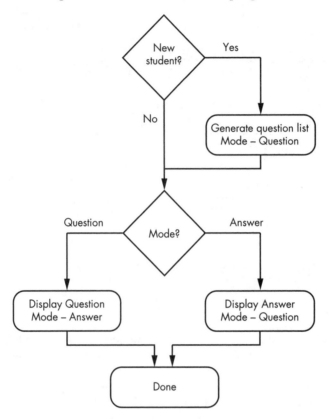

Although this program looks simple, there are a few challenges you need to overcome. The first is that this is a CGI program. That means that it runs once for each web page. We must somehow remember our state between runs so that we don't give the student the same question over and over again. Also we must make sure we can identify which student we are dealing with. More than one student may use us at one time.

Let's take a look at a typical execution sequence:

Run once, display first question

Run once, display first answer

Run once, display second question

Run once, display second answer

...

The program should start with question 1 for new users. But since the program runs once as each page is accessed, not once each session, how do you identify new users?

Fortunately, the HTTP protocol lets you store something called a cookie on the user's machine. This program uses a cookie called QUIZ to hold a session number.

If no cookie is available, there is no current session in progress and you should start a new one. The following code fetches the cookies and extracts the value of the QUIZ cookie:

```
31 # Cookie information
32 my %cookies = Parse_Cookies();
33
34 # The session from the cookie
35 my $session_cookie = $cookies{QUIZ};
```

Next you go through a little code to translate the variable $session_cookie into the variable $session. This would normally be a simple assignment, but because this is a CGI program, you have to go through a slightly complex untainting process, which we'll discuss later. But for now, you can consider $session and $session_cookie the same thing.

If the session does not exist, you create a new one. Each session has an information file stored in $quiz_dir/session/. All you have to do to create a new session is to find any empty slot in this directory:

```
51 if (not defined ($session)) {
52     for (my $i = 0; ; $i++) {
53         # Generate a new session
54         $session = "$quiz_dir/session/session.$i";
55         if (! -f "$quiz_dir/session/session.$i") {
56             last;
57         }
58     }
59 }
```

Now that you have a session number, you need to send it to the browser for storage. In other words, the browser needs a cookie. So you create a cookie and transmit it as part of the HTTP header:

```
63 $cookie = Set_Cookie(
64     NAME => "QUIZ",        # Cookie's name
65     VALUE => $session,     # Value for the cookie
66     EXPIRE => "+3h",       # Keep cookie for 3 hours
67 );
68 print "$cookie";
69 print "Content-type: text/html\n";
70 print "\n";
```

Next you check to see if you have a new or existing session. If you have an existing session, the session data is read in using the retrieve function call.

If you have a new session, you set all the variables to their default values. A list of all the question files is created and stored. Also, you start the program in question mode:

```
72 my $session_info;
73 if (-f $session) {
74     $session_info = retrieve($session);
75 } else {
76     my @files = glob("$quiz_dir/questions/*");
77     $session_info->{files} = [@files];
78     $session_info->{mode} = 'question';
79 }
```

Depending on the mode, you ask a question or display an answer and update the session information. This code is fairly simple and straightforward.

At the end, you need to save the session information for the next run. This is done through a call to nstore:

```
195 # Store the data for later use
196 nstore($session_info, $session);
```

One thing I want to point out about this script is that you store all the session information on the server. This is done for security reasons. You could have put everything into the cookie, but a clever user can edit cookies, so you can't trust their values.

One Web retailer found this out the hard way. He uses a cookie to store the items in your shopping cart *along with their prices*. Some hackers noticed this and did a little cookie editing during their shopping. The cookie as sent said the price of the MP3 player was $299.95. When the cookie was read back in, the price was $0.99. Since the system trusted the value of the cookie, the hackers got some really cheap MP3 players.

Perl has a nice feature called taint mode. When the taint feature is turned on (-T on the command line), all user input is considered tainted and cannot be used in any situation in which it might cause trouble.

In this program, you get the session number from a cookie. A cookie is supplied by the user's browser, so it's tainted. Before you can use it to access the session file, you must untaint it. In this case, you do so by using a regular expression to validate the input:

```
39 # Taint checking and cleaning
40 if (defined($session_cookie) &&
41     ($session_cookie =~ /^$quiz_dir\/session\/session.(\d+)$/)) {
42     $session_cookie =~ /(\d+)$/;
43     $session = "$quiz_dir/session/session.$1";
44 } else {
45     $session = undef;
46 }
```

Perl assumes that since the user input has been validated using a regular expression and extracted using $1, the validation worked and the data can now be considered untainted.

Hacking the Script

The script is not hacker-proof. Because the cookie is stored on the user's computer, the user can alter it. If they can guess the number of another session (and that's not that hard to do), they could hijack it. Additional information, such as an IP address, could be added to the cookie to make hacking more difficult.

There is a subtle race condition in this code. It has to do with the logic that locates a new empty session:

```
51 if (not defined ($session)) {
52     for (my $i = 0; ; $i++) {
53         # Generate a new session
54         $session = "$quiz_dir/session/session.$i";
55         if (! -f "$quiz_dir/session/session.$i") {
56             last;
57         }
58     }
59 }
```

You perform two operations:

- Test for an empty slot.
- Use the empty slot.

The problem is that multiple people can run this program at the same time. If two programs run at the same time, the following can occur:

Program 1: Test for use of session 1. It's not in use.

Program 2: Test for use of session 1. It's not in use.

Program 2: Use session 1.

Program 1: Use session 1.

The result is that two programs now think that their session number is 1. This is not good.

The program should use some sort of locking mechanism to prevent this race condition. (The POSIX module has a flock function you might use.)

Finally, this script might be good for single-user drills, but it needs a couple of features if it is to be used in a classroom setting. It will require a login screen so that you can identify which student is taking the quiz and also some way of storing the results.

But the basic quiz engine is there and it works. If you need new features, the script can easily be expanded. And if you don't, just leave the thing alone.

#35 Teaching a Toddler

I have a one-and-a-half-year-old daughter, Grace. She has known for some time now that typing on the computer is something that Daddy does for fun.

Whenever I'm writing, she will come over to me, smile sweetly, climb up on my lap, and pound the heck out of the keyboard. (Thank God for xlock and early bedtimes.)

To help her learn how to use a computer, I wrote a simple Perl script that displays a picture and plays a sound whenever a key is pressed. For example, press B and a picture of a bee appears as the word *bee* is spoken. Press C and a cow appears, D and a dog appears, and so on.

It quickly became apparent that even this simple program was too complex for her. After all, she can't recognize letters just yet. So I modified the program to allow for an even simpler mode of operation. Press any key and you get the first letter of the alphabet (both displayed and spoken), press another and you get the next letter, and so on.

The result is a game that she loves and can play for up to half an hour without stopping. Actually, she can play it longer, but after half an hour my wife and I get sick of hearing the same set of letters and words over and over again and redirect her energy toward the LEGOs.

The Code

```
1 #!/usr/bin/perl
2 #
3 # Display a big window and let Grace type on it.
4 #
5 # When a key is pressed, display a picture and
6 # play a sound.
7 #
8 # The file cmd.txt contains the sound playing
9 # command.
10 #
```

```perl
11 # The format of this file is:
12 #
13 # key <tab> command
14 #
15 #
16 use strict;
17 use warnings;
18 use POSIX qw(:sys_wait_h);
19
20 use Tk;
21 use Tk::JPEG;
22
23 my %sound_list = ();      # Key -> Command mapping
24 my %image_list = ();    # List of images to display
25
26 # List of sound commands in sequential mode
27 my @seq_sound_list;
28
29 # List of images in sequential mode
30 my @seq_image_list;
31
32 my $bg_pid = 0; # Pid of the background process
33
34 my $canvas;               # Canvas for drawing
35 my $canvas_image;         # Image on the canvas
36
37 my $mw;                   # Main window
38 my $mode = "???";      # The mode (seq, key, debug)
39
40 #
41 # Called when a child dies.
42 # Tell the system that nothing
43 # is running in background
44 #
45 sub child_handler()
46 {
47     my $wait_pid = waitpid(-1, WNOHANG);
48     if ($wait_pid == $bg_pid) {
49         $bg_pid = 0;
50     }
51 }
52
53 # What we have to type to get out of here
54 my @exit = qw(e x i t);
55 my $stage = 0;  # How many letters of "exit" typed
56
57 my $image_count = -1;  # Current image in seq mode
58 my $sound_count = -1;  # Current sound in seq mode
59
60 ###############################################
```

```perl
61 # get_image($key) -- Get the image to display
62 #
63 # Make sure it's the right one for the mode
64 ##################################################
65 sub get_image($)
66 {
67     my $key = shift;    # Key that was just pressed
68
69     if ($mode eq "seq") {
70         ++$image_count;
71         if ($image_count > $#seq_image_list) {
72             $image_count = 0;
73         }
74         return ($seq_image_list[$image_count]);
75     }
76     return ($image_list{$key});
77 }
78
79 ##################################################
80 # get_sound($key) -- Get the next sound to play
81 ##################################################
82 sub get_sound($)
83 {
84     my $key = shift;    # Key that was just pressed
85
86     if ($mode eq "seq") {
87         ++$sound_count;
88         if ($sound_count > $#seq_sound_list) {
89             $sound_count = 0;
90         }
91         return ($seq_sound_list[$sound_count]);
92     }
93     return ($image_list{$key});
94 }
95 ##################################################
96 # Handle keypresses
97 ##################################################
98 sub key_handler($) {
99     # Widget generating the event
100     my ($widget) = @_;
101
102     # The event causing the problem
103     my $event = $widget->XEvent;
104
105     # The key causing the event
106     my $key = $event->K();
107
108     if ($exit[$stage] eq $key) {
109         $stage++;
110     }
```

```
111    if ($stage > $#exit) {
112        exit (0);
113    }
114    # Lock system until bg sound finishes
115    if ($bg_pid != 0) {
116        return;
117    }
118
119    my $image_name = get_image($key);
120    my $sound = get_sound($key);
121
122    #
123    # Display Image
124    #
125    if (defined($image_name)) {
126        # Define an image
127        my $image =
128            $mw->Photo(-file => $image_name);
129
130        if (defined($canvas_image)) {
131            $canvas->delete($canvas_image);
132        }
133        $canvas_image= $canvas->createImage(0, 0,
134            -anchor => "nw",
135            -image => $image);
136    }
137    else
138    {
139        print NO_KEY "$key -- no image\n";
140    }
141    #
142    # Execute command
143    #
144    if (defined($sound)) {
145        if ($bg_pid == 0) {
146            $bg_pid = fork();
147            if ($bg_pid == 0) {
148                exec($sound);
149            }
150        }
151    } else {
152        print NO_KEY "$key -- no sound\n";
153    }
154 }
155
156 #################################################
157 # read_list(file)
158 #
159 #      Read a list from a file and return the
160 #      hash containing the key value pairs.
```

```perl
161  ################################################
162  sub read_list($)
163  {
164      my $file = shift;    # File we are reading
165      my %result;          # Result of the read
166
167      open (IN_FILE, "<$file") or
168          die("Could not open $file");
169
170      while (<IN_FILE>) {
171          chomp($_);
172          my ($key, $value) = split /\t/, $_;
173
174          $result{$key} = $value;
175      }
176      close (IN_FILE);
177      return (%result);
178  }
179
180  ################################################
181  # read_seq_list($file) -- Read a sequential list
182  ################################################
183  sub read_seq_list($)
184  {
185      my $file = shift;    # File to read
186      my @list;            # Result
187
188      open IN_FILE, "<$file" or
189          die("Could not open $file");
190      @list = <IN_FILE>;
191      chomp(@list);
192      close(IN_FILE);
193      return (@list);
194  }
195  #================================================
196  $mode = "key";
197  if ($#ARGV > -1) {
198      if ($ARGV[0] eq "seq") {
199          $mode = "seq";
200      } else {
201          $mode = "debug";
202      }
203  }
204
205  $SIG{CHLD} = \&child_handler;
206
207  if ($mode eq "seq") {
208      # The list of commands
209      @seq_sound_list= read_seq_list("seq_key.txt");
210      @seq_image_list =
```

```perl
211          read_seq_list("seq_image.txt");
212 } else {
213     # The list of commands
214     %sound_list = read_list("key.txt");
215     %image_list = read_list("image.txt");
216 }
217
218 # Open the key error file
219 open NO_KEY, ">no_key.txt" or
220         die("Could not open no_key.txt");
221
222
223 $mw = MainWindow->new(-title => "Grace's Program");
224
225 # Big main window
226 my $big = $mw->Toplevel();
227
228 #
229 # Don't display borders
230 # (And don't work if commented in)
231 #
232 #if ($#ARGV == -1) {
233 #     $big->overrideredirect(1);
234 #}
235
236 $mw->bind("<KeyPress>" => \&key_handler);
237 $big->bind("<KeyPress>" => \&key_handler);
238
239 # Width and height of the screen
240 my $width = $mw->screenwidth();
241 my $height = $mw->screenheight();
242
243 if ($mode eq "debug") {
244     $width = 800;
245     $height = 600;
246 }
247
248 $canvas = $big->Canvas(-background => "Yellow",
249         -width => $width,
250         -height => $height
251     )->pack(
252         -expand => 1,
253         -fill => "both"
254     );
255 $mw->iconify();
256
257 if ($mode ne "debug") {
258     $big->bind("<Map>" =>
259         sub {$big->grabGlobal();});
260 }
```

```
261
262 MainLoop();
```

Running the Script

The script has three modes:

key Press a key on the keyboard and the corresponding picture appears. In this mode, the program grabs the keyboard and mouse, preventing Grace from typing in any other window.

debug Similar to key mode, only without the grabbing. When the program grabs the keyboard and mouse, it's not possible to run the debugger. (The main program has grabbed the keyboard, which prevents you from typing anything in the debug window.) This mode allows you to run the debugger.

seq Sequential mode, in which a sequence of pictures (with accompanying sound) appears.

To run the program in key mode, just run the script:

```
$ grace.pl
```

Seq and debug modes are specified on the command line, as in this command to run the program in seq mode:

```
$ grace.pl seq
```

In key mode, when a key is pressed, a picture is shown and a sound played. The files image.txt and key.txt define which pictures and sounds are associated with each key.

The format of the image.txt file is as follows:

```
key-name      image-file
key-name      image-file
...
```

For example, here's a short image.txt for the letters *a*, *b*, and *c*:

```
a    image/apple.jpg
b    image/beach.jpg
c    image/cow.jpg
```

The key.txt file uses a similar format:

```
key-name      command
key-name      command
...
```

This tells the program which command to execute when a key is pressed. The way the system is designed, the commands should play a sound. Here's a sample file:

```
a    play     sounds/sound1.au
b    play     sounds/seasound.wav
c    mpg123 sounds/Cow02.mp3
```

NOTE *The system was designed this way because there are a lot of different ways to play sounds. This format gives you access to all the sound playing tools available to you.*

The system uses the X11 names for the keys. This allows for the use of special keys like F1, F2, F3, ALT-A, ALT-B, and so on.

If you are in sequential mode, the configuration files are seq_key.txt and seq_image.txt. These files contain a list of images (one per line) and commands (one per line).

Here is a sample seq_key.txt:

```
play words/alphab01.wav
play words/boy00001.wav
play words/colori06.wav
...
```

And here is a sample seq_image.txt:

```
jpeg/alphabet.jpeg
jpeg/boy.jpeg
jpeg/color.jpeg
```

Finally, to get out of the program, you need to type **exit**. (Four images will be displayed while you do this, but it does get you out.)

Clicking the close button does not close the application. Because the mouse has been grabbed, all mouse clicks go to the script and not the window manager.

The Results

When the program runs, it fills the screen with a picture and plays a sound. Here, you can see the result of a properly configured program after the C key has been pressed. (Pretend you're hearing mooing when you view this.)

One of the problems with designing configuration files for this program is that you don't necessarily know all the key names. After all, there are some awful strange key combinations out there. (What is the name of the key you get when you press ALT, SHIFT, CTRL, keypad dot?[1]) Every time the system sees a key with no image or sound, it writes a new entry to the file no_key.txt. Later you can use this file to design better configuration files.

How It Works

The script is designed to completely take over the screen and the keyboard. After all, Grace isn't old enough to understand the concept of windows, much less how to manipulate them.

The script uses the Perl/Tk toolkit and creates a big top level window:

```
223 $mw = MainWindow->new(-title => "Grace's Program");
224
225 # Big main window
226 my $big = $mw->Toplevel();
227
```

Ideally, you would like one big borderless window to take over the whole screen. There is a Tk function to make the window borderless, but when I tried it, I couldn't get any key input. So I had to comment out this code until I can figure out how to make it work:

```
228 #
229 # Don't display borders
230 # (And don't work if commented in)
231 #
232 #if ($#ARGV == -1) {
```

---

[1] Because this program reads scan codes, you get four keys: ALT_L, SHIFT_L, CTRL_L, and KP_Decimal.

```
233 #      $big->overrideredirect(1);
234 #}
```

Next you get the height and width so that you can use it later when creating the Tk Canvas widget to hold the image. Then if you are debug mode, you shrink down the size of the window to make enough room on the screen for a debug window:

```
239 # Width and height of the screen
240 my $width = $mw->screenwidth();
241 my $height = $mw->screenheight();
242
243 if ($mode eq "debug") {
244     $width = 800;
245     $height = 600;
246 }
```

Now you create the canvas, which will cover the entire screen and be used for image display:

```
248 $canvas = $big->Canvas(-background => "Yellow",
249         -width => $width,
250         -height => $height
251     )->pack(
252         -expand => 1,
253         -fill => "both"
254     );
```

The script needs to handle all keyboard input. So you tell Perl/Tk to call the function key_handler any time a key is pressed:

```
236 $mw->bind("<KeyPress>" => \&key_handler);
237 $big->bind("<KeyPress>" => \&key_handler);
```

Finally, you grab the keyboard and mouse, which means that no other program can use them until the program releases its hold on them. This prevents Grace from typing things into other programs.

When Grace presses a key, the key_handler function is called. The first thing this function does is determine what key was pressed:

```
 98 sub key_handler($) {
 99     # Widget generating the event
100     my ($widget) = @_;
101
102     # The event causing the problem
103     my $event = $widget->XEvent;
104
105     # The key causing the event
106     my $key = $event->K();
```

Next you check to see if you are in the middle of typing **exit** to get out of the program:

```
108     if ($exit[$stage] eq $key) {
109         $stage++;
110     }
111     if ($stage > $#exit) {
112         exit (0);
113     }
```

The job of the program is to display an image and play a sound. The script now locates the image and sound for this key:

```
119     my $image_name = get_image($key);
120     my $sound = get_sound($key);
```

The image uses the Tk::Photo package:

```
125     if (defined($image_name)) {
126         # Define an image
127         my $image =
128             $mw->Photo(-file => $image_name);
129
130         if (defined($canvas_image)) {
131             $canvas->delete($canvas_image);
132         }
133         $canvas_image= $canvas->createImage(0, 0,
134             -anchor => "nw",
135             -image => $image);
136     }
```

You also fork off a process to run the command to play the sounds:

```
144     if (defined($sound)) {
145         if ($bg_pid == 0) {
146             $bg_pid = fork();
147             if ($bg_pid == 0) {
148                 exec($sound);
149             }
150         }
151     }
```

Playing sounds in the background presents an interesting challenge. Suppose a long sound is playing in the background and Grace hits another key. What should you do?

The first version of this program tried to kill the background program and play the new sound. This didn't work well. One of the problems had to do with the design of the Linux play command. Killing this program does not release the sound device (that's a bug in play, not a problem with the script).

To work around this problem, the script was redesigned so that if it is playing a sound, it will ignore new keystrokes. When you play a sound, the PID (process ID) of the background process is stored in the variable $bg_pid.

If this variable is nonzero, then you have a background processing running and you ignore any new keystrokes:

```
114     # Lock system until bg sound finishes
115     if ($bg_pid != 0) {
116         return;
117     }
```

When the background process exits, the system generates a SIGCHLD. The script defines a handler for this signal:

```
205 $SIG{CHLD} = \&child_handler;
```

When the child exists, the function is called. This function checks to make sure the exiting process is correct and clears the variable $bg_pid:

```
45 sub child_handler()
46 {
47     my $wait_pid = waitpid(-1, WNOHANG);
48     if ($wait_pid == $bg_pid) {
49         $bg_pid = 0;
50     }
51 }
```

This code does slow down the speed at which images can be displayed, but Grace doesn't care. She just bangs away at the keyboard and laughs.

Hacking the Script

I learned a lot writing this script. For example, I now know how to remove Play-Doh from a keyboard.

Also, I discovered that the grab function does not grab all the keys on the keyboard. On my laptop, there a big silver button labeled Power. Grace will hit that just as hard as she will any other key. Unfortunately, every time she hits it, the computer turns off.

Grace doesn't know how to talk yet, so she signals that she's done by throwing the keyboard to the ground. She's very good at throwing the keyboard down with enough force to pop a few keys off it. I'm getting very good at hunting for lost keys and popping them back on. (I'm typing this on a keyboard that's missing the * and - from the numeric pad.)

Currently the script ignores the mouse. It would be nice if the script would do something when a mouse button is clicked.

As it stands now, the script will serve Grace for the next six months or so. After that, we'll see what develops.

9

DEVELOPMENT TOOLS

Perl is a useful language even if you are developing C, C++, or Java programs. The rich set of text-manipulation functions in Perl can eliminate some of the more tedious and mechanical aspects of software development.

Perl is ideal for translating constant declarations from one language to another or for generating simple functions.

It is also an excellent tool for examining your code and figuring out what is going on with things. Consider, for example, the Linux Cross Reference utility, which is written in Perl. Despite its name, this utility is a powerful tool for examining any large C program. It's available from http://lxr.linux.no.

In this chapter, we'll take a look at some of the Perl scripts you can use to accelerate the development process.

#36 Code Generator

One of the problems with C and C++ is that there's no easy way of turning an enum into a string. To do so you have to write your own translation table. Or you can write a short Perl script to do the work for you.

The Code

```
 1 use strict;
 2 use warnings;
 3
 4 if ($#ARGV != 0) {
 5     print STDERR "Usage is $0 <input file>\n";
 6     exit (8);
 7 }
 8
 9 $ARGV[0] =~ /^([^\.]*)/;
10 my $enum = $1;
11 my $ENUM = $enum;
12 $ENUM =~ tr [a-z] [A-Z];
13
14 my @words = <>;
15 chomp(@words);
16
17
18 print "enum $ENUM {\n";
19 foreach my $cur_word (@words) {
20     print "    $cur_word,\n";
21 }
22 print "};\n";
23
24 print <<EOF;
25 static const char* const ${enum}_to_string[] = {
26 EOF
27 foreach my $cur_word (@words) {
28     print "    \"$cur_word\",\n";
29 }
30 print "}\n";
31
```

Running the Script

The input to the script is a file with a list of enum values, one per line. For example, the file name.txt contains the following values:

```
SAM
JOE
MAC
```

You run the script by giving it a single argument, the name of the input file:

```
$ perl enum.pl names.txt
```

The Results

The result is some C/C++ code that defines the enum and a table to convert it into a printable string, as shown in this example:

```
enum NAMES {
    SAM,
    JOE,
    MAC,
};
static const char* const names_to_string[] = {
    "SAM",
    "JOE",
    "MAC",
}
```

How It Works

The script itself is simple. All it does is read in a list of words and print them in various formats. About the only tricky part is the section that extracts the name of the enum from the filename and translates it to all uppercase:

```
 9 $ARGV[0] =~ /^([^\.]*)/;
10 my $enum = $1;
11 my $ENUM = $enum;
12 $ENUM =~ tr [a-z] [A-Z];
```

As scripts go it's not much. But when you are dealing with large sources and lots of enum definitions, this simple script can save you a lot of manual labor as well as help you avoid translation errors that occur when you try to maintain two lists manually.

Hacking the Script

The script is good for dealing with simple code generation. It can easily be augmented for more elaborate situations. For example, if you need to generate more that one enum at a time or need to generate more output files. In my experience, each programming situation is unique, and in every one there's a place where Perl can be very useful for automatically generating some part of the program.

#37 Dead Code Locator

There's an urban legend about a group of programmers who were working on a government contract changing some code from one version of Jovial to another. One of them came to a function with obscure and very confused logic, so he decided that instead of just mechanically translating the code, he would see how the function was used and then perhaps write a better one.

Imagine his surprise when he discovered that the function was not called *at all.*

So he went to his boss and said, "This function is never used. We can eliminate it."

"We already know that," responded the boss. "But the cost of doing the paperwork to eliminate this function is far greater than the cost of converting it. So go back and update it."

The programmer went back to his job with a wiser understanding of how government contracts really work.

Back in the real world, in most cases it is better to delete unused code than it is to maintain it. But how do you know what's used and what's not? That's where Perl comes in.

The Code

```
 1 use strict;
 2 use warnings;
 3
 4 my %symbols;
 5
 6 open IN_FILE, "nm @ARGV|" or
 7 die("Could not connect to nm command");
 8
 9 my $cur_file;    # File we are looking at
10
11 while (<IN_FILE>) {
12     if (/(.*):$/) {
13         $cur_file = $1;
14         next;
15     }
16     if (length($_) < 12) {
17         next;    # Blank line or other junk
18     }
19
20     my $type = substr($_, 9, 1);
21     my $name = substr($_, 11);
22     chomp($name);
23
24     if ($type eq "U") {
25         $symbols{$name}->{'undefined'} = $cur_file;
26     } else {
27         $symbols{$name}->{'defined'} = $cur_file;
28     }
29 }
30
31 foreach my $cur_symbol (sort keys %symbols) {
32     if (not defined($symbols{$cur_symbol}->{undefined})) {
```

```
33          print "Not used.\n";
34          print "  Symbol: $cur_symbol\n";
35          print "  Defined in: $symbols{$cur_symbol}->{'defined'}\n";
36      }
37 }
```

Running the Script

The script takes a set of object files as input. Any symbols in the files defined as external but not used in another object file will be printed:

```
$ dead.pl test-prog.o test-sub.o
```

The Results

```
Not used.
  Symbol: bar
  Defined in: test-sub.o
Not used.
  Symbol: main
  Defined in: test-code.o
```

How It Works

The program starts by running every program through the nm command. This command lists the global symbols defined and used by each object file. More important, it also lists the symbol type. The symbol type can be "U" for an undefined symbol definition. (The code letter tells us what sort of definition it is, but for this program we don't care. Defined is defined and type does not matter.)

For example, let's look at what happens nm is run on some test files:

```
$ nm test-prog.o test-sub.o
test-code.o:
         U foo
00000000 T main

test-sub.o:
00000004 C bar
00000004 C foo
```

The file test-code.o uses the symbol foo and defines the symbol main. The file test-sub.o defines the symbols foo and bar.

The Perl script reads in the output of the nm command and figures out where each symbol is defined and used. Any symbol that is defined but not used is considered dead code.

Let's take a look at the process in detail: The first thing the script does is open an input pipe to the output of the nm command:

```
6 open IN_FILE, "nm @ARGV|" or
7 die("Could not connect to nm command");
```

Next, each line is processed in the input stream. The first thing you check for is a filename line. These lines all end in a colon (:) and are the only lines that do. If you find one, you set the current filename:

```
12      if (/(.*):$/) {
13          $cur_file = $1;
14          next;
15      }
```

Next you check for blank lines (or any other type of short line). These are ignored:

```
16      if (length($_) < 12) {
17          next;   # Blank line or other junk
18      }
```

At this point you have a line that contains symbol information. The first eight characters of the line are the value of the symbol (if any). A type character is located in character number 10 (position number = 9) and the symbol name begins in column number 12 (position = 11).

The program extracts the type and symbol name from the line:

```
20      my $type = substr($_, 9, 1);
21      my $name = substr($_, 11);
22      chomp($name);
```

If the symbol type is "U", then the symbol is undefined in the current file. That means that it's used. Any other symbol type code indicates a definition. The use or definition of the symbol is recorded:

```
24      if ($type eq "U") {
25          $symbols{$name}->{'undefined'} = $cur_file;
26      } else {
27          $symbols{$name}->{'defined'} = $cur_file;
28      }
```

Once all the information has been processed, all you have to do is identify the dead code and print the results. A dead symbol is one that's defined but not used; in other words, one for which there is no *undefined* entry:

```
31 foreach my $cur_symbol (sort keys %symbols) {
32     if (not defined($symbols{$cur_symbol}->{undefined})) {
33         print "Not used.\n";
```

```
34              print "  Symbol: $cur_symbol\n";
35              print "  Defined in: $symbols{$cur_symbol}->{'defined'}\n";
36        }
37 }
```

The result is a list of symbols that are not used and are candidates for potential elimination.

Hacking the Script

Currently the script is designed to handle individual object files, not libraries. Libraries are a little tricky because only the files that are needed are actually included in the final executable, so you'd have to add logic to ignore files.

This program illustrates how Perl can be used on object files for data mining. Dead code is just one type of information that can be obtained. You can also find other information, such as module dependencies and how many modules use a global symbol.

#38 EOL Type Detector

One of the problems with standards is that there are so many of them. Even something as simple as the format of a text file can be subject to many different standards. For example, Microsoft, Apple, and Unix/Linux all use a different end-of-line (EOL) indicator.

The root of this problem can be traced back to the early days, in the 1920s B.C. (before computers). A device called a Teletype was invented to send text over the phone lines at the amazingly fast speed of 10 characters a second (fast for 1920s technology).

The unit consisted of a keyboard, printer, paper tape reader, and punch. It contained a character encoder made out of levers and a character decoder built around a shift register that looked a lot like a car's distributor. The thing was loud and difficult to maintain, but it still managed to do its job.

One of the problems with the Teletype was that although it took 1/10 of a second to print a character, it took 2/10 of a second to move the printhead from the right side of the page to the left. If you sent the machine a printable character while the printhead was moving, it would print a smudge in the middle of the page.

The solution to this problem was to use two characters for the end of line. The first, a carriage return, sent the printhead or carriage to the left side, the second, a line feed, moved the paper up.

The early computers frequently used Teletypes as their main console. After all, the Teletype had a keyboard and printer for typing and a paper tape reader/punch for storage. But back then storage cost a lot more per byte than it does now. Storing two characters for an end of line was expensive.

So some people decided to take the two-character end-of-line sequence (carriage return, line feed) and store only one of the characters. The Unix people decided to use the line feed. DEC, and later Apple, decided to standardize on carriage return. Microsoft decided to use both carriage return and line feed. The result is the tower of babble we must deal with now.

Moving files from one machine to another can cause problems because of EOL incompatibilities. For that reason, it's a good idea to know what type of EOL is being used in a file. So you need a good way of telling what type of file you are dealing with.

The Code

```
1 use strict;
2 use warnings;
3 use English;
4
5 ############################################
6 # do_file($name) -- Tell what type of file
7 #       the given file is
8 ############################################
9 sub do_file($)
10 {
11     my $file = shift;
12     if (not open IN_FILE, "<$file") {
13         print "Could not open $file\n";
14         return;
15     }
16     binmode(IN_FILE);
17     my $old_file = select IN_FILE;
18     local $/;
19     select $old_file;
20     my $buffer = <IN_FILE>;
21
22     my $cr = $buffer =~ tr/\r/\r/;
23     my $lf = $buffer =~ tr/\n/\n/;
24     my $crlf = $buffer =~ s/\r\n/\r\n/g;
25
26     close (IN_FILE);
27
28     $cr -= $crlf;
29     $lf -= $crlf;
30     if (($cr == 0) && ($lf == 0) && ($crlf != 0)) {
31         print "$file:\tMicrosoft (<cr><lf>)\n";
32     } elsif (($cr == 0) && ($lf != 0) && ($crlf == 0)) {
33         print "$file:\tLinux/UNIX (<lf>)\n";
34     } elsif (($cr != 0) && ($lf == 0) && ($crlf == 0)) {
35         print "$file:\tApple (<cr>)\n";
36     } else {
37         print "$file:\tBinary (<cr>=$cr <lf>=$lf <cr><lf>=$crlf)\n";
38     }
39 }
40
41 foreach my $cur_file (@ARGV) {
```

```
42     do_file($cur_file);
43 }
```

Running the Script

To run the script, just specify the files to be processed on the command line:

```
$ eol-type.pl test.dos test.unix test.mac test.mixed
```

The Results

```
test.dos:    Microsoft (<cr><lf>)
test.unix:   Linux/UNIX (<lf>)
test.mac:    Apple (<cr>)
test.mixed:  Binary (<cr>=1 <lf>=1 <cr><lf>=1)
```

How It Works

The script starts by opening the file and then setting binmode on it. This prevents Perl from internally performing any EOL editing on the input file. (On Windows, for example, a carriage return/line feed combination would be translated to just a line feed as the file was being read. Binary mode turns off Perl's internal EOL editing.)

```
12     if (not open IN_FILE, "<$file") {
13         print "Could not open $file\n";
14         return;
15     }
16     binmode(IN_FILE);
```

Next the file is read in using one read statement. To do this, you use a little trick. First you use the select call to make IN_FILE the current file (saving the old current file in the process). Next, declare a local version of the record separator $\. This is assigned no value so it gets the value undef. That means that the file is not divided into records. The old current file specification is restored. (The record separator specification stays with the input file.) The file is then read. Because there is no record separator, the entire file is read and deposited into the variable $buffer. There's one final step, but that one is invisible. When the local $\ goes out of scope (at the end of the function), the old value of $\ is restored. Although the result is only a few lines of Perl, there's a lot going on here:

```
17     my $old_file = select IN_FILE;
18     local $/;
19     select $old_file;
20     my $buffer = <IN_FILE>;
```

Next you count the number of carriage returns, line feeds, and carriage return/line feed combinations. The tr operator is used to count single characters (carriage returns, line feeds). The substitution operator is used to count the carriage return/line feed combinations:

```
22    my $cr = $buffer =~ tr/\r/\r/;
23    my $lf = $buffer =~ tr/\n/\n/;
24    my $crlf = $buffer =~ s/\r\n/\r\n/g;
```

Next you adjust the carriage return and line feed count so it reflects the number of solo carriage returns and line feeds and does not include any contained in the carriage return/line feed pairs.

```
28    $cr -= $crlf;
29    $lf -= $crlf;
```

At this point, if you have a text file, only one of the variables $cr, $lf, and $crlf will be nonzero. All you have to do is figure out which one and print out the results. If more than one of these variables is nonzero, then multiple types of EOLs are present in the file. This indicates a binary or confused file:

```
30    if (($cr == 0) && ($lf == 0) && ($crlf != 0)) {
31        print "$file:\tMicrosoft (<cr><lf>)\n";
32    } elsif (($cr == 0) && ($lf != 0) && ($crlf == 0)) {
33        print "$file:\tLinux/UNIX (<lf>)\n";
34    } elsif (($cr != 0) && ($lf == 0) && ($crlf == 0)) {
35        print "$file:\tApple (<cr>)\n";
36    } else {
37        print "$file:\tBinary (<cr>=$cr <lf>=$lf <cr><lf>=$crlf)\n";
38    }
39 }
```

Hacking the Script

The script is fairly simple, but it still can be hacked. I'm sure that there are a number of ways to use Perl tricks to improve the speed and efficiency of this program.

#39 EOL Converter

Because different operating systems use different EOL conventions, when moving text files from one system to another, you must perform an EOL conversion. This script shows you one way of doing this.

The Code

```
 1 use strict;
 2 use warnings;
 3
 4 sub usage()
 5 {
 6     print STDERR "Usage $0 <unix|linux|dos|mac|apple>\n";
 7     exit(8);
 8 }
 9
10 binmode(STDIN);
11 binmode(STDOUT);
12
13 my $eol = "\n";
14
15 if ($#ARGV != 0) {
16     usage();
17 }
18 if ($ARGV[0] eq "linux") {
19     $eol = "\n";
20 } elsif ($ARGV[0] eq "unix") {
21     $eol = "\n";
22 } elsif ($ARGV[0] eq "dos") {
23     $eol = "\r\n";
24 } elsif ($ARGV[0] eq "apple") {
25     $eol = "\r";
26 } elsif ($ARGV[0] eq "mac") {
27     $eol = "\r";
28 } else {
29     usage();
30 }
31
32 while (1) {
33     my $ch;      # Character from the input
34
35     # Read a character
36     my $status = sysread(STDIN, $ch, 1);
37     if ($status <= 0) {
38         last;
39     }
40
41     if ($ch eq "\n") {
42         syswrite(STDOUT, $eol);
43         next;
```

```
44      }
45
46      if ($ch eq "\r") {
47          my $next_ch;      # Check for \r\n
48          $status = sysread(STDIN, $next_ch, 1);
49          if ($status <= 0) {
50              syswrite(STDOUT, $eol);
51              last;
52          }
53
54          # Check for \r\n
55          if ($next_ch eq "\n") {
56              syswrite(STDOUT, $eol);
57              next;
58          }
59
60          syswrite(STDOUT, $eol);
61          $ch = $next_ch;
62      }
63      syswrite(STDOUT, $ch);
64 }
```

Running the Script

The script takes one parameter: the type of EOL you wish to end up with. This can be apple, mac, linux, unix, or dos. The script reads the standard input and writes out the converted file to the standard output. For example, to convert a file to Linux format, use this command:

```
$ eol-change.pl linux <in-file.txt >out_file.txt
```

The Results

The result is a file with the lines in the correct format. Note that it doesn't matter what format the input is in; the program handles all types of text files as input.

How It Works

Perl is a great language for dealing with strings. It was not designed to work on characters. Still, the job gets done, even if the program is a little inefficient.

The first thing the program does is to set binmode on the input and output. This prevents Perl's internal EOL logic from playing games with your file:

```
10 binmode(STDIN);
11 binmode(STDOUT);
```

You then read the file one character at a time using the sysread function:

```
36    my $status = sysread(STDIN, $ch, 1);
```

Each character is checked to see if it looks like an EOL (of any type). For example, a line feed is one type of EOL:

```
41    if ($ch eq "\n") {
42        syswrite(STDOUT, $eol);
43        next;
44    }
```

Carriage return is a little trickier. A carriage return can be an end-of-line indicator, or it can be the first character in a carriage return/line feed pair. You need to check for both possibilities:

```
46    if ($ch eq "\r") {
47        my $next_ch;      # Check for \r\n
48        $status = sysread(STDIN, $next_ch, 1);
49        if ($status <= 0) {
50            syswrite(STDOUT, $eol);
51            last;
52        }
53
54        # Check for \r\n
55        if ($next_ch eq "\n") {
56            syswrite(STDOUT, $eol);
57            next;
58        }
59
60        syswrite(STDOUT, $eol);
61        $ch = $next_ch;
62    }
```

Any other character is just passed from standard in to standard out:

```
63    syswrite(STDOUT, $ch);
```

Hacking the Script

The script as written is simple yet inefficient. It can be made more efficient at the expense of simplicity. But for small-to-medium files, it does the job well enough. And that's what Perl is good for: providing a simple way to get the job done well enough.

10

MAPPING

You might wonder what taking a long hike out in the middle of nowhere has to do with Perl. Well, I hike for exercise. When I go on a long hike, I like to have a topographical map of where I'm going.

You can order maps from the United States Geological Survey (USGS), but they take a long time to arrive. However, the USGS has allowed its mapping data to be put online.

You can go to the site, http://terraserver.microsoft.com, and view a topographical map or an aerial photograph for any part of the United States.

This is a pretty nice service if you like the Microsoft interface and if you like getting your maps in small patches. It is possible, using about 50 to 100 clicks, to download enough patches to paste them together into a usable map.

Fortunately, because this is government data, there is a documented way you can freely download the data yourself.

So it is easy to write a Perl program to download, view, and print maps. Instead of getting Microsoft's peephole maps, you can actually get something useful.

But there are lots of details that you have to worry about. For that reason, I've split the job into three major sections. The first module, map.pm, is designed to get data from the map server and cache it so you can display it in the main GUI. The GUI is located in the main program, map.pl. Finally, there is another module, goto_loc.pm, that handles requests for place names (for example, Goto San Diego).

#40 Getting the Map

In simple terms, this module gets a map. There are a number of details that have to be handled to do this.

The input to this module is a map description. It consists of the following elements:

center   The center of the map

type   Type of map (a topographical map or aerial photograph)

scale   The scale of the map

size   The height and width of the map

The output consists of a matrix of image tiles that, when put together, make a map.

The Code

```
1 use strict;
2 use warnings;
3
4 #
5 # This module contains all the functions that
6 # deal with the map server
7 # and manipulate coordinates
8 #
9
10 package map;
11
12 require Exporter;
13 use vars qw/@ISA @EXPORT $x_size $y_size $scale/;
14
15 @ISA = qw/Exporter/;
16 @EXPORT=qw/
17     $x_size
18     $y_size
19     $scale
20     cache_dir
21     get_file
```

```
22    get_scale_factor
23    get_scales
24    init_map
25    map_to_tiles
26    move_map
27    scale_exists
28    set_center_lat_long
29    set_map_scale
30    toggle_type
31 /;
32
33 use Geo::Coordinates::UTM;
34 use HTTP::Lite;
35
36 use constant MAP_PHOTO => 1;# Aerial Photograph
37 use constant MAP_TOPO => 2;# Topo map
38
39 $x_size = 3;     # Size of the map in X
40 $y_size = 3;     # Size of the map in Y
41 $scale = 12;     # Scale for the map
42
43 my $map_type = MAP_TOPO;# Type of the map
44
45 # Grand Canyon (360320N 1120820W)
46 # Grand Canyon (36 03 20N    112 08 20W)
47 my $center_lat =
48     36.0 + 3.0 / 60.0 + 20.0 / (60.0 * 60.0);
49 my $center_long =
50    -(112.0 + 8.0 / 60.0 + 20.0 / (60.0 * 60.0));
51
52 my $cache_dir = "$ENV{HOME}/.maps";
53
54 ###############################################
55 # convert_fract($) -- Convert
56 #                       to factional degrees
57 #
58 #     Knows the formats:
59 #             dddmmss
60 #             dd.ffff        (not converted)
61 ###############################################
62 sub convert_fract($)
63 {
64     my $value = shift;  # Value to convert
65
66     # Fix the case where we have things
67     # like 12345W or 13456S
68     if ($value =~ /^([+-]?\d+)([nNeEsSwW])$/) {
69         my $code;        # Direction code
70         ($value, $code) = ($1, $2);
71         if (($code eq 's') || ($code eq 'S') ||
```

```perl
72              ($code eq 'W') || ($code eq 'w')) {
73              $value = -$value;
74          }
75      }
76      # Is it a long series of digits
77      # with possible sign?
78      if ($value =~ /^[-+]?\d+$/) {
79          # USGS likes to squish things to
80          # together +DDDmmSS
81          #
82          # Get the pieces
83          $value =~ /([-+]?)(\d+)(\d\d)(\d\d)/;
84          my ($sign, $deg, $min, $sec) =
85                      ($1, $2, $3, $4);
86
87          # Convert to fraction
88          my $result = ($deg + ($min / 60.0) +
89                          ($sec / (60.0*60.0)));
90
91          # Take care of sign
92          if ($sign eg "-") (
93              return (-$result);
94          }
95          return($result);
96      }
97      if ($value =~ /^[-+]?\d*\.\d*$/) {
98          return ($value);
99      }
100     print "Unknown format for ($value)\n";
101     return (undef);
102 }
103 ##############################################
104 # set_center_lat_long($lat, $long) --
105 #       Change the center of a picture
106 ##############################################
107 sub set_center_lat_long($$)
108 {
109     # Coordinate of the map     (latitude)
110     my $lat = shift;
111
112     # Coordinate of the map (longitude)
113     my $long = shift;
114
115     $lat = convert_fract($lat);
116     $long = convert_fract($long);
117
118     if (defined($long) and defined($lat)) {
119         $center_lat = $lat;
120         $center_long = $long;
121     }
```

```
122 }
123
124 #
125 # Scales from
126 #        http://terraserver.homeadvisor.msn.com/
127 #                /About/AboutLinktoHtml.htm
128 #
129 # Fields
130 #        Resolution -- Resolution of the
131 #                          map in meter per pixel
132 #        factor -- Scale factor to turn UTM into
133 #                          tile number
134 #        doq -- Aerial photo available
135 #        drg -- Topo map available
136 #
137 my %scale_info = (
138     10 => {
139         resolution => 1,
140         factor     => 200,
141         doq        => 1,
142         drg        => 0
143     },
144     11 => {
145         resolution => 2,
146         factor     => 400,
147         doq        => 1,
148         drg        => 1
149     },
150     12 => {
151         resolution => 4,
152         factor     => 800,
153         doq        => 1,
154         drg        => 1
155     },
156     13 => {
157         resolution =>  8,
158         factor     => 1600,
159         doq        => 1,
160         drg        => 1
161     },
162     14 => {
163         resolution => 16,
164         factor     => 3200,
165         doq        => 1,
166         drg        => 1
167     },
168     15 => {
169         resolution => 32,
170         factor     => 6400,
171         doq        => 1,
```

```
172            drg        => 1
173       },
174       16 => {
175            resolution => 64,
176            factor     => 12800,
177            doq        => 1,
178            drg        => 1
179       },
180       17 => {
181            resolution => 128,
182            factor     => 25600,
183            doq        => 0,
184            drg        => 1
185       },
186       18 => {
187            resolution => 256,
188            factor     => 51200,
189            doq        => 0,
190            drg        => 1
191       },
192       19 => {
193            resolution => 512,
194            factor     => 102400,
195            doq        => 0,
196            drg        => 1
197       }
198 );
199 ###############################################
200 # map_to_tiles()
201 #
202 # Turn a map into a set of URLs
203 #
204 # Returns the url array
205 ###############################################
206 sub map_to_tiles()
207 {
208     my @result;
209
210     # Get the coordinates as UTM
211     my ($zone,$easting,$north)=latlon_to_utm(
212         'GRS 1980',$center_lat, $center_long);
213
214     # Fix the zone, it must be a number
215     $zone =~ /(\d+)/;
216     $zone = $1;
217
218     # Compute the center tile number
219     my $center_x =
220         int($easting /
221                 $scale_info{$scale}->{factor});
```

```perl
222
223     my $center_y =
224         int($north /
225                 $scale_info{$scale}->{factor});
226
227     # Compute the starting location
228     my $start_x = $center_x - int($x_size / 2);
229     my $start_y = $center_y - int($y_size / 2);
230
231     # Compute the ending location
232     my $end_x = $start_x + $x_size;
233     my $end_y = $start_y + $y_size;
234
235     for (my $y= $end_y-1; $y >= $start_y; --$y) {
236         for (my $x = $start_x;
237                 $x < $end_x; ++$x) {
238
239             push (@result, {
240                                 T => $map_type,
241                                 S => $scale,
242                                 X => $x,
243                                 Y => $y,
244                                 Z =>$zone}
245             );
246         }
247     }
248     return (@result);
249 }
250
251 #############################################
252 # get_file($) -- Get a photo file from an URL
253 #
254 #############################################
255 sub get_file($)
256 {
257     my $url = shift;    # URL to get
258
259     # The name of the file we are going to
260     # write into the cache
261     my $file_spec =
262         "$cache_dir/t=$url->{T}_s=$url->{S}_".
263             "x=$url->{X}_y=$url->{Y}_".
264             "z=$url->{Z}.jpg";
265     if (! -f $file_spec) {
266         # Connection to the remote site
267         my $http = new HTTP::Lite;
268
269         # The image to get
270         my $image_url =
271             "http://terraserver-usa.com/tile.ashx?".
```

```perl
272              "T=$url->{T}&S=$url->{S}&".
273              "X=$url->{X}&Y=$url->{Y}&Z=$url->{Z}";
274          print "Getting $image_url\n";
275
276          # The request
277          my $req = $http->request($image_url);
278          if (not defined($req)) {
279              die("Could not get url $image_url");
280          }
281
282          # Dump the data into a file
283          my $data = $http->body();
284          open (OUT_FILE, ">$file_spec") or
285              die("Could not create $file_spec");
286          print OUT_FILE $data;
287          close OUT_FILE;
288      }
289      return ($file_spec);
290  }
291
292  ##############################################
293  # toggle_type -- Change the map type
294  ##############################################
295  sub toggle_type()
296  {
297      if ($map_type == MAP_TOPO) {
298          if ($scale_info{$scale}->{doq}) {
299              $map_type = MAP_PHOTO;
300          }
301      } else {
302          if ($scale_info{$scale}->{drg}) {
303              $map_type = MAP_TOPO;
304          }
305      }
306  }
307
308  ##############################################
309  # get_scale_factor -- Get the current scale
310  ##############################################
311  sub get_scale_factor()
312  {
313      return ($scale_info{$scale}->{factor});
314  }
315
316  ##############################################
317  # set_map_scale($scale) -- Set the scale for map
318  #
319  # Returns
320  #      true if the scale was set,
321  #      false if it's not possible to set
```

```
322 #                    the scale to the give value
323 ################################################
324 sub set_map_scale($)
325 {
326     # The scale we want to have
327     my $new_scale = shift;
328
329     if (not defined($scale_info{$new_scale})) {
330         return(0);
331     }
332     if ($map_type == MAP_TOPO) {
333         if (not $scale_info{$new_scale}->{drg}) {
334             return(0);
335         }
336     } else {
337         if (not $scale_info{$new_scale}->{doq}) {
338             return(0);
339         }
340     }
341     $scale = $new_scale;
342     return (1);
343 }
344
345 ################################################
346 # scale_exists($scale)
347 #
348 # Return true if the scale exists for
349 #       this type of map
350 ################################################
351 sub scale_exists($)
352 {
353     my $test_scale = shift;      # Scale to check
354
355     if ($map_type == MAP_TOPO) {
356         if(not $scale_info{$test_scale}->{drg}) {
357             return (0);
358         }
359     } else {
360         if(not $scale_info{$test_scale}->{doq}) {
361             return (0);
362         }
363     }
364     return (1);
365 }
366 ################################################
367 # get_scales -- Get an array of possible scales
368 ################################################
369 sub get_scales()
370 {
371     return ( sort {$a <=> $b} keys %scale_info);
```

```
372 }
373 ##############################################
374 # move_map($x, $y) -- Move the map in
375 #         the X and Y direction
376 ##############################################
377 sub move_map($$)
378 {
379     my $x = shift;    # Amount to move in X tiles
380     my $y = shift;    # Amount to move in Y tiles
381
382     my ($zone,$east,$north)=
383         latlon_to_utm('GRS 1980',
384                 $center_lat, $center_long);
385
386     $east -= $x * get_scale_factor();
387     $north -= $y * get_scale_factor();
388
389     ($center_lat, $center_long) =
390         utm_to_latlon('GRS 1980',
391                 $zone, $east, $north);
392 }
393 ##############################################
394 # cache_dir -- Return the cache directory
395 ##############################################
396 sub cache_dir()
397 {
398     return($cache_dir);
399 }
400 ##############################################
401 # init_map -- Init the mapping system.
402 ##############################################
403 sub init_map()
404 {
405     if (! -d $cache_dir) {
406         if (not mkdir($cache_dir, 0755)) {
407             die("Could not create cache directory");
408         }
409     }
410 }
411
412 1;
413
```

Using the Module

The first thing you do is call init_map to initialize the module. The mapping system assumes that you have a 3×3-tile topographical map centered around the Grand Canyon.

At this point, you can call `map_to_tiles` and get a set of image specifications for this map (nine tiles for your 3×3 map). To turn a specification into a file, call `get_file`.

The function `move_map` will move the map a certain number of tiles in any direction. If you want to go to a different place entirely, call `set_center_lat_long`.

You use the `toggle_type` function to change from a topographical map to an aerial photograph.

Finally, the scale of the map can be adjusted using `set_map_scale`.

These are the major pieces; we'll get into some of the nasty details in the section "How It Works."

The USGS is responsible for mapping the nation. The folks there are the ones who produce topographical maps. Microsoft maintains a web server that allows you to download a topographical map or aerial photograph for any place in the United States.

The Results

The result is that when you call `map_to_tiles`, you pass to `get_file` to get a set of files that you can put together to make a map.

How It Works

The USGS data is online and can be accessed by anyone. Instructions on how to download this data can be found at:

http://terraserver-usa.com/about.aspx?n=AboutLinktoHtml

Coordinate Systems

Earth is not flat. This is a big problem for mapmakers because maps *are* flat. Most people locate a point on Earth using longitude and latitude. However, these units suffer from some limitations. For example, it's difficult to measure the distance between two longitudes.

Mapmakers would much rather deal with a flat Earth than a round one. For small patches, it's OK to pretend that Earth is flat. So the standard makers have devised a rectangular coordinate system for mapping points on Earth called the Universal Transverse Mercator (UTM) system. There are several different versions of this coordinate system out there and each one uses its own ellipsoid for coordinate conversion. The United States Geological Survey uses the North American Datum of 1983 (NAD83) version.

Perl has a module to convert longitude/latitude to UTM. But there's a problem. This module has no provision for the NAD83 ellipsoid. Turns out that that NAD83 is the same as an earlier standard, the Geodetic Reference System 1980 (GRS 1980). (It took me about three weeks of searching the Web to discover that GRS 1980 and NAD83 are the same. Obviously, Perl programmers aren't the only ones who can be a bit cryptic.)

Figuring out the language the various mapping agencies are using and all the abbreviations is half the battle. The other half is Perl code.

Downloading Map Tiles

From the TerraServer you can download a 200×200-pixel tile containing a map or aerial photograph of any place in the United States. But you need to know the name of the tile. The first step in the process is to turn the longitude/latitude coordinate into the UTM coordinate used by the server:

```
210     # Get the coordinates as UTM
211     my ($zone,$easting,$north)=latlon_to_utm(
212         'GRS 1980',$center_lat, $center_long);
```

To download a tile, you need to know five numbers:

X The easting number divided by a scale factor

Y The northing number divided by a scale factor

Z The zone number

S The scale factor

T The map type (1=Topographical, 2= Aerial Photograph, 3=Urban Aerial Photographs)

Table 10-1 shows the various scale factors for each zoom level.

Table 10-1: Conversion Factors[1]

Theme	Scale Value	Resolution (Meters per Pixel)	UTM Multiplier
Urban	8	0.25	50
Urban	9	0.5	100
DOQ, Urban	10	1	200
DOQ, DRG, Urban	11	2	400
DOQ, DRG, Urban	12	4	800
DOQ, DRG, Urban	13	8	1,600
DOQ, DRG, Urban	14	16	3,200
DOQ, DRG, Urban	15	32	6,400
DOQ, DRG, Urban	16	64	12,800
DOQ, DRG, Urban	17	128	25,600
DOQ, DRG, Urban	18	256	51,200

[1] From the API specification: http://terraserver-usa.com/about.aspx?n=AboutLinktoHtml

The TerraServer contains three types of data. The first, digital raster graphic (DRG), is a topographical map. The next, digital orthophoto quadrangle (DOQ), is an aerial photograph. Finally there is Urban, which indicates a USGS Urban Area photograph. This script does not handle Urban images because they cover only a limited area and because at the time the script was originally written, this type of data was not available.

So let's see what it takes to create a map of the Grand Canyon. You start with the coordinates of the visitor's center in the park:

36°03'20"N 112°08'20"W

Now you need to get the S, T, X, Y, and Z values for the tile. You want a topographical map, so the type is 1 (T=1), and you want the highest resolution possible. For topographical maps, that is 1 meter per pixel. Looking through the table, you can see that the scale factor is 11 (S=11).

When you convert the longitude/latitude to UTM, you get this:

Zone	12S
Easting	397424
Northing	3990710

The TerraServer wants the zone without the north/south indicator, so the zone is 12 (Z=12).

The table shows that the scale factor is 800. Dividing that into the easting, you get 496 (X=496). Performing a similar conversion on the northing gives you a Y of 4988. As a result, the full URL for the map tile is http://terraserver-usa.com/tile.ashx?T=2&S=12&X=496&Y=4988&Z=12.

NOTE *The X- and Y-coordinate numbers are consecutive. So by decrementing the X number by 1, you get the tile to the left of the current tile, incrementing the Y number by 1 gives the tile below the current tile, and so on.*

Getting the Data

The get_file function is responsible for turning a tile specification into an image file. The module HTTP::Lite is used to fetch the file.

The first thing you do is create a HTTP::Lite object for downloading:

```
266         # Connection to the remote site
267         my $http = new HTTP::Lite;
```

Next you turn your tile specification into a URL:

```
269         # The image to get
270         my $image_url =
271             "http://terraserver-usa.com/tile.ashx?".
272             "T=$url->{T}&S=$url->{S}&".
273             "X=$url->{X}&Y=$url->{Y}&Z=$url->{Z}";
```

The next step is to create an HTTP request to get the data:

```
276         # The request
277         my $req = $http->request($image_url);
278         if (not defined($req)) {
```

```
279              die("Could not get url $image_url");
280         }
```

This gets all sorts of information about the page. All you want is the data, so you take the body of the page and dump it to a file. It is this file that you give back to the user as the image file they want:

```
282         # Dump the data into a file
283         my $data = $http->body();
284         open (OUT_FILE, ">$file_spec") or
285             die("Could not create $file_spec");
286         print OUT_FILE $data;
287         close OUT_FILE;
288    }
```

Moving the Map

You allow the map to be panned to the left or right. The move_map function moves the map by tiles. But you store your center point as longitude/latitude. Changing the center is not as simple as just adding in a constant to these values.

The problem is that longitude curves. So in order to recenter, you need a rectangular coordinate system, in this case UTM. The amount to move is determined by the scale factor. The move_map function schanges the center point by one tile in the X or Y direction or both. Each parameter to this function can have the value 1, 0, or −1. The result of this function is a new map with a different center point.

```
373 ##############################################
374 # move_map($x, $y) -- Move the map in
375 #       the X and Y direction
376 ##############################################
377 sub move_map($$)
378 {
379     my $x = shift;    # Amount to move in X tiles
380     my $y = shift;    # Amount to move in Y tiles
381
382     my ($zone,$east,$north)=
383         latlon_to_utm('GRS 1980',
384                 $center_lat, $center_long);
385
386     $east -= $x * get_scale_factor();
387     $north -= $y * get_scale_factor();
388
389     ($center_lat, $center_long) =
390         utm_to_latlon('GRS 1980',
391                 $zone, $east, $north);
392 }
```

Hacking the Script

This module was created by the process of successive experimentation: try something, see if works, try something else, see if it works, add a little to the code, and so on. In other words, there's not a whole lot of design that went into this module.

As a result, the API is a little more complex and cluttered than it needs to be. The code could use a little cleaning up. But then again, this is *Wicked Cool Perl Scripts*, not *Clean Pretty Perl Scripts*, so have fun.

#41 Map Generator

With this program, the user can view and print topographical maps and aerial photographs of any place in the United States. Its job is to take the data from the mapping module and display it in a way you can use it.

The Code

```perl
 1 use strict;
 2 use warnings;
 3
 4 use Tk;
 5 use Geo::Coordinates::UTM;
 6 use HTTP::Lite;
 7 use Tk::Photo;
 8 use Tk::JPEG;
 9 use Tk::LabEntry;
10 use Tk::BrowseEntry;
11 use Image::Magick;
12
13 use map;
14 use goto_loc;
15
16 my $tk_mw;        # Main window
17 my $tk_canvas;    # Canvas on the main window
18 my $tk_nav;       # Navigation window
19
20 my $goto_long = 0; # Where to go from the entry
21 my $goto_lat = 0;
22
23 # The buttons to display the scale
24 my @tk_scale_buttons;
25
26 ###############################################
27 # do_error -- Display an error dialog
28 ###############################################
29 sub do_error($)
30 {
31     # Error message to display
```

```perl
32      my $msg = shift;
33
34      $tk_mw->messageBox(
35          -title => "Error",
36          -message => $msg,
37          -type => "OK",
38          -icon => "error"
39      );
40  }
41
42  ##################################################
43  # get_photo($) -- Get a photo from a URL
44  ##################################################
45  sub get_photo($)
46  {
47      my $url = shift;     # Url to get
48
49      # File containing the data
50      my $file_spec = get_file($url);
51
52      my $tk_photo =
53          $tk_mw->Photo(-file => $file_spec);
54
55      return ($tk_photo);
56  }
57
58  ##################################################
59  # paint_map(@maps)
60  #
61  # Paint a bitmap on the canvas
62  ##################################################
63  sub paint_map(@)
64  {
65      my @maps = @_;       # List of maps to display
66
67      # Delete all the old map items
68      $tk_canvas->delete("map");
69
70      for (my $y = 0; $y < $y_size; ++$y) {
71          for (my $x = 0; $x < $x_size; ++$x) {
72              my $url = shift @maps;# Get the URL
73              # Turn it into a photo
74              my $photo = get_photo($url);
75              $tk_canvas->createImage(
76                  $x * 200, $y * 200,
77                  -tags => "map",
78                  -anchor => "nw",
79                  -image => $photo);
80          }
81      }
```

```perl
82      $tk_canvas->configure(
83          -scrollregion => [
84                  $tk_canvas->bbox("all")]);
85  }
86
87  ################################################
88  # show_map -- Show the current map
89  ################################################
90  sub show_map()
91  {
92      my @result = map_to_tiles();
93      # Repaint the screen
94      paint_map(@result);
95  }
96  ################################################
97  # do_move($x, $y) -- Move the map in
98  #        the X and Y direction
99  ################################################
100 sub do_move($$)
101 {
102     my $x = shift;      # Amount to move in X tiles
103     my $y = shift;      # Amount to move in Y tiles
104
105     move_map($x, $y);
106     show_map();
107 }
108 ################################################
109 # change_type -- Toggle the type of the map
110 ################################################
111 sub change_type() {
112     toggle_type();
113     set_scale($scale);
114     show_map()
115 }
116 ################################################
117 # set_scale($new_scale) --
118 #        Change the scale to a new value
119 ################################################
120 sub set_scale($) {
121     # The scale we want to have
122     my $new_scale = shift;
123
124     if (not set_map_scale($new_scale)) {
125         return;
126     }
127     $scale = $new_scale;
128     for (my $i = 0;
129         $i <= $#tk_scale_buttons; ++$i) {
130
131         if (($i + 10) == $scale) {
```

```
132              $tk_scale_buttons[$i]->configure(
133                  -background => "green"
134              );
135          } else {
136              # The background
137              my $bg = "white";
138              if (not scale_exists($i + 10)) {
139                  $bg = "gray";
140              }
141              $tk_scale_buttons[$i]->configure(
142                  -background => $bg
143              );
144          }
145      }
146      show_map();
147 }
148 ################################################
149 # change_canvas_size --
150 #       Change the size of the canvas
151 ################################################
152 sub change_canvas_size()
153 {
154      if ($x_size <= 0) {
155          $x_size = 1;
156      }
157      if ($y_size <= 0) {
158          $y_size = 1;
159      }
160      $tk_canvas->configure(
161          -width => $x_size * 200,
162          -height => $y_size * 200);
163      show_map();
164 }
165 # The name of the image file to save
166 my $save_image_name = "map_image";
167
168 my $tk_save_image;        # The save image popup
169
170 use Image::Magick;
171 ################################################
172 # do_save_image --
173 #       Save the image as a file
174 #       (actually do the work)
175 ################################################
176 sub do_save_image()
177 {
178      if ($save_image_name !~ /\.(jpg|jpeg)$/) {
179          $save_image_name .= ".jpg";
180      }
181
```

```perl
182     # List of tiles to write
183     my @tiles = map_to_tiles();
184
185     # The image array
186     my $images = Image::Magick->new();
187
188     # Load up the image array
189     foreach my $cur_tile (@tiles) {
190         # The file containing the tile
191         my $file = get_file($cur_tile);
192
193         # The result of the read
194         my $result = $images->Read($file);
195         if ($result) {
196             print
197                 "ERROR: for $file -- $result\n";
198         }
199     }
200
201     # Put them together
202     my $new_image = $images->Montage(
203         geometry => "200x200",
204         tile => "${x_size}x$y_size");
205
206     my $real_save_image_name = $save_image_name;
207     if ($save_image_name =~ /%d/) {
208         for (my $i = 0; ; ++$i) {
209             $real_save_image_name =
210                 sprintf($save_image_name, $i);
211             if (! -f $real_save_image_name) {
212                 last;
213             }
214         }
215     }
216     # Save them
217     $new_image->Write($real_save_image_name);
218     $tk_save_image->withdraw();
219     $tk_save_image = undef;
220 }
221
222 ################################################
223 # save_image -- Display the save image popup
224 ################################################
225 sub save_image()
226 {
227     if (defined($tk_save_image)) {
228         $tk_save_image->deiconify();
229         $tk_save_image->raise();
230         return;
231     }
```

```perl
232     $tk_save_image = $tk_mw->Toplevel(
233         -title => "Save Image");
234
235     $tk_save_image->LabEntry(
236         -label => "Name: ",
237         -labelPack => [ -side => 'left'],
238         -textvariable => \$save_image_name
239     )->pack(
240         -side => "top",
241         -expand => 1,
242         -fill => 'x'
243     );
244     $tk_save_image->Button(
245         -text => "Save",
246         -command => \&do_save_image
247     )->pack(
248         -side => 'left'
249     );
250     $tk_save_image->Button(
251         -text => "Cancel",
252         -command =>
253             sub {$tk_save_image->withdraw();}
254     )->pack(
255         -side => 'left'
256     );
257 }
258 ###############################################
259 # print_image --
260 #       Print the image to the default printer
261 #       (Actually save it as postscript)
262 ###############################################
263 sub print_image()
264 {
265     # List of tiles to write
266     my @tiles = map_to_tiles();
267
268     # The image array
269     my $images = Image::Magick->new();
270
271     # Load up the image array
272     foreach my $cur_tile (@tiles) {
273         # The file containing the tile
274         my $file = get_file($cur_tile);
275
276         # The result of the read
277         my $result = $images->Read($file);
278         if ($result) {
279             print
280                 "ERROR: for $file -- $result\n";
281         }
```

```
282     }
283
284     # Put them together
285     my $new_image = $images->Montage(
286         geometry => "200x200",
287         tile => "${x_size}x$y_size");
288
289     my $print_file;       # File name for printing
290
291     for (my $i = 0; ; ++$i) {
292         if (! -f "map.$i.ps") {
293             $print_file = "map.$i.ps";
294             last;
295         }
296     }
297     # Save them
298     $new_image->Set(page => "Letter");
299     $new_image->Write($print_file);
300     $tk_mw->messageBox(
301         -title => "Print Complete",
302         -message =>
303       "Print Done.  Output file is $print_file",
304         -type => "OK",
305         -icon => "info"
306     );
307 }
308 ################################################
309 # goto_lat_long -- Goto the given location
310 ################################################
311 sub goto_lat_long()
312 {
313     set_center_lat_long($goto_lat, $goto_long);
314 }
315
316
317 ################################################
318 # scroll_listboxes -- Scroll all the list boxes
319 #       (taken from the O'Reilly book
320 #       with little modification)
321 ################################################
322 sub scroll_listboxes
323 {
324     my ($sb, $scrolled, $lbs, @args) = @_;
325
326     $sb->set(@args);
327     my ($top, $bottom) = $scrolled->yview();
328     foreach my $list (@$lbs) {
329         $list->{tk_list}->yviewMoveto($top);
330     }
331 }
```

```perl
332
333 # Mapping from direction to image names
334 my %images = (
335     ul => undef,
336     u => undef,
337     ur => undef,
338     l => undef,
339     r => undef,
340     dl => undef,
341     d => undef,
342     dr => undef,
343 );
344
345 my @key_bindings = (
346     {
347         key => "<Key-j>",
348         event => sub{do_move(0, +1)}
349     },
350     {
351         key => "<Key-k>",
352         event => sub{do_move(0, -1)}
353     },
354     {
355         key => "<Key-h>",
356         event => sub{do_move(+1, 0)}
357     },
358     {
359         key => "<Key-l>",
360         event => sub{do_move(-1, 0)}
361     },
362     {
363         key => "<Key-p>",
364         event => \&print_image
365     },
366     {
367         key => "<Key-q>",
368         event => sub { exit(0)}
369     },
370     {
371         key => "<Key-x>",
372         event => sub { exit(0)}
373     },
374     {
375         key => "<Key-s>",
376         event => \&save_image
377     },
378 );
379
380 ##############################################
381 # build_gui -- Create all the GUI elements
```

```
382 ##############################################
383 sub build_gui()
384 {
385     $tk_mw = MainWindow->new(
386         -title => "Topological Map");
387
388     my $tk_scrolled = $tk_mw->Scrolled(
389         'Canvas',
390         -scrollbars => "sw"
391     )->pack(
392         -fill => "both",
393         -expand => 1,
394         -anchor => 'n',
395         -side => 'top'
396     );
397
398     $tk_canvas =
399         $tk_scrolled->Subwidget('canvas');
400     $tk_canvas->configure(
401         -height => 600,
402         -width => 600
403     );
404     $tk_canvas->CanvasBind("<Button-1>",
405         sub {set_scale($scale-1)});
406
407     $tk_canvas->CanvasBind("<Button-2>",
408         sub {set_scale($scale+1)});
409
410     $tk_canvas->CanvasBind("<Button-3>",
411         sub {set_scale($scale+1)});
412
413     foreach my $cur_image (keys %images) {
414         # The file to put in the image
415         my $file_name = "arrow_$cur_image.jpg";
416
417         # Create the image
418         $images{$cur_image} = $tk_mw->Photo(
419             -file => $file_name);
420     }
421     $tk_mw->Button(-image => $images{ul},
422         -command => sub {do_move(-1, 1)} )->grid(
423             $tk_mw->Button(
424                 -image => $images{u},
425                 -command => sub {do_move(0, 1)}
426             ),
427             $tk_mw->Button(
428                 -image => $images{ur},
429                 -command => sub {do_move(1, 1)}
430             ),
431         -sticky => "nesw"
```

```
432    );
433    $tk_mw->Button(-image => $images{l},
434        -command => sub {do_move(-1, 0)} )->grid(
435            $tk_scrolled,
436            $tk_mw->Button(
437                -image => $images{r},
438                -command => sub {do_move(1, 0)}
439            ),
440        -sticky => "nesw"
441    );
442    $tk_mw->Button(
443        -image => $images{dl},
444        -command => sub {do_move(-1, -1)}
445    )->grid(
446        $tk_mw->Button(
447            -image => $images{d},
448            -command => sub {do_move(0, -1)}
449        ),
450        $tk_mw->Button(
451            -image => $images{dr},
452            -command => sub {do_move(1, -1){
453        ),
454        -sticky => "nesw"
455    );
456    $tk_mw->gridColumnconfigure(1, -weight => 1);
457    $tk_mw->gridRowconfigure(1, -weight => 1);
458
459    # TODO: Is there some way of
460    # making this on top?
461    $tk_nav = $tk_mw->Toplevel(
462        -title => "Map Control");
463
464    # Map the keys
465    foreach my $bind (@key_bindings) {
466        $tk_mw->bind($bind->{key},
467                $bind->{event});
468
469        $tk_nav->bind($bind->{key},
470                $bind->{event});
471    }
472
473    # The item to set the scale
474    my $tk_scale_frame = $tk_nav->Frame();
475    $tk_scale_frame->pack(
476        -side => 'top',
477        -anchor => 'w'
478    );
479
480    $tk_scale_frame->Button(
481            -text => "+",
```

```perl
482             -command => sub {set_scale($scale-1)}
483         )->pack(
484             -side => 'right'
485         );
486
487     # Go through each scale and produce
488     # a button for it.
489     foreach my $info (get_scales()) {
490         push(@tk_scale_buttons,
491             $tk_scale_frame->Button(
492                 -bitmap => "transparent",
493                 -width => 10,
494                 -height => 20,
495                 -command =>
496                         sub {set_scale($info);}
497             )->pack(
498                 -side => 'right'
499             ));
500     }
501
502     $tk_scale_frame->Button(
503         -text => "-",
504         -command => sub {set_scale($scale+1) }
505     )->pack(
506         -side => 'right'
507     );
508
509     $tk_nav->Button(
510         -text => "Toggle Type",
511         -command => \&change_type
512     )->pack(
513         -side => "top",
514         -anchor => "w"
515     );
516
517
518     # The frame for the X size adjustment
519     my $tk_map_x = $tk_nav->Frame()->pack(
520             -side => "top",
521             -fill => "x",
522             -expand => 1
523         );
524
525     $tk_map_x->Label(
526             -text => "Map Width"
527         )->pack(
528             -side => "left"
529         );
530
531     $tk_map_x->Button(
```

```
532             -text => "+",
533             -command => sub {
534                 $x_size++, change_canvas_size()
535             }
536         )->pack(
537             -side => "left"
538         );
539     $tk_map_x->Button(
540             -text => "-",
541             -command => sub {
542                 $x_size--, change_canvas_size()
543             }
544         )->pack(
545             -side => "left"
546         );
547
548     # The frame for the Y size adjustment
549     my $tk_map_y = $tk_nav->Frame()->pack(
550         -side => "top",
551         -fill => "x",
552         -expand => 1
553     );
554     $tk_map_y->Label(
555         -text => "Map Height"
556     )->pack(
557         -side => "left"
558     );
559     $tk_map_y->Button(
560         -text => "+",
561         -command =>
562             sub {$y_size++, change_canvas_size()}
563     )->pack(
564         -side => "left"
565     );
566     $tk_map_y->Button(
567         -text => "-",
568         -command =>
569             sub {$y_size--, change_canvas_size()}
570     )->pack(
571         -side => "left"
572     );
573     $tk_nav->Button(
574         -text => "Save Image",
575         -command => \&save_image
576     )->pack(
577         -side => "top",
578         -anchor => "w"
579     );
580     $tk_nav->Button(
581         -text => "Print",
```

```perl
582         -command => \&print_image
583     )->pack(
584         -side => "top",
585         -anchor => "w"
586     );
587
588     # The frame for the lat/log goto button
589     my $tk_lat_long = $tk_nav->Frame(
590     )->pack(
591         -side => "top",
592         -expand => 1,
593         -fill => "x"
594     );
595
596     $tk_lat_long->Label(
597         -text => "Latitude:"
598     )->pack(
599         -side => "left"
600     );
601     $tk_lat_long->Entry(
602         -textvariable => \$goto_lat,
603         -width => 10
604     )->pack(
605         -side => "left"
606     );
607     $tk_lat_long->Label(
608         -text => "Longitude"
609     )->pack(
610         -side => "left"
611     );
612     $tk_lat_long->Entry(
613         -textvariable => \$goto_long,
614         -width => 10
615     )->pack(
616         -side => "left"
617     );
618
619     $tk_lat_long->Button(
620         -text => "Goto Lat / Long",
621         -command => \&goto_lat_long
622     )->pack(
623         -side => "left"
624     );
625     $tk_nav->Button(
626         -text => "Goto Location",
627         -command => sub { goto_loc($tk_mw);}
628     )->pack(
629         -side => "top",
630         -anchor => "w"
631     );
```

```
632     $tk_nav->Button(
633         -text => "Exit",
634         -command => sub {exit(0);}
635     )->pack(
636         -side => "top",
637         -anchor => "w"
638     );
639
640     $tk_nav->bind('<Destroy>', sub { exit(0);});
641     $tk_nav->raise();
642 }
643
644 init_map();
645 build_gui();
646
647 # Grand Canyon (360320N 1120820W)
648 set_center_lat_long(360320, -1120820);
649 set_scale(12);
650
651 show_map();
652 $tk_nav->raise();
653
654 MainLoop();
```

Running the Script

When the script starts, it displays a map window and a control window.

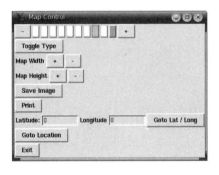 

A detailed view of the control panel can be seen in the following figure.

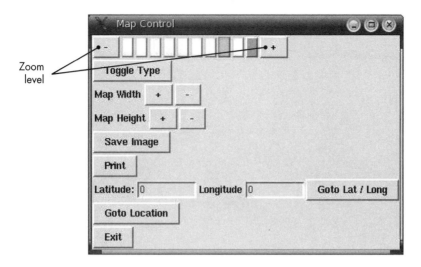

Zoom level

The controls in this GUI are as follows:

Zoom Level

Controls the zoom level of the map. Pressing + increases the zoom level. Similarly, – decreases it. Click any of the buttons in between to set the zoom level to the corresponding level. (Not all zoom levels are available for each map type.)

Toggle Type

Changes the map type from topographical map to aerial photograph and back.

Map Width

Increases or decreases the map width by one tile (200 pixels).

Map Height

Increases or decreases the map height by one tile (200 pixels).

Save Image

Saves the image to a file. (The program prompts you for the file name.)

Print

Saves the image as a PostScript file suitable for printing.

Goto Lat/Long

Takes you to the given latitude and longitude.

Goto Location

Displays a dialog you can use to select a location by name (i.e., Grand Canyon or San Diego, CA).

Exit

Gets you out of the program.

You can toggle between topographical maps and aerial photographs.

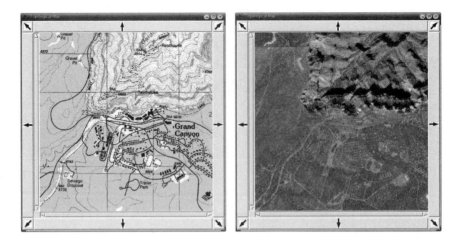

You use the arrows at the edge of the map to scroll the view in any direction.

Clicking the Goto Location button brings up a dialog in which you select a named location to go to. This will be discussed in the next section.

How It Works

The basic algorithm is fairly simple: get the needed tiles and paint them on the screen. Sounds simple, but there are hundreds of details and lots of controls to worry about.

Displaying the Map

To display a map, you first get the specification for the tiles that are to be displayed and then send them off to be painted on the screen:

```
87 ###############################################
88 # show_map -- Show the current map
89 ###############################################
90 sub show_map()
91 {
92     my @result = map_to_tiles();
93     # Repaint the screen
94     paint_map(@result);
95 }
```

The paint_map function goes through each tile on the screen:

```
70     for (my $y = 0; $y < $y_size; ++$y) {
71         for (my $x = 0; $x < $x_size; ++$x) {
```

The tile is turned into a Tk::photo and the system paints it on the canvas:

```
72              my $url = shift @maps;# Get the URL
73              # Turn it into a photo
74              my $photo = get_photo($url);
75              $tk_canvas->createImage(
76                  $x * 200, $y * 200,
77                  -tags => "map",
78                  -anchor => "nw",
79                  -image => $photo);
```

The get_photo function is responsible for turning a tile specification into a Tk::photo you can display. It uses the map.pm module to get the image file containing the tile and the Tk::photo module to turn it into a displayable Tk object:

```
42  ###############################################
43  # get_photo($) -- Get a photo from a URL
44  ###############################################
45  sub get_photo($)
46  {
47      my $url = shift;     # Url to get
48
49      # File containing the data
50      my $file_spec = get_file($url);
51
52      my $tk_photo =
53          $tk_mw->Photo(-file => $file_spec);
54
55      return ($tk_photo);
56  }
```

Saving the Map

To save an image, you need to take all your tiles and put them together to form one big image. The Image::Magick package provides you with the tools to do this. This module includes a rich set of image manipulation functions that allow you to do just about anything to an image.

The first step in putting your tiles together is to create the image object:

```
185     # The image array
186     my $images = Image::Magick->new();
```

Next you read in all the tiles and store them in the image:

```
188     # Load up the image array
189     foreach my $cur_tile (@tiles) {
190         # The file containing the tile
```

```
191        my $file = get_file($cur_tile);
192
193        # The result of the read
194        my $result = $images->Read($file);
195        if ($result) {
196            print
197                "ERROR: for $file -- $result\n";
198        }
199    }
```

You use the Montage function to put them together. This function creates a montage of all the images that have been loaded in the object. In this case, the geometry of each cell in the montage is 200×200 pixels (the tile size) and number of rows and columns of the composition are determined by the number of rows and columns in the main map window ($x_size, $y_size).

```
201    # Put them together
202    my $new_image = $images->Montage(
203        geometry => "200x200",
204        tile => "${x_size}x$y_size");
```

The last step is to write out the result:

```
216    # Save them
217    $new_image->Write($real_save_image_name);
```

Printing the Map

Actually, the script does not print the map. Instead, it creates a PostScript file that the user can print. The code to create the PostScript is very similar to the image save code except that, instead of writing a JPEG file, it writes a PostScript file.

Hacking the Script

The original purpose of this program was to provide me with maps for hiking. It would be nice to be able to annotate the images with information.

In particular, it would be nice to be able to trace a trail on an aerial photograph and have the same line show up on the topographical map.

Also, an interface to a GPS system would be nice so that you could download GPS tracks and have them drawn on the maps as well.

If you wanted to get really fancy, the USGS has digital elevation data available that would allow you to convert the aerial photographs into 3D images. I'm not sure why you'd want to do that, but it would be really wicked and very cool.

#42 The Location Finder

When the mapping program was first written, you could get a map of any place in the United States. This was useful if you knew the coordinates, but you couldn't tell the system to give you a map of Lake Dixon by name. That's where the location finder comes in.

The Code

```
1 use strict;
2 use warnings;
3
4 #
5 # This module contains the info needed to go
6 # to a named location
7 #
8
9
10 package goto_loc;
11
12 use Tk;
13 use Geo::Coordinates::UTM;
14 use HTTP::Lite;
15 use Tk::Photo;
16 use Tk::JPEG;
17 use Tk::LabEntry;
18 use Tk::BrowseEntry;
19 use Image::Magick;
20
21 use map;
22
23 require Exporter;
24 use vars qw/@ISA @EXPORT/;
25
26 @ISA = qw/Exporter/;
27 @EXPORT=qw/goto_loc/;
28
29 my $tk_goto_loc;# Goto location popup window
30 my $place_name; # Name of the place to go to
31 my $state;      # State containing the place name
32
33 my $tk_mw;      # Main window
34
35 #
36 # The scrolling lists of data
37 #
```

```perl
38 # Fields
39 #    name --   The title of the data
40 #    index --  Index into the data fields for
41 #                 the place data
42 #    width --  Width of the field
43 #
44 my @data_list = (
45    {                           # 0
46        name => "Name",
47        index => 2,
48        width => 30
49    },
50    {                           # 1
51        name => "Type",
52        index => 3,
53        width => 10,
54    },
55    {                           # 2
56        name => "County",
57        index => 4,
58        width => 20,
59    },
60    {                           # 3
61        name => "Latitude",
62        index => 7,
63        width => 10,
64    },
65    {                           # 4
66        name => "Longitude",
67        index => 8,
68        width => 10,
69    },
70    {                           # 5
71        name => "Elevation",
72        index => 15,
73        width => 9,
74    }
75 );
76
77 # List of states and two character abbreviations
78 my @state_list = (
79    "AK = Alaska",
80    "AL = Alabama",
81    "AR = Arkansas",
82    "AS = American Samoa",
83    "AZ = Arizona",
84    "CA = California",
85    "CO = Colorado",
86    "CT = Connecticut",
87    "DC = District of Columbia",
```

```
88      "DE = Delaware",
89      "FL = Florida",
90      "FM = Federated States of Micronesia",
91      "GA = Georgia",
92      "GU = Guam",
93      "HI = Hawaii",
94      "IA = Iowa",
95      "ID = Idaho",
96      "IL = Illinois",
97      "IN = Indiana",
98      "IT = All Indian Tribes",
99      "KS = Kansas",
100     "KY = Kentucky",
101     "LA = Louisiana",
102     "MA = Massachusetts",
103     "MD = Maryland",
104     "ME = Maine",
105     "MH = Marshall Island",
106     "MI = Michigan",
107     "MN = Minnesota",
108     "MO = Missouri",
109     "MP = Northern Mariana Islands",
110     "MS = Mississippi",
111     "MT = Montana",
112     "NC = North Carolina",
113     "ND = North Dakota",
114     "NE = Nebraska",
115     "NH = New Hampshire",
116     "NJ = New Jersey",
117     "NM = New Mexico",
118     "NV = Nevada",
119     "NY = New York",
120     "OH = Ohio",
121     "OK = Oklahoma",
122     "OR = Oregon",
123     "PA = Pennsylvania",
124     "PR = Puerto Rico",
125     "PW = Palau, Republic of",
126     "RI = Rhode Island",
127     "SC = South Carolina",
128     "SD = South Dakota",
129     "TN = Tennessee",
130     "TX = Texas",
131     "UT = Utah",
132     "VA = Virginia",
133     "VI = Virgin Islands",
134     "VT = Vermont",
135     "WA = Washington",
136     "WI = Wisconsin",
137     "WV = West Virginia",
```

```perl
138     "WY = Wyoming"
139 );
140
141 # The window with the places in it
142 my $tk_place_where;
143
144
145 ##############################################
146 # jump_to_loc --
147 #       Jump to the location specified
148 #       in the list box
149 ##############################################
150 sub jump_to_loc()
151 {
152     my $cur_selection =
153         $data_list[0]->{tk_list}->curselection();
154
155     if (not defined($cur_selection)) {
156         do_error(
157         "You need to select an item to jump to"
158         );
159         return;
160     }
161     # Where we're jumping to
162     my $lat =
163         $data_list[3]->{tk_list}->get(
164             $cur_selection->[0]);
165
166     my $long =
167         $data_list[4]->{tk_list}->get(
168             $cur_selection->[0]);
169
170     set_center_lat_long($lat, $long);
171     ::show_map();
172 }
173
174 ##############################################
175 # select_boxes -- Called when a Listbox
176 #                 gets a selection
177 #
178 #       So make everybody walk in lock step
179 ##############################################
180 sub select_boxes($)
181 {
182     # The widget in which someone selected
183     my $tk_widget = shift;
184
185     my $selected = $tk_widget->curselection();
186
187     foreach my $cur_data (@data_list) {
```

```perl
188          $cur_data->{tk_list}->selectionClear(
189              0, 'end');
190
191          $cur_data->{tk_list}->selectionSet(
192              $selected->[0]);
193      }
194 }
195
196 ##############################################
197 # Given a state name, return the
198 #        file with the information in it
199 ##############################################
200 sub info_file($)
201 {
202      my $state = shift;  # State we have
203
204      # The file we need for this state
205      my $file_spec = cache_dir()."/${state}_info.txt";
206      return ($file_spec);
207 }
208
209 ##############################################
210 # get_place_file($) --
211 #        Get a place information file
212 #        for the give state
213 ##############################################
214 sub get_place_file($)
215 {
216      my $state = shift;  # URL to get
217
218      # The file we need for this state
219      my $file_spec = info_file($state);
220
221      if (! -f $file_spec) {
222          # Connection to the remote site
223          my $http = new HTTP::Lite;
224
225          # The image to get
226          my $place_url =
227            "http://geonames.usgs.gov/".
228            "stategaz/${state}_DECI.TXT";
229          print "Getting $place_url\n";
230
231          # The request
232          my $req = $http->request($place_url);
233          if (not defined($req)) {
234              die("Could not get url $place_url");
235          }
236
237          # Dump the data into a file
```

```
238        my $data = $http->body();
239        open (OUT_FILE, ">$file_spec") or
240            die("Could not create $file_spec");
241        print OUT_FILE $data;
242        close OUT_FILE;
243    }
244    return ($file_spec);
245 }
246
247 ##############################################
248 # do_goto_loc -- Goto a given location
249 ##############################################
250 sub do_goto_loc()
251 {
252    if ((not defined($state)) ||
253        ($state eq "")) {
254        do_error("No state selected");
255        return;
256    }
257    if (not defined($place_name)) {
258        do_error("No place name entered");
259        return;
260    }
261    if ($place_name =~ /^\s*$/) {
262        do_error("No place name entered");
263        return;
264    }
265
266    # The state as two character names
267    my $state2 = substr($state, 0, 2);
268    get_place_file($state2);
269
270    # The file containing the state information
271    my $state_file = info_file($state2);
272
273    open IN_FILE, "<$state_file" or
274        die("Could not open $state_file");
275
276    my @file_data = <IN_FILE>;
277    chomp(@file_data);
278    close(IN_FILE);
279
280    #TODO: Check to see if anything matched,
281    # if not error
282
283    if (defined($tk_place_where)) {
284        $tk_place_where->deiconify();
285        $tk_place_where->raise();
286    } else {
287        # The pick a place screen
```

```
288          $tk_place_where = $tk_mw->Toplevel(
289               -title => "Goto Selection");
290
291          # Frame in which we place our places
292          my $tk_place_frame =
293               $tk_place_where->Frame();
294
295          # The scrollbar for the place list
296          my $tk_place_scroll =
297               $tk_place_where->Scrollbar()->pack(
298                   -side => 'left',
299                   -fill => 'y'
300               );
301
302          # Loop through each item and construct it
303          foreach my $cur_data (@data_list) {
304               $cur_data->{tk_frame} =
305                   $tk_place_frame->Frame();
306
307               $cur_data->{tk_frame}->Label(
308                   -text => $cur_data->{name}
309               )->pack(
310                   -side => 'top'
311               );
312               $cur_data->{tk_list} =
313                   $cur_data->{tk_frame}->Listbox(
314                   -width => $cur_data->{width},
315                   -selectmode => 'single',
316                   -exportselection => 0
317               )->pack(
318                   -side => "top",
319                   -expand => 1,
320                   -fill => "both"
321               );
322               $cur_data->{tk_list}->bind(
323                   "<<ListboxSelect>>",
324                   \&select_boxes);
325
326               $cur_data->{tk_frame}->pack(
327                   -side => "left"
328               );
329
330               # Define how things scroll
331               $cur_data->{tk_list}->configure(
332                   -yscrollcommand =>
333                       [ \&scroll_listboxes,
334                       $tk_place_scroll,
335                       $cur_data->{tk_list},
336                       \@data_list]);
337          }
```

```
338
339          # define how the scroll bar works
340          $tk_place_scroll->configure(
341              -command => sub {
342                  foreach my $list (@data_list) {
343                      $list->{tk_list}->yview(@_);
344                  }
345              }
346          );
347          # Put the frame containing the list
348          # on the screen
349          $tk_place_frame->pack(
350              -side => 'top',
351              -fill => 'both',
352              -expand => 1);
353
354          $tk_place_where->Button(
355              -text => "Go To",
356              -command => \&jump_to_loc
357          )->pack(
358              -side => 'left'
359          );
360          $tk_place_where->Button(
361              -text => "Close",
362              -command => sub {
363                  $tk_place_where->withdraw();
364              }
365          )->pack(
366              -side => 'left'
367          );
368      }
369
370      foreach my $cur_result (@file_data) {
371          # Split the data up into fields
372          # See http://gnis.usgs.gov for field list
373          my @data = split /\|/, $cur_result;
374          if ($data[2] !~ /$place_name/i) {
375              next;
376          }
377          foreach my $cur_data (@data_list) {
378              $cur_data->{tk_list}->insert('end',
379                  $data[$cur_data->{index}]);
380          }
381      }
382      foreach my $cur_data (@data_list) {
383          $cur_data->{tk_list}->selectionSet(0);
384      }
385  }
386
```

```perl
387  ##########################################
388  # goto_loc -- Goto a named location
389  #        (popup the window to ask the name)
390  ##########################################
391  sub goto_loc($)
392  {
393      $tk_mw = shift;
394
395      if (defined($tk_goto_loc)) {
396          $tk_goto_loc->deiconify();
397          $tk_goto_loc->raise();
398          return;
399      }
400      $tk_goto_loc = $tk_mw->Toplevel(
401          -title => "Goto Location");
402
403      #TODO: Add label
404      $tk_goto_loc->BrowseEntry(
405          -variable => \$state,
406          -choices => \@state_list,
407      )->pack(
408          -side => "top",
409      );
410
411      #TODO: Add place type
412      $tk_goto_loc->LabEntry(
413          -label => "Place Name: ",
414          -labelPack => [ -side => 'left'],
415          -textvariable => \$place_name
416      )->pack(
417          -side => "top",
418          -expand => 1,
419          -fill => 'x'
420      );
421      $tk_goto_loc->Button(
422          -text => "Locate",
423          -command => \&do_goto_loc
424      )->pack(
425          -side => 'left'
426      );
427      $tk_goto_loc->Button(
428          -text => "Cancel",
429          -command =>
430                  sub {$tk_goto_loc->withdraw();}
431      )->pack(
432          -side => 'left'
433      );
434  }
435
436  1;
```

Running the Script

If you click Goto Location, the program calls the goto_loc function in this module. This displays a dialog that asks you for the name of the location and the state in which it's located.

It then displays a list of all the locations that match that name and you select the correct one.

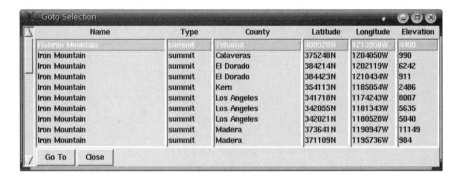

One final note: The program caches the image files and other information files in $HOME/.maps. It never removes any files from this cache, so you'll need to clean out this directory every so often.

How It Works

The USGS maintains a gazetteer containing the names of all the significant and most of the insignificant places in the United States. The actual URL for this information is http://geonames.usgs.gov/stategaz.

For each state, there is a data file containing the place names. For example, the information on California can be found at http://geonames.usgs.gov/stategaz/CA_DECI.TXT.

This is a text file with pipe (|) separated fields, something Perl eats for lunch. Here are the first few lines of the California file:

```
664200|CA|10 Mg Walteria 1049 Dam|dam|Los Angeles|06|037|334718N|1182012W|
33.78833|-118.33667||||||||Torrance
1664803|CA|101 Ranch|locale|Madera|06|039|370852N|1194019W|37.14778|-
119.67194||||||||O'Neals
1663277|CA|10th and Western 5-004 Dam|dam|Los Angeles|06|037|341042N|1181654W|
34.17833|-118.28167||||||||Burbank
```

```
1655057|CA|2 S Ranch 3220 Dam|dam|Shasta|06|089|403942N|1215706W|40.66167|-
121.95167|||||||Whitmore
238384|CA|2 Schali Drain|canal|Imperial|06|025|324616N|1152028W|32.77111|-
115.34111|||||||Holtville East
```

To process this file, all you have to do is split out the fields and match them against the name the user specified in the search dialog. When the user selects one of the items you found, you can recenter the map at that location.

The Scrolling List

The GUI is a little tricky. One of its major features is a scrolling list of place names. Actually, the dialog contains six lists that all scroll together. Also, the currently selected item is synchronized between these lists.

The first step in displaying this dialog is to create the window to hold the list:

```
287     # The pick a place screen
288     $tk_place_where = $tk_mw->Toplevel(
289             -title => "Goto Selection");
290
291     # Frame in which we place our places
292     my $tk_place_frame =
293             $tk_place_where->Frame();
```

Next, the scrollbar is added to the edge of the frame. You'll be using one scrollbar for all six lists:

```
295     # The scrollbar for the place list
296     my $tk_place_scroll =
297         $tk_place_where->Scrollbar()->pack(
298             -side => 'left',
299             -fill => 'y'
300         );
```

Each column of the data is placed in its own list. (The lists don't have their own scroll bar; you will be using the common scroll bar you just created.) Each list is placed in its own Tk Frame widget:

```
302     # Loop through each item and construct it
303     foreach my $cur_data (@data_list) {
304         $cur_data->{tk_frame} =
305             $tk_place_frame->Frame();
306
307         $cur_data->{tk_frame}->Label(
308             -text => $cur_data->{name}
309         )->pack(
310             -side => 'top'
311         );
312         $cur_data->{tk_list} =
```

```
313              $cur_data->{tk_frame}->Listbox(
314                  -width => $cur_data->{width},
315                  -selectmode => 'single',
316                  -exportselection => 0
317              )->pack(
318                  -side => "top",
319                  -expand => 1,
320                  -fill => "both"
321              );
```

There is one "feature" of the Tk GUI that's not well documented and
caused me a lot of trouble. When I first wrote this code, only one of the six
columns would have a selection in it. And if I selected something in column
2, the selection in column 1 went away.

There was no apparent reason for this and it took a lot of time for me to
find the problem. By default, a Tk::ListBox exports the current selection to
the clipboard. What's this got to do with the disappearing selections? When
one item gets exported to the clipboard, any other item that may have been
exported is cleared.

As a result, I would select something in column 1. It would be high-
lighted and go to the clipboard. Then I'd highlight something in column 2.
Since column 1's selection was on the clipboard, the data on the clipboard
and column 1's selection would be cleared.

The solution was to tell the system to leave the clipboard alone. The
actual code is as follows:

```
316                  -exportselection => 0
```

After you create your list box, you need to tell it to call the select_boxes
function when something is selected. That way, when you select something in
column 1, all the other columns will follow suit:

```
322          $cur_data->{tk_list}->bind(
323              "<<ListboxSelect>>",
324              \&select_boxes);
```

You also need to tell the system that when one list box scrolls, it needs to
call the function scroll_listboxes to scroll them all:

```
330          # Define how things scroll
331          $cur_data->{tk_list}->configure(
332              -yscrollcommand =>
333                  [ \&scroll_listboxes,
334                  $tk_place_scroll,
335                  $cur_data->{tk_list},
336                  \@data_list]);
337      }
```

The last little bit of code tells the scroll bar to scroll all six lists when it gets moved:

```
339     # define how the scroll bar works
340     $tk_place_scroll->configure(
341         -command => sub {
342             foreach my $list (@data_list) {
343                 $list->{tk_list}->yview(@_);
344             }
345         }
346     );
```

The last little bit of code is called when someone scrolls. Its job is to make sure that all six list boxes scroll the same:

```
317 ################################################
318 # scroll_listboxes -- Scroll all the list boxes
319 #       (taken from the O'Reilly book
320 #       with little modification)
321 ################################################
322 sub scroll_listboxes
323 {
324     my ($sb, $scrolled, $lbs, @args) = @_;
325
326     $sb->set(@args);
327     my ($top, $bottom) = $scrolled->yview();
328     foreach my $list (@$lbs) {
329         $list->{tk_list}->yviewMoveto($top);
330     }
331 }
```

Hacking the Script

There are a lot of online databases popping up on the Web. This script exploits one of them, the USGS place name database. But it could be expanded to take advantage of some of the other ones available.

Also, the GUI can be used to select something by name. It would be nice to expand this to allow for a type (lake, point, city) to be used as well.

#43 Hacking the Grand Canyon

I wrote this program to provide myself with maps when I hiked the Grand Canyon. I produced high-resolution maps and aerial photographs for every mile I was going to hike.

I made my map set using the OpenOffice.org presentation program (Impress). I started by importing a map into a slide. I then traced out my route using a red line from the drawing tool.

Next I duplicated the slide. On the second slide, I replaced the topographical map with an aerial photograph. This gave me an aerial photograph with the trail drawn on it.

The Grand Canyon is an interesting place. For the most part, you don't need a map to see where you are going. The first day, I looked down and saw 10 switchbacks below me. The next day, I looked up and saw 20 switchbacks way above me.

The trip went very well. The only surprise was that, although they recommend that you leave the bottom at 6:00 AM, the store that sells sack lunches to the hikers opens at 8:00 AM. (We brought along lots of trail snacks, so this was not a problem.)

I also learned that the bottom of the Grand Canyon is one of the few places where it's difficult to hack Perl.

11

REGULAR EXPRESSION GRAPHER

Regular expressions are among Perl's most powerful features. But they are also the most cryptic. After all, it's hard at first glance to tell what /\s*(\S+)(\d+)/ really means. But it turns out that the regular expression matcher is a simple state machine whose input and processing can easily be represented graphically, as shown.

Regular Expression: \/s*(\S+)(\d+)/

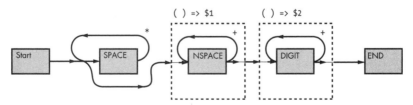

From this you can see that the regular expression consists of three major parts (excluding the start and end nodes) and that it stores results into $1 and $2. We'll go into what all those lines and symbols mean later, but this example shows how something complex and cryptic can be made simple and understandable if you present it in the right manner.

#44 Regular Expression Parser

In order to be able to graph a regular expression, you first must figure out what's in it. That's the job of the parse.pm module.

The Code

```
 1 #
 2 # parse_re -- Parse a regular expression
 3 #
 4 use strict;
 5 use warnings;
 6
 7 package parse;
 8 require Exporter;
 9
10 use English;
11
12 use vars qw/@ISA @EXPORT/;
13
14 @ISA = qw/Exporter/;
15 @EXPORT = qw/parse_re/;
16
17 ##############################################
18 # parse_re -- Parse a regular expression
19 #     and return an array of parsed data
20 ##############################################
21 sub parse_re($)
22 {
23     # The regular expression to use
24     my $quote_re = shift;
25
26     $quote_re =~ s/\\/\\\\/g;
27
28     # The command to get the debug output
29     my $cmd = <<EOF ;
30 perl 2>&1 <<SHELL_EOF
31 use re 'debug';
32 /$quote_re/;
33 SHELL_EOF
34 EOF
35
36     # The raw debug output
```

```
37     my @raw_debug = `$cmd`;
38
39     if ($main::opt_d) {
40         print @raw_debug;
41     }
42
43     if ($CHILD_ERROR != 0) {
44     my $cmd = <<EOF ;
45 perl 2>&1 <<SHELL_EOF
46 use re 'debug';
47 /ERROR/;
48 SHELL_EOF
49 EOF
50         @raw_debug = `$cmd`;
51         if ($CHILD_ERROR != 0) {
52             die("Could not run perl");
53         }
54     }
55
56     my @re_debug = ();   # The regular expression
57     push(@re_debug, {
58             node => 0,
59             type => "Start",
60             next => 1
61             });
62     foreach my $cur_line (@raw_debug) {
63         if ($cur_line =~ /^Compiling/) {
64             next;
65         }
66         if ($cur_line =~ /^\s*size/) {
67             next;
68         }
69     #                     +++-------------------------------- Spaces
70     #                     ||| +++--------------------------- Digits
71     #                     |||+|||+------------------------- Group $1
72     #                     ||||||||                          (Node)
73     #                     ||||||||
74     #                     ||||||||+------------------------- Colon
75     #                     |||||||||+++---------------------- Spaces
76     #                     ||||||||||||
77     #                     |||||||||||| +++------------------ Word chars
78     #                     ||||||||||||+|||+----------------- Group $2
79     #                     ||||||||||||||||||                (Type)
80     #                     ||||||||||||||||||
81     #                     ||||||||||||||||||+++------------- Spaces
82     #                     |||||||||||||||||||||
83     #                     ||||||||||||||||||||| ++---------- Any chars
84     #                     |||||||||||||||||||||+||+--------- Group $3
85     #                     ||||||||||||||||||||||||||         (arg)
86     #                     |||||||||||||||||||||||||-------- Lit <>
```

```
87      #                    |||||||||||||||||||||||
88      #                    |||||||||||||||||||||||+++---------- Spaces
89      #                    |||||||||||||||||||||||||
90      #                    |||||||||||||||||||||||||||  ++----- Any char str
91      #                    |||||||||||||||||||||||||||++ || ++-- Lit ()
92      #                    ||||||||||||||||||||||||||| || ||   (next state)
93      #                    ||||||||||||||||||||||||||||+||+||-- Group $4
94      if ($cur_line =~ /\s*(\d+):\s*(\w+)\s*(.*)\s*\((.*)\)\)/) {
95          push(@re_debug, {
96                  node => $1,
97                  type => $2,
98                  raw_type => $2,
99                  arg => $3,
100                 next => $4
101                 });
102         next;
103     }
104     if ($cur_line =~ /^anchored/) {
105         next;
106     }
107     if ($cur_line =~ /^Freeing/) {
108         last;
109     }
110 }
111 return (@re_debug);
112 }
```

Executing the Module

The module contains one function, parse_re, which takes a regular expression as input and outputs an array containing a parsed version of the expression.

The Results

The expression /a*b/ results in the following array:

```
0   HASH(0x84c1b54)
    'next' => 1
    'node' => 0
    'type' => 'Start'
1   HASH(0x804c43c)
    'arg' => ''
    'next' => 4
    'node' => 1
    'raw_type' => 'STAR'
    'type' => 'STAR'
2   HASH(0x80761ac)
    'arg' => '<a>'
    'next' => 0
```

```
        'node' => 2
        'raw_type' => 'EXACT'
        'type' => 'EXACT'
3   HASH(0x84c1bfc)
        'arg' => '<b>'
        'next' => 6
        'node' => 4
        'raw_type' => 'EXACT'
        'type' => 'EXACT'
4   HASH(0x84c1c50)
        'arg' => ''
        'next' => 0
        'node' => 6
        'raw_type' => 'END'
        'type' => 'END'
```

Each part of the array has the following elements:

type, raw_type   The type of the node. (See the Perl documentation perlre for a list of types.) The raw_type is never changed, while subsequent code can change the value of type as needed.

arg   The argument for this node. For example, if this node is an exact match, this field will contain the text to be matched.

node   The node number.

next   New node number of the next node (if any).

How It Works

The script runs the code through the regular expression debugger. For example, if the regular expression is /a*b/, the function creates and executes the following Perl mini-script:

```
use re 'debug';
/a*b/;
```

The first line causes the system to output a lot of debugging information as Perl compiles the regular expression. In this example, the debugger outputs the following:

```
Compiling REx `a*b'
size 6 Got 52 bytes for offset annotations.
first at 1
synthetic stclass `ANYOF[ab]'.
    1: STAR(4)
    2:   EXACT <a>(0)
    4: EXACT <b>(6)
    6: END(0)
floating `b' at 0..2147483647 (checking floating) stclass `ANYOF[ab]' minlen 1
```

```
Offsets: [6]
    2[1] 1[1] 0[0] 3[1] 0[0] 4[0]
Freeing REx: `"a*b"'
```

It's only the numbered lines we are interested in (the ones that begin
with STAR and end with END). These are parsed by a large regular expression
and the results stuffed in the @re_debug array.

#45 Laying Out the Graph

You have the basic information about the regular expression. The next step
is to lay things out. The size.pm module has two functions: it decides how big
each element of the graph is and it decides where each element goes.

The Code

```
 1 use strict;
 2 use warnings;
 3
 4 package size;
 5 require Exporter;
 6
 7 use vars qw/@ISA @EXPORT format_re/;
 8
 9 @ISA = qw/Exporter/;
10 @EXPORT = qw/convert_re &BOX_FONT_SIZE
11    &X_CHAR_SIZE &X_MARGIN &Y_NODE_SIZE
12    &X_MARGIN &Y_MARGIN &MARGIN
13    &X_NODE_SIZE Y_NODE_SIZE
14    &X_BRANCH_MARGIN &Y_BRANCH_MARGIN
15    &X_TEXT_OFFSET &Y_TEXT_OFFSET
16    @format_re layout_array &BOX_MARGIN/;
17
18 #
19 # Constants that control the layout
20 #
21 # Margin around the graph
22 use constant MARGIN => 100;
23
24 # Size of a node (X Space)
25 use constant X_NODE_SIZE => 60;
26
27 # Size of a node (Y Space)
28 use constant Y_NODE_SIZE => 40;
29 #------------------------------------------
30 # layout the "ANYOF" node  (ANYOF + text)
31 #------------------------------------------
32 # Size of a character in X dimensions
33 use constant X_CHAR_SIZE => 7;
```

```perl
34
35  #-------------------------------------------
36  # OPEN    the open (
37  #-------------------------------------------
38  # Size of the box around a group
39  use constant BOX_MARGIN => 50;
40
41  # Height of the font used to label boxes
42  use constant BOX_FONT_SIZE => 15;
43
44  # Space between nodes (X)
45  use constant X_MARGIN => 50;
46
47  # Vertical spacing
48  use constant Y_MARGIN => 10;
49
50  # Padding for PLUS style nodes (left, right)
51  use constant PLUS_PAD => 10;
52
53  # Space between branches (x)
54  use constant X_BRANCH_MARGIN => 20;
55
56  # Space between branches (y)
57  use constant Y_BRANCH_MARGIN => 20;
58
59  # Space text over this far
60  use constant X_TEXT_OFFSET => 3;
61  use constant Y_TEXT_OFFSET => 3;
62
63  # The regular expression debugging information
64  my $re_debug;
65
66  sub size_array(\@);
67  ######################################
68  # size_text -- Compute the size of a
69  #        text type node
70  ######################################
71  sub size_text($)
72  {
73      # Node we want layout information for
74      my $node = shift;
75
76      # Get the size of the string argument
77      my $length = length($node->{node}->{arg});
78      if ($length < 10) {
79          $length = 10;
80      }
81      $node->{x_size} =
82          $length * X_CHAR_SIZE + X_MARGIN;
83
```

```
84      $node->{y_size} = Y_NODE_SIZE;
85 }
86 #############################################
87 # size_start -- Layout a start node
88 #############################################
89 sub size_start($)
90 {
91      # Node we want layout information for
92      my $node = shift;
93
94      $node->{x_size} = X_NODE_SIZE + X_MARGIN;
95      $node->{y_size} = Y_NODE_SIZE;
96 }
97 #------------------------------------------
98 # layout the end node
99 #------------------------------------------
100 sub size_end($)
101 {
102      # Node we want layout information for
103      my $node = shift;
104
105      $node->{x_size} = X_NODE_SIZE;
106      $node->{y_size} = Y_NODE_SIZE;
107 }
108 #------------------------------------------
109 # layout the "EXACT" node   (EXACT + text)
110 #------------------------------------------
111 sub size_exact($)
112 {
113      # Node we want layout information for
114      my $node = shift;
115
116      $node->{x_size} = X_NODE_SIZE + X_MARGIN;
117      $node->{y_size} = Y_NODE_SIZE;
118 }
119
120 #################################################
121 # size_open -- Size the open ( -- Actually
122 #       the entire (....) expression
123 #################################################
124 sub size_open($)
125 {
126      # The node we want to size
127      my $node = shift;
128
129      # Compute the size of the children
130      my ($x_size, $y_size) =
131          size_array(@{$node->{children}});
132
133      # We add X_MARGIN because we
```

```perl
134     # must for all nodes
135     #
136     # We subtract X_MARGIN because one too many
137     # is added in our children
138     #
139     # Result is nothing
140
141     $node->{x_size} = $x_size + BOX_MARGIN;
142
143     $node->{y_size} =
144         $y_size + BOX_MARGIN + BOX_FONT_SIZE;
145 }
146 #-------------------------------------------
147 # size_plus -- Compute the size of
148 #               a plus/star type node
149 #-------------------------------------------
150 sub size_plus($)
151 {
152     # Node we want layout information for
153     my $node = shift;
154
155     # Compute the size of the children
156     my ($x_size, $y_size) =
157         size_array(@{$node->{children}});
158
159     # Arc size is based on the
160     # Y dimension of the children
161     $node->{arc_size} =
162         int($y_size/4) + PLUS_PAD;
163
164     $node->{child_x} = $x_size - X_MARGIN;
165
166     $node->{x_size} =
167         $node->{child_x} +
168         $node->{arc_size} * 2 + X_MARGIN;
169
170     $node->{y_size} =
171         $y_size + $node->{arc_size} * 2;
172 }
173 #-------------------------------------------
174 # size_star -- Compute the size of
175 #       a star type node
176 #-------------------------------------------
177 sub size_star($)
178 {
179     # Node we want layout information for
180     my $node = shift;
181
182     # Compute the size of the children
183     my ($x_size, $y_size) =
```

```perl
184        size_array(@{$node->{children}});
185
186    # Arc size is based on the
187    # Y dimension of the children
188    $node->{arc_size} =
189        int($y_size/4) + PLUS_PAD;
190
191    $node->{child_x} = $x_size - X_MARGIN;
192
193    $node->{x_size} = $node->{child_x} +
194        $node->{arc_size} * 5 + X_MARGIN;
195
196    $node->{y_size} = $y_size +
197        $node->{arc_size} * 2 + Y_MARGIN;
198 }
199 #-------------------------------------------
200 # layout a branch node
201 #-------------------------------------------
202 sub size_branch($)
203 {
204    # Node we want layout information for
205    my $node = shift;
206
207    my $x_size = 0;     # Current X size
208    my $y_size = 0;     # Current Y size
209
210    foreach my $cur_choice (
211            @{$node->{choices}}) {
212
213        # The size of the current choice
214        my ($x_choice, $y_choice) =
215            size_array(@{$cur_choice});
216
217        if ($x_size < $x_choice) {
218            $x_size = $x_choice;
219        }
220        if ($y_size != 0) {
221            $y_size += Y_BRANCH_MARGIN;
222        }
223        $cur_choice->[0]->{row_y_size} =
224            $y_choice;
225
226        $y_size += $y_choice;
227    }
228    $x_size += 2 * X_BRANCH_MARGIN + X_MARGIN;
229    $node->{x_size} = $x_size;
230    $node->{y_size} = $y_size;
231 }
232 # Functions used to compute the sizes
233 # of various elements
```

```perl
234 my %compute_size = (
235     "ANYOF" => \&size_text,
236     "BOL" => \&size_exact,
237     "SPACE" => \&size_exact,
238     "NSPACE" => \&size_exact,
239     "DIGIT" => \&size_exact,
240     "BRANCH"=> \&size_branch,
241     "END"   => \&size_end,
242     "EOL" => \&size_exact,
243     "EXACT" => \&size_exact,
244     "IFMATCH"  => \&size_open,
245     "OPEN"  => \&size_open,
246     "PLUS"  => \&size_plus,
247     "REF"   => \&size_exact,
248     "REG_ANY" => \&size_exact,
249     "STAR"  => \&size_star,
250     "Start" => \&size_start,
251     "UNLESSM"  => \&size_open
252 );
253 #############################################
254 # do_size($cur_node) --
255 #       Compute the size of a given node
256 #############################################
257 sub do_size($);
258 sub do_size($)
259 {
260     my $cur_node = shift;
261
262     if (not defined(
263             $compute_size{
264                 $cur_node->{node}->{type}}))) {
265
266         die("No compute function for ".
267             "$cur_node->{node}->{type}");
268         exit;
269     }
270     $compute_size{
271         $cur_node->{node}->{type}}($cur_node);
272 }
273 #############################################
274 # $new_index = parse_node($index,
275 #               $array, $next, $close)
276 #
277 #       -- Parse a single regular expression node
278 #       -- Stop when next (or end) is found
279 #       -- Or when a close ")" is found
280 #############################################
281 sub parse_node($$$$);
282 sub parse_node($$$$)
283 {
```

```perl
284     # Index into the array
285     my $index = shift;
286
287     # Array to put things on
288     my $array = shift;
289
290     my $next = shift;              # Next node
291
292     # Looking for a close?
293     my $close = shift;
294
295     my $min_flag = 0;             # Minimize flag
296     while (1) {
297         if (not defined($re_debug->[$index])) {
298             return ($index);
299         }
300         if (defined($next)) {
301             if ($next <=
302                 $re_debug->[$index]->{node}) {
303
304                 return ($index);
305             }
306         }
307         if ($re_debug->[$index]->{type} =~
308             /CLOSE(\d+)/) {
309             if (defined($close)) {
310                 if ($1 == $close) {
311                     return ($index + 1);
312                 }
313             }
314         }
315         if ($re_debug->[$index]->{type} eq
316             "MINMOD") {
317             $min_flag = 1;
318             $index++;
319             next;
320         }
321 #-----------------------------------------
322         if (($re_debug->[$index]->{type} eq
323              "IFMATCH") ||
324             ($re_debug->[$index]->{type} eq
325              "UNLESSM")) {
326             if ($re_debug->[$index]->{arg} !~
327                 /\[(.*?)\]/) {
328                 die("IFMATCH/UNLESSM funny ".
329                     "argument ".
330                     "$re_debug->[$index]->{arg}");
331             }
332             # Ending text (= or !=)
333             my $equal = "!=";
```

```
334
335             if ($re_debug->[$index]->{type} eq
336                 "IFMATCH") {
337                 $equal = "=";
338             }
339             # Flag indicating the next look ahead
340             my $flag = $1;
341
342             # Text to label this box
343             my $text;
344
345             if ($flag eq "-0") {
346                 $text = "$equal ahead";
347             } elsif ($flag eq "-0") {
348                 $text = "$equal behind";
349             } elsif ($flag eq "-1") {
350                 $text = "$equal behind";
351             } else {
352                 die("Unknown IFMATCH/UNLESSM ".
353                         "flag text $flag");
354                 exit;
355             }
356             push(@{$array}, {
357                 node => $re_debug->[$index],
358                 text => $text,
359                 children => []
360             });
361
362             $index = parse_node($index+1,
363                 $$array[$#$array]->{children},
364                 $re_debug->[$index]->{next},
365                 undef);
366         next;
367     }
368 #----------------------------------------
369     if ($re_debug->[$index]->{type} =~
370             /OPEN(\d+)/) {
371
372         my $paren_count = $1;
373         $re_debug->[$index]->{type} = "OPEN";
374         push(@{$array}, {
375             node => $re_debug->[$index],
376             paren_count => $paren_count,
377             text => "( ) => \$$paren_count",
378             children => []
379         });
380
381         $index = parse_node($index+1,
382             $$array[$#$array]->{children},
383             undef, $paren_count);
```

```
384             next;
385         }
386 #----------------------------------------
387         if ($re_debug->[$index]->{type} =~
388             /REF(\d+)/) {
389
390             my $ref_number = $1;
391             $re_debug->[$index]->{type} = "REF";
392             push(@{$array}, {
393                 node => $re_debug->[$index],
394                 ref => $ref_number,
395                 children => []
396             });
397
398             ++$index;
399             next;
400         }
401 #----------------------------------------
402         if ($re_debug->[$index]->{type} eq
403             "BRANCH") {
404
405             push(@{$array}, {
406                 node => $re_debug->[$index],
407                 choices => []
408             });
409
410             my $choice_index = 0;
411             while (1) {
412                 # Next node in this series
413                 my $next =
414                     $re_debug->[$index]->{next};
415
416                 $$array[$#$array]->
417                     {choices}[$choice_index] = [];
418
419                 $index = parse_node($index+1,
420                     $$array[$#$array]->
421                         {choices}[$choice_index],
422                     $next, undef);
423
424                 if (not defined(
425                         $re_debug->[$index])) {
426                     last;
427                 }
428
429                 if ($re_debug->[$index]->{type} ne
430                         "BRANCH") {
431                     last;
432                 }
433                 $choice_index++;
```

```
434             }
435             next;
436         }
437 #-------------------------------------------
438         if (($re_debug->[$index]->{type} eq
439             "CURLYX") |
440         ($re_debug->[$index]->{type} eq
441             "CURLY")) {
442
443         # Min number of matches
444         my $min_number;
445
446         # Max number of matches
447         my $max_number;
448
449         if ($re_debug->[$index]->{arg} =~
450                 /{(\d+),(\d+)}/) {
451             $min_number = $1;
452             $max_number = $2;
453         } else {
454             die("Funny CURLYX args ".
455                 "$re_debug->[$index]->{arg}");
456             exit;
457         }
458
459         my $star_flag = ($min_number == 0);
460
461         my $text = "+";
462         if ($min_number == 0) {
463             $text = "*";
464         }
465         if (($max_number != 32767) ||
466                 ($min_number > 1)) {
467
468             $text =
469                 "{$min_number, $max_number}";
470             if ($max_number == 32767) {
471                 $text = "min($min_number)";
472             }
473         }
474         # Node that's enclosed
475         # inside this one
476         my $child = {
477             node => {
478                 type =>
479                     ($star_flag) ?
480                         "STAR" : "PLUS",
481                 raw_type =>
482                     $re_debug->[$index]->{type},
483                 arg =>
```

```
484                        $re_debug->[$index]->{arg},
485                next =>
486                        $re_debug->[$index]->{next},
487                text_label =>
488                        $text
489             },
490          min_flag => $min_flag,
491          children => [],
492      };
493
494      push(@{$array}, $child);
495
496      $index = parse_node($index+1,
497              $child->{children},
498              $re_debug->[$index]->{next},
499              undef);
500      next;
501   }
502 #-----------------------------------------
503      if ($re_debug->[$index]->{type} eq
504          "CURLYM") {
505
506      my $paren_count;    # () number
507
508      # Min number of matches
509      my $min_number;
510
511      # Max number of matches
512      my $max_number;
513
514      if ($re_debug->[$index]->{arg} =~
515          /\[(\d+)\]\s*{(\d+),(\d+)}/) {
516          $paren_count = $1;
517          $min_number = $2;
518          $max_number = $3;
519      } else {
520          die("Funny CURLYM args ".
521              "$re_debug->[$index]->{arg}");
522          exit;
523      }
524      # Are we doing a * or +
525      # (anything else is just too hard)
526
527      my $star_flag = ($min_number == 0);
528
529      # The text for labeling this node
530      my $text = "+";
531      if ($min_number == 0) {
532          $text = "*";
533      }
```

```perl
534        if (($max_number != 32767) ||
535                 ($min_number > 1)) {
536
537           $text =
538              "{$min_number, $max_number}";
539
540           if ($max_number == 32767) {
541               $text = "min($min_number)";
542           }
543        }
544
545        # Node that's enclosed
546        # inside this one
547        my $child = {
548            node => {
549                type =>
550                    ($star_flag) ?
551                        "STAR" : "PLUS",
552                raw_type =>
553                    $re_debug->[$index]->{type},
554                arg =>
555                    $re_debug->[$index]->{arg},
556                next =>
557                    $re_debug->[$index]->{next},
558                text_label =>
559                    $text
560            },
561            min_flag => $min_flag,
562            children => [],
563        };
564        $min_flag = 0;
565
566        # The text for labeling this node
567        $text = "( ) => \$$paren_count";
568        if ($paren_count == 0) {
569            $text = '( ) [no $x]';
570        }
571        push(@{$array},
572        {
573            node => {
574                type =>
575                    "OPEN",
576                raw_type =>
577                    $re_debug->[$index]->{type},
578                arg =>
579                    $re_debug->[$index]->{arg},
580                next =>
581                    $re_debug->[$index]->{next}
582            },
583            paren_count => $paren_count,
```

```
584                 text => $text,
585                 children => [$child]
586             });
587
588         $index = parse_node($index+1,
589                 $child->{children},
590                 $re_debug->[$index]->{next},
591                 undef);
592         next;
593     }
```

```
594 #----------------------------------------
595     if ($re_debug->[$index]->{type} eq
596             "STAR") {
597         push(@{$array},
598             {
599                 node => {
600                     %{$re_debug->[$index]},
601                     -text_label => "+"
602                 },
603                 min_flag => $min_flag,
604                 children => []
605             });
606         $min_flag = 0;
607
608         # Where we go for the next state
609         my $star_next;
610
611         if (defined($next)) {
612             $star_next = $next;
613         } else {
614             $star_next =
615                 $re_debug->[$index]->{next};
616         }
617
618         $index = parse_node($index+1,
619             $$array[$#$array]->{children},
620             $star_next, undef);
621         next;
622     }
623 #----------------------------------------
624     if ($re_debug->[$index]->{type} eq
625             "PLUS") {
626         push(@{$array},
627             {
628                 node => {
629                     %{$re_debug->[$index]},
630                     text_label => "+"
631                 },
632                 min_flag => $min_flag,
```

```
633                    children => []
634                });
635            $min_flag = 0;
636            $index = parse_node($index+1,
637                $$array[$#$array]->{children},
638                $re_debug->[$index]->{next},
639                undef);
640            next;
641        }
642 #----------------------------------------
643        # Ignore a couple of nodes
644        if ($re_debug->[$index]->{type} eq
645                "WHILEM") {
646            ++$index;
647            next;
648        }
649        if ($re_debug->[$index]->{type} eq
650                "SUCCEED") {
651            ++$index;
652            next;
653        }
654        if ($re_debug->[$index]->{type} eq
655                "NOTHING") {
656            ++$index;
657            next;
658        }
659        if ($re_debug->[$index]->{type} eq
660                "TAIL") {
661            ++$index;
662            next;
663        }
664        push(@$array, {
665            node => $re_debug->[$index]});
666
667        if ($re_debug->[$index]->{type} eq "END") {
668            return ($index+1);
669        }
670        $index++;
671
672    }
673 }
674
675 ##############################################
676 # size_array(\@array) -- Compute the size of
677 #                        an array of nodes
678 #
679 # Returns
680 #        (x_size, y_size) -- Size of the elements
681 #
```

```
682 #        x_size -- Size of all the elements in X
683 #                 (We assume they are
684 #                          laid out in a line)
685 #        y_size -- Biggest Y size
686 #                          (side by side layout)
687 ################################################
688 sub size_array(\@)
689 {
690     # The array
691     my $re_array = shift;
692
693     # Size of the array in X
694     my $x_size = 0;
695
696     # Size of the elements in Y
697     my $y_size = 0;
698
699     foreach my $cur_node(@$re_array) {
700         do_size($cur_node);
701         $x_size += $cur_node->{x_size};
702         if ($y_size < $cur_node->{y_size}) {
703             $y_size = $cur_node->{y_size};
704         }
705     }
706     return ($x_size, $y_size);
707 }
708 ################################################
709 # layout_array($x_start, $y_start,
710 #       $y_max, \@array)
711 #
712 # Layout an array of nodes
713 ################################################
714 sub layout_array($$$\@)
715 {
716     # Starting point in X
717     my $x_start = shift;
718
719     # Starting point in Y
720     my $y_start = shift;
721
722     # largest Y value
723     my $y_max = shift;
724
725     # The data
726     my $re_array = shift;
727
728     foreach my $cur_node (@$re_array) {
729         $cur_node->{x_loc} = $x_start;
730         $cur_node->{y_loc} = $y_start +
```

```
731              int(($y_max -
732                   $cur_node->{y_size})/2);
733          $x_start += $cur_node->{x_size};
734      }
735  }
736
737  ################################################
738  # convert_re -- Convert @re_debug -> @format_re
739  #
740  # The formatted re node contains layout
741  # information as well as information on
742  # nodes contained
743  # inside the current one.
744  ################################################
745  sub convert_re($)
746  {
747      # The regular expression information
748      $re_debug = shift;
749
750      # Clear out old data
751      @format_re = ();
752
753      parse_node(0, \@format_re, undef, undef);
754      #
755      # Compute sizes of each node
756      #
757      my ($x_size, $y_size) =
758          size_array(@format_re);
759
760      #
761      # Compute the location of each node
762      #
763      layout_array(MARGIN,
764          MARGIN, $y_size,
765          @format_re
766      );
767      return (MARGIN + $x_size, MARGIN + $y_size);
768  }
769
```

Running the Script

The convert_re function takes as input the raw regular expression from the parse.pm mode. It converts the raw tree into something a little more formatted and then computes the size of each node (the x_size and y_size fields).

Finally, the code places each node on the output plot (computes the x_loc and y_loc fields).

How It Works

Let's start with a simple regular expression, /test/. The debug output for this regular expression is as follows:

```
1: EXACT <test>(3)
3: END(0)
```

These tell you that the first step (line 1) checks for an exact match of the data test. The next step is in line 3. It is the END step, indicating the end of this expression.

The convert_re turns this into an array, @format_re, which looks like the following figure.

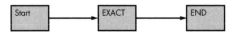

Once you have parsed the expression, you need to lay it out on the graph. The program goes through each node and asks it to compute its size. Since you are dealing with simple nodes, the algorithm is fairly simple. The start and end node have a fixed size. The EXACT node's size is based on the text that's matched.

All the nodes in the graph go through a straight line. So the layout of the nodes is fairly simple.

Now let's look at a more complex expression:

```
/ab*c/
```

The parser output looks like this:

```
1: EXACT <a>(3)
3: STAR(6)
4: EXACT <b>(0)
6: EXACT <c>(8)
8: END(0)
```

The key item in this list is line 3:

```
3: STAR(6)
```

This tells you that the * operator applies to all the nodes from here up to node 6 (node 6 is not included). The parser turns this into an array of elements:

```
EXACT<a>
START -- and whatever the star operates on
EXACT<b>
```

The STAR node contains not only the star operator, but also all the nodes affected by the star. In this case, it's EXACT<b>.

Graphically, your parsed tree looks like the following figure.

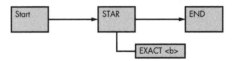

Now one of the key things to notice about this arrangement is that everything is still in a straight line if you consider the STAR node and its children as one entity. Actually, that's the method used by both the layout and drawing logic.

The layout logic tells STAR, "Give me the size of yourself and your children so I can compute the straight line layout." Using this system, the main layout and drawing logic is fairly simple. Everything is drawn in a straight line, although occasionally some of the nodes have to do something recursive. But that complexity and vertical stuff is hidden from the top-level logic.

This makes the layout code fairly simple. You first compute the size of each item in the top row:

```
675 ################################################
676 # size_array(\@array) -- Compute the size of
677 #                        an array of nodes
678 #
679 # Returns
680 #      (x_size, y_size) -- Size of the elements
681 #
682 #      x_size -- Size of all the elements in X
683 #               (We assume they are
684 #                        laid out in a line)
685 #      y_size -- Biggest Y size
686 #                        (side by side layout)
687 ################################################
688 sub size_array(\@)
689 {
690     # The array
691     my $re_array = shift;
692
693     # Size of the array in X
694     my $x_size = 0;
695
696     # Size of the elements in Y
697     my $y_size = 0;
698
699     foreach my $cur_node(@$re_array) {
700         do_size($cur_node);
701         $x_size += $cur_node->{x_size};
```

```
702        if ($y_size < $cur_node->{y_size}) {
703            $y_size = $cur_node->{y_size};
704        }
705    }
706    return ($x_size, $y_size);
707 }
```

This also computes the sizes of any children.

Next you lay them out using a similar method:

```
714 sub layout_array($$$\@)
715 {
716    # Starting point in X
717    my $x_start = shift;
718
719    # Starting point in Y
720    my $y_start = shift;
721
722    # largest Y value
723    my $y_max = shift;
724
725    # The data
726    my $re_array = shift;
727
728    foreach my $cur_node (@$re_array) {
729        $cur_node->{x_loc} = $x_start;
730        $cur_node->{y_loc} = $y_start +
731            int(($y_max -
732                $cur_node->{y_size})/2);
733        $x_start += $cur_node->{x_size};
734    }
735 }
```

Now let's take a closer look at how the size logic works for the STAR
node. The graph of a typical STAR node can be seen in the following figure.

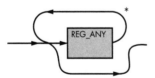

The key features of this are that a STAR node consists of a child or set of
children in the middle and a bunch of lines and arrows surrounding it. So
the code first sizes the children and then adds in the size for the various lines
that are drawn.

```
177 sub size_star($)
178 {
```

```
179      # Node we want layout information for
180      my $node = shift;
181
182      # Compute the size of the children
183      my ($x_size, $y_size) =
184          size_array(@{$node->{children}});
185
186      # Arc size is based on the
187      # Y dimension of the children
188      $node->{arc_size} =
189          int($y_size/4) + PLUS_PAD;
190
191      $node->{child_x} = $x_size - X_MARGIN;
192
193      $node->{x_size} = $node->{child_x} +
194          $node->{arc_size} * 5 + X_MARGIN;
195
196      $node->{y_size} = $y_size +
197          $node->{arc_size} * 2 + Y_MARGIN;
198 }
```

Now let's take on a slightly more complex regular expression:

```
/a|b|c/
```

The debug output from the parser looks like this:

```
 1: BRANCH(4)
 2: EXACT <a>(10)
 4: BRANCH(7)
 5: EXACT <b>(10)
 7: BRANCH(10)
 8: EXACT <c>(10)
10: END(0)
```

The parse tree for this regular expression is illustrated in the following figure.

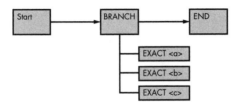

Again, you can lay things out in a straight line if you consider the BRANCH node as a single entity. Because each node is responsible for the layout and drawing of its children, you can do this, thus simplifying the code greatly.

So by being careful with your design and using recursion, you can greatly simplify the algorithm used to lay out and draw the graph. Unfortunately, because there are many details to worry about, you still have a lot of code to deal with.

Hacking the Script

Perl's regular expressions contain a very rich set of operators. I'm sure that there are some that this script doesn't know how to handle. Fortunately, the layout engine is mostly table driven, so it shouldn't be too hard to add new elements as needed.

#46 Drawing the Image

After you lay out the elements, you need to create the image. That's the job of the draw.pm module.

The Code

```
 1 use strict;
 2 use warnings;
 3
 4 package draw;
 5 use GD;
 6 use GD::Arrow;
 7
 8 use size;
 9
10 require Exporter;
11 use vars qw/@ISA @EXPORT $image $color_black/;
12
13 @ISA = qw/Exporter/;
14 @EXPORT = qw/draw_re $image $color_black/;
15
16 # Thickness of the lines
17 use constant THICKNESS => 3;
18
19 # Offset for line 2 of a 2 line text field
20 use constant X_LINE2_OFFSET => 10;
21
22 # Offset for line 2 of a 2 line text field
23 use constant Y_LINE2_OFFSET => 15;
24
25 #
26 # Image variables
27 #
28 my $color_white;        # White color
29 my $color_green;        # Green color
30 my $color_blue;         # Blue color
```

```
31 my $color_light_green;  # Light green color
32 ###############################################
33 # filled_rectangle -- Draw a filled rectangle at
34 #                 the given location
35 ###############################################
36 sub filled_rectangle($$$$$)
37 {
38     # Corners of the rectangle
39     my $x1 = shift;
40     my $y1 = shift;
41     my $x2 = shift;
42     my $y2 = shift;
43
44     my $color = shift;  # Color for drawing
45
46     if ($main::opt_d) {
47         print
48         "Rectangle($x1,$y1,$x2, $y2, $color)\n";
49     }
50     $image->filledRectangle(
51                 $x1, $y1, $x2, $y2,
52                 $color);
53     $image->setThickness(1);
54     $image->rectangle(
55                 $x1, $y1, $x2, $y2,
56                 $color_black);
57 }
58
59 ###############################################
60 # arrow -- Draw an arrow from x1,y1 -> x2,y2
61 #
62 # All arrows are black
63 ###############################################
64 sub arrow($$$$) {
65     my $x1 = shift;      # Start of arrow
66     my $y1 = shift;
67     my $x2 = shift;      # End of arrow
68     my $y2 = shift;
69
70     if ($main::opt_d) {
71         print "Arrow($x1, $y1, $x2, $y2)\n";
72     }
73     # For some reason arrows
74     # tend to point backwards
75     my $arrow = GD::Arrow::Full->new(
76         -X1 => $x2,
77         -Y1 => $y2,
78         -X2 => $x1,
79         -Y2 => $y1,
80         -WIDTH => THICKNESS-1);
```

```
 81     $image->setThickness(1);
 82     $image->filledPolygon($arrow, $color_black);
 83 }
 84
 85 ###########################################
 86 # The "PLUS" node
 87 #
 88 #
 89 #      0  1  2     1p 2p  3p (p = +size of child)
 90 #      v  v  v L3 v  v    v
 91 #      .  ---------   .   .
 92 #      . /.    .  .\ .   .
 93 #      ./ .    .  . \  .
 94 # a2  < .    .  . > a1.
 95 #      .\ .    .  . /.  .
 96 #      . \+-------+/    .
 97 # L1--->| child |----->+ L2
 98 #      .  +-------+  .   .
 99 #
100 # Arc start, end, centers
101 #
102 #         a1 / 270  - 180 / (ap*2, y-a)
103 #         a2 /  90  - 180 / (a0, y-2a), (a2, y-2a)
104 #
105 #         L1 (a3, y+2a) (a3p, y+2a)
106 ###########################################
107
108 #-------------------------------------------
109 # Draw the plus type node
110 #-------------------------------------------
111 sub draw_plus($)
112 {
113     # The node we are drawing
114     my $cur_node = shift;
115
116     layout_array(
117         $cur_node->{x_loc} +
118             $cur_node->{arc_size} * 1,
119         $cur_node->{y_loc},
120         $cur_node->{y_size},
121         @{$cur_node->{children}});
122
123     draw_node_array($cur_node->{children});
124
125     # The place we start drawing from (X)
126     my $from_x = $cur_node->{x_loc};
127
128     # The current middle of the item (Y)
129     my $y = $cur_node->{y_loc} +
130         int($cur_node->{y_size}/2);
```

```perl
131
132     # Size of an arc
133     my $arc_size = $cur_node->{arc_size};
134
135     # Size of the child
136     my $child_x = $cur_node->{child_x};
137
138     # Debugging
139     if (0) {
140         for (my $debug_x = 0;
141              $debug_x < 5;
142              $debug_x++) {
143             $image->line(
144                     $from_x +
145                         $arc_size * $debug_x,
146                     $y - $arc_size*2,
147                     $from_x +
148                         $arc_size * $debug_x,
149                     $y + $arc_size*2,
150                     $color_black
151                     );
152         }
153
154         for (my $debug_x = 3;
155              $debug_x < 7;
156              $debug_x++) {
157             $image->line(
158                     $from_x + $child_x +
159                         $arc_size * $debug_x,
160                             $y - $arc_size*2,
161                     $from_x + $child_x +
162                         $arc_size * $debug_x,
163                             $y + $arc_size*2,
164                     $color_green
165                 );
166         }
167     }
168
169     my $flip = 1;        # Flipping factor
170     if ($cur_node->{min_flag}) {
171         $flip = -1;
172     }
173
174     $image->setThickness(THICKNESS);
175     # First arc (a1)
176     $image->arc(
177             $from_x + $child_x + $arc_size,
178             $y - $arc_size * $flip,
179             $arc_size *2, $arc_size *2,
180             270, 90,
```

```
181              $color_black);
182
183     $image->arc(
184              $from_x + $arc_size * 1,
185                  $y - $arc_size * $flip,
186              $arc_size *2, $arc_size *2,
187              90, 270,
188              $color_black);
189
190     # Draw (L1)
191     arrow(
192              $from_x, $y,
193              $from_x + $arc_size * 1, $y
194     );
195
196     # Draw (L2)
197     arrow(
198              $from_x + $child_x + $arc_size * 1,
199              $y,
200              $from_x + $child_x + $arc_size * 2,
201              $y
202     );
203
204     # Draw (L3)
205     arrow(
206              $from_x + $child_x + $arc_size * 1,
207              $y - $arc_size * 2,
208              $from_x + $arc_size * 1,
209              $y - $arc_size * 2
210     );
211
212
213     # Text to display for the current node
214     my $text = $cur_node->{node}->{text_label};
215     if ($cur_node->{min_flag}) {
216         $text .= "?";
217     }
218
219     $image->string(
220              gdMediumBoldFont,
221              $from_x + $child_x + $arc_size * 2,
222                  $y - $arc_size * 2,
223              $text,
224              $color_blue);
225
226     $cur_node->{left_x} = $from_x;
227     $cur_node->{left_y} = $y;
228
229     $cur_node->{right_x} =
230         $from_x + $cur_node->{child_x} +
```

```
231                    $cur_node->{arc_size} * 2;
232
233     $cur_node->{right_y} = $y;
234 }
235 ##########################################
236 # The "STAR" node
237 #
238 #
239 #                         (p = +size of child)
240 #     0  1  2    3        p3 p4  p5
241 #     v  v  v    v  L2 v  v  v
242 #     .  ----------------   .   .
243 #     . /.  .    .        .\ .   .
244 #     ./ .  .    .         . \   .
245 # a6  <  .  .    .     a5 .  >   .
246 #     .\ .  .    .         . /.  .
247 #     . \. . .  +------+/      .
248 # L3----------->| child |- .    +
249 #     . .\ . j  +------+  .a4/.
250 #     . . \a1   .         . ./ .
251 #     . . \     .         ./ .
252 #     . . |     .        . |   .
253 #     . . .\    .        . /   .
254 #     . . a2\   .       ./a3  .
255 #     . . .  \---------
256 #          ^     ^    L1
257 #          2     3
258 #
259 # Arc / swing / center
260 #       a1 / 270 - 0   / (a1,  y + a)
261 #       a2 /  90 - 180 / (a3,  y + a)
262 #       a3 /   0 - 90  / (p3,  y + a)
263 #       a4 / 180 - 270  / (a4p, y)
264 #
265 #       a5 / 270 - 90  / (p3, y-a)
266 #       a6 /  90 - 270 / (a1, y-a)
267 #
268 #    L1 (a3, y+2a) (a3p, y+2a)
269 ##########################################
270
271 #----------------------------------------
272 # Draw the star type node
273 #----------------------------------------
274 sub draw_star($)
275 {
276     # The node we are drawing
277     my $cur_node = shift;
278
279     layout_array(
280         $cur_node->{x_loc} +
```

```
281            $cur_node->{arc_size} * 3,
282        $cur_node->{y_loc},
283        $cur_node->{y_size},
284        @{$cur_node->{children}});
285
286    # The place we start drawing from (X)
287    my $from_x = $cur_node->{x_loc};
288
289    # The current middle of the item (Y)
290    my $y = int($cur_node->{y_loc} +
291        $cur_node->{y_size}/2);
292
293    # Size of an arc
294    my $arc_size = $cur_node->{arc_size};
295
296    # Size of the child
297    my $child_x = $cur_node->{child_x};
298
299    # Debugging
300    if (0) {
301        for (my $debug_x = 0;
302                $debug_x < 5;
303                $debug_x++) {
304            $image->line(
305                    $from_x +
306                    $arc_size * $debug_x,
307                        $y - $arc_size*2,
308                    $from_x +
309                        $arc_size * $debug_x,
310                    $y + $arc_size*2,
311                    $color_black
312                );
313        }
314
315        for (my $debug_x = 3;
316                $debug_x < 7;
317                $debug_x++) {
318            $image->line(
319                    $from_x + $child_x +
320                        $arc_size * $debug_x,
321                                $y - $arc_size*2,
322                    $from_x + $child_x +
323                        $arc_size * $debug_x,
324                                $y + $arc_size*2,
325                    $color_green
326                );
327        }
328    }
329
330    my $flip = 1;        # Flipping factor
```

```
331     if ($cur_node->{min_flag}) {
332         $flip = -1;
333     }
334
335     $image->setThickness(THICKNESS);
336     if ($flip == 1) {
337         # First arc (a1)
338         $image->arc(
339                 $from_x + $arc_size,
340                 $y + $arc_size,
341                 $arc_size * 2, $arc_size * 2,
342                 270,  0,
343                 $color_black);
344
345         # Second arc (a2)
346         $image->arc(
347                 $from_x + $arc_size * 3,
348                 $y + $arc_size,
349                 $arc_size * 2, $arc_size * 2,
350                 90, 180,
351                 $color_black);
352     } else {
353         # First arc (a1)
354         $image->arc(
355                 $from_x + $arc_size,
356                 $y - $arc_size,
357                 $arc_size * 2, $arc_size * 2,
358                 0, 90,
359                 $color_black);
360
361         # Second arc (a2)
362         $image->arc(
363                 $from_x + $arc_size * 3,
364                 $y - $arc_size,
365                 $arc_size * 2, $arc_size * 2,
366                 180, 270,
367                 $color_black);
368     }
369
370     if ($flip > 0)  {
371         # Third arc (a3)
372         $image->arc(
373                 $from_x + $child_x +
374                     $arc_size * 3,
375                 $y + $arc_size,
376                 $arc_size * 2, $arc_size * 2,
377                 0, 90,
378                 $color_black);
379
380         # Fourth arc (a4)
```

```
381      $image->arc(
382              $from_x + $child_x +
383                  $arc_size * 5,
384              $y + $arc_size,
385              $arc_size * 2, $arc_size * 2,
386              180, 270,
387              $color_black);
388  } else {
389      # Third arc (a3)
390      $image->arc(
391              $from_x + $child_x +
392                      $arc_size * 3,
393              $y - $arc_size,
394              $arc_size * 2, $arc_size * 2,
395              270, 0,
396              $color_black);
397
398      # Fourth arc (a4)
399      $image->arc(
400              $from_x + $child_x +
401                  $arc_size * 5,
402              $y - $arc_size,
403              $arc_size * 2, $arc_size * 2,
404              90, 180,
405              $color_black);
406  }
407
408  # Fifth arc (a5)
409  $image->arc(
410          $from_x + $child_x + $arc_size * 3,
411              $y - $arc_size * $flip,
412          $arc_size * 2, $arc_size * 2,
413          270, 90,
414          $color_black);
415
416  # Sixth arc (a6)
417  $image->arc(
418          $from_x + $arc_size,
419              $y - $arc_size * $flip,
420          $arc_size * 2, $arc_size * 2,
421          90, 270,
422          $color_black);
423
424  # L1
425  arrow(
426          $from_x + $arc_size * 3,
427              $y + $arc_size * 2 * $flip,
428          $from_x + $arc_size * 3 + $child_x,
429              $y + $arc_size * 2 * $flip);
430
```

```
431    # L2
432    arrow(
433            $from_x + $arc_size * 3 + $child_x,
434                $y - $arc_size * 2 * $flip,
435            $from_x + $arc_size * 1,
436                $y - $arc_size * 2 * $flip);
437
438    # Draw (L3)
439    arrow(
440            $from_x, $y,
441            $from_x + $arc_size * 3, $y);
442
443
444    $image->string(
445            gdMediumBoldFont,
446            $from_x + $child_x + $arc_size * 4,
447                $y - $arc_size * 2,
448            ($cur_node->{min_flag}) ? "*?" : "*",
449            $color_black);
450
451
452    draw_node_array($cur_node->{children});
453
454    $cur_node->{left_x} = $from_x;
455    $cur_node->{left_y} = $y;
456
457    $cur_node->{right_x} =
458        $from_x + $cur_node->{child_x} +
459        $cur_node->{arc_size} * 5;
460
461    $cur_node->{right_y} = $y;
462 }
463
464 #############################################
465 # Branch nodes
466 #############################################
467 #-------------------------------------------
468 # draw_branch -- Draw a branch structure
469 #-------------------------------------------
470 sub draw_branch($)
471 {
472    # Node we want layout information for
473    my $cur_node = shift;
474
475    # Location where we draw the branches
476    my $x_loc = $cur_node->{x_loc} +
477        X_BRANCH_MARGIN;
478
479    my $y_loc = $cur_node->{y_loc};
480
```

```
481    foreach my $cur_child (
482            @{$cur_node->{choices}}
483        ) {
484        layout_array(
485            $x_loc + X_BRANCH_MARGIN,
486            $y_loc,
487            $cur_child->[0]->{row_y_size},
488            @{$cur_child});
489
490        $y_loc += $cur_child->[0]->{row_y_size} +
491                Y_BRANCH_MARGIN;
492        draw_node_array($cur_child);
493    }
494
495    # Largest right x of any node
496    my $max_x = 0;
497
498    foreach my $cur_child (
499            @{$cur_node->{choices}}) {
500
501        # Last node on the string of children
502        my $last_node =
503            $cur_child->[$#{$cur_child}];
504
505        if ($last_node->{right_x} > $max_x) {
506            $max_x = $last_node->{right_x};
507        }
508    }
509    foreach my $cur_child (
510            @{$cur_node->{choices}}
511        ) {
512        # Last node on the
513        # string of children
514        my $last_node =
515            $cur_child->[$#{$cur_child}];
516
517        if ($last_node->{right_x} < $max_x) {
518            $image->line(
519                    $last_node->{right_x},
520                    $last_node->{right_y},
521                    $max_x,
522                    $last_node->{right_y},
523                    $color_black);
524        }
525    }
526
527    my $left_x = $cur_node->{x_loc};
528    my $right_x = $cur_node->{x_loc} +
529        $cur_node->{x_size} - X_MARGIN;
530
```

```perl
531     my $y = $cur_node->{y_loc} +
532         ($cur_node->{y_size} / 2);
533
534     foreach my $cur_child (
535                 @{$cur_node->{choices}}
536         ) {
537         # Create a branch line to the item
538         # in the list of nodes
539         $image->line(
540                 $left_x, $y,
541                 $cur_child->[0]->{left_x},
542                 $cur_child->[0]->{left_y},
543                 $color_black);
544
545         # The last node on the list
546         my $last_child =
547             $cur_child->[$#$cur_child];
548
549         # Line from the last node
550         # to the collection point
551         $image->line(
552                 $max_x, $last_child->{right_y},
553                 $right_x, $y,
554                 $color_black);
555     }
556
557     $cur_node->{left_x} = $left_x;
558     $cur_node->{left_y} = $y;
559
560     $cur_node->{right_x} = $right_x;
561     $cur_node->{right_y} = $y;
562 }
563
564
565
566 ##########################################
567 # draw a start or end node
568 ##########################################
569 sub draw_start_end($)
570 {
571     my $cur_node = shift;
572     my $node_number = $cur_node->{node}->{node};
573
574     filled_rectangle(
575             $cur_node->{x_loc},
576             $cur_node->{y_loc},
577             $cur_node->{x_loc} + X_NODE_SIZE,
578             $cur_node->{y_loc} + Y_NODE_SIZE,
579             $color_green);
580
```

```
581     $cur_node->{text} = $image->string(
582             gdSmallFont,
583             $cur_node->{x_loc} + X_TEXT_OFFSET,
584             $cur_node->{y_loc} + Y_TEXT_OFFSET,
585
586             $cur_node->{node}->{type},
587             $color_black);
588
589     $cur_node->{left_x} = $cur_node->{x_loc};
590
591     $cur_node->{left_y} =
592         $cur_node->{y_loc} + Y_NODE_SIZE / 2;
593
594     $cur_node->{right_x} =
595         $cur_node->{x_loc} + X_NODE_SIZE;
596
597     $cur_node->{right_y} =
598         $cur_node->{y_loc} + Y_NODE_SIZE / 2;
599 }
600
601 #-------------------------------------------
602 # draw_exact($node) -- Draw a "EXACT" re node
603 #-------------------------------------------
604 sub draw_exact($)
605 {
606     my $cur_node = shift;        # The node
607     my $node_number = $cur_node->{node}->{node};
608
609     filled_rectangle(
610             $cur_node->{x_loc},
611             $cur_node->{y_loc},
612             $cur_node->{x_loc} +
613                 $cur_node->{x_size} -
614                 X_MARGIN,
615             $cur_node->{y_loc} + Y_NODE_SIZE,
616             $color_green);
617
618     $image->string(
619             gdSmallFont,
620             $cur_node->{x_loc} + X_TEXT_OFFSET,
621             $cur_node->{y_loc} + Y_TEXT_OFFSET,
622             "$cur_node->{node}->{type}",
623             $color_black);
624
625     $image->string(
626             gdSmallFont,
627             $cur_node->{x_loc} +
628                 X_TEXT_OFFSET + X_LINE2_OFFSET,
629             $cur_node->{y_loc} +
630                 Y_TEXT_OFFSET + Y_LINE2_OFFSET,
```

```
631                 "$cur_node->{node}->{arg}",
632             $color_black);
633
634     $cur_node->{left_x} = $cur_node->{x_loc};
635
636     $cur_node->{left_y} =
637         $cur_node->{y_loc} + Y_NODE_SIZE / 2;
638
639     $cur_node->{right_x} =
640         $cur_node->{x_loc} + X_NODE_SIZE;
641
642     $cur_node->{right_y} =
643         $cur_node->{y_loc} + Y_NODE_SIZE / 2;
644 }
645 #-------------------------------------------
646 # draw_ref($node) -- Draw a "REF" re node
647 #-------------------------------------------
648 sub draw_ref($)
649 {
650     my $cur_node = shift;          # The node
651     my $node_number = $cur_node->{node}->{node};
652
653     filled_rectangle(
654             $cur_node->{x_loc},
655             $cur_node->{y_loc},
656             $cur_node->{x_loc} + X_NODE_SIZE,
657             $cur_node->{y_loc} + Y_NODE_SIZE,
658             $color_light_green);
659
660     $cur_node->{text} = $image->String(
661             gdSmallFont,
662             $cur_node->{x_loc} + X_TEXT_OFFSET,
663             $cur_node->{y_loc} + Y_TEXT_OFFSET,
664             "Back Reference:\n".
665             "  $cur_node->{node}->{ref}",
666             $color_black);
667
668     $cur_node->{left_x} = $cur_node->{x_loc};
669
670     $cur_node->{left_y} =
671         $cur_node->{y_loc} + Y_NODE_SIZE / 2;
672
673     $cur_node->{right_x} =
674         $cur_node->{x_loc} + X_NODE_SIZE;
675
676     $cur_node->{right_y} =
677         $cur_node->{y_loc} + Y_NODE_SIZE;
678 }
679 #-------------------------------------------
680 # draw the () stuff
```

```
681  #-------------------------------------------
682  sub draw_open($$)
683  {
684      my $cur_node = shift;        # The node
685
686      $image->setStyle(
687          $color_black, $color_black,
688                  $color_black, $color_black,
689                  $color_black,
690          $color_white, $color_white,
691                  $color_white, $color_white,
692                  $color_white
693      );
694      $image->rectangle(
695              $cur_node->{x_loc},
696                  $cur_node->{y_loc} +
697                  BOX_FONT_SIZE,
698              $cur_node->{x_loc} +
699                  $cur_node->{x_size} -
700                  X_MARGIN,
701              $cur_node->{y_loc} +
702                  $cur_node->{y_size},
703              gdStyled);
704
705      $image->string(
706              gdSmallFont,
707              $cur_node->{x_loc},
708              $cur_node->{y_loc},
709              $cur_node->{text},
710              $color_black);
711
712      layout_array(
713          $cur_node->{x_loc} +
714                  BOX_MARGIN/2,
715          $cur_node->{y_loc} +
716                  BOX_MARGIN/2 + BOX_FONT_SIZE,
717          $cur_node->{y_size} -
718                  BOX_MARGIN - BOX_FONT_SIZE,
719          @{$cur_node->{children}});
720
721      draw_node_array($cur_node->{children});
722
723      $cur_node->{left_x} = $cur_node->{x_loc};
724      $cur_node->{left_y} = $cur_node->{y_loc} +
725          ($cur_node->{y_size} + BOX_FONT_SIZE)/2;
726
727      $cur_node->{right_x} = $cur_node->{x_loc} +
728          $cur_node->{x_size} - X_MARGIN;
729
730      $cur_node->{right_y} = $cur_node->{left_y};
```

```perl
731
732     # Child we are drawing arrows to / from
733     my $child = $cur_node->{children}->[0];
734     $image->line(
735             $cur_node->{left_x},
736             $cur_node->{left_y},
737             $child->{left_x},
738             $child->{left_y},
739             $color_black
740     );
741     $child =
742         $cur_node->{children}->[
743             $#{$cur_node->{children}}
744         ];
745
746     $image->line(
747             $child->{right_x},
748             $child->{right_y},
749             $cur_node->{right_x},
750             $cur_node->{right_y},
751             $color_black
752     );
753 }
754
755 my %draw_node = (
756     "ANYOF" => \&draw_exact,
757     "BOL"   => \&draw_start_end,
758     "EOL"   => \&draw_start_end,
759     "SPACE"   => \&draw_start_end,
760     "NSPACE"   => \&draw_start_end,
761     "DIGIT"   => \&draw_start_end,
762     "BRANCH"=> \&draw_branch,
763     "END"   => \&draw_start_end,
764     "EXACT" => \&draw_exact,
765     "IFMATCH"  => \&draw_open,
766     "OPEN"  => \&draw_open,
767     "PLUS"  => \&draw_plus,
768     "REF"   => \&draw_ref,
769     "REG_ANY" => \&draw_start_end,
770     "STAR"  => \&draw_star,
771     "Start" => \&draw_start_end,
772     "UNLESSM"  => \&draw_open
773 );
774
775 #############################################
776 # draw_node_array -- draw an array of nodes
777 #############################################
778 sub draw_node_array($)
779 {
780     my $array = shift;
```

```
781    #
782    # Draw Nodes
783    #
784    foreach my $cur_node (@$array) {
785        if (not defined(
786            $draw_node{
787                $cur_node->{node}->{type}})) {
788
789            die("No draw function for ".
790                "$cur_node->{node}->{type}");
791        }
792        $draw_node{
793            $cur_node->{node}->{type}}(
794                $cur_node
795            );
796    }
797    #
798    # Loop through all the things
799    # (except the last) and
800    # draw arrows between them
801    #
802    for (my $index = 0;
803        $index < $#$array;
804        ++$index) {
805
806        my $from_x = $array->[$index]->{right_x};
807        my $from_y = $array->[$index]->{right_y};
808
809        my $to_x = $array->[$index+1]->{left_x};
810        my $to_y = $array->[$index+1]->{left_y};
811
812        arrow(
813            $from_x, $from_y,
814            $to_x, $to_y
815        );
816    }
817 }
818 #############################################
819 # draw_re -- Draw the image
820 #############################################
821 sub draw_re($)
822 {
823    # Formatted expression
824    my $format_re = shift;
825
826    # Background color
827    $color_white =
828        $image->colorAllocate(255,255,255);
829    $color_black = $image->colorAllocate(0,0,0);
830    $color_green=$image->colorAllocate(0,255, 0);
```

```
831     $color_blue=$image->colorAllocate(0, 0, 255);
832     $color_light_green =
833             $image->colorAllocate(0, 128, 0);
834     # Draw the top level array
835     #   (Which recursively draws
836     #     all the enclosed elements)
837     draw_node_array($format_re);
838     # Make all the canvas visible
839 }
```

Running the Script

The function draw_re takes a formatted regular expression and produces an image. The image is stored in a global variable, $image, so that the caller can then do what they want with it.

How It Works

Drawing is a pretty straightforward operation. The shapes are mostly simple and the layout has already been done. The same recursive system you used for laying out the nodes work for drawing. For example, if you are to draw a STAR node, you tell the children to draw themselves and then you draw the lines around them.

The drawing consists of squares, lines, text, and arcs. Squares, lines, and text are simple to draw. Unfortunately, nobody has found a good way of specifying arcs. As a result, it's easy to draw arcs backwards, upside down, flipped, offset, and generally screwed. Let's take a look at the STAR node again.

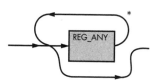

This element has six, count them, six arcs. Getting each one specified perfectly is difficult. To make things easier, the STAR node was laid out as a text graph before the code was generated as illustrated in the next code example. This gave me the ability to see where things should go before committing them to code. Also, I was able to record my notes and measurements, which helped in computing exactly where everything should go. (It also helped me find out what was going on when things went wrong.)

In some cases, the comments for a drawing function are bigger than the code. But the planning helps tremendously when it comes time to commit the drawing to code.

```
235 ##########################################
236 # The "STAR" node
```

```
237 #
238 #
239 #                          (p = +size of child)
240 #      0  1  2   3         p3 p4  p5
241 #      v  v  v   v    L2   v  v   v
242 #      .  ------------------  .   .
243 #      . /.  .   .          .\ .  .
244 #      ./ .  .   .          . \   .
245 # a6  <  .  .   .     a5 .  >    .
246 #      .\ .  .   .          . /.  .
247 #      . \. . .   +-------+/     .
248 #  L3----------->| child |- .    +
249 #      . .\ . j  +-------+ .a4/.
250 #      . . \a1   .         . . / .
251 #      . .  \    .         . ./  .
252 #      . .  |    .         . |   .
253 #      . .  .\   .         . /   .
254 #      . . a2\   .         ./a3  .
255 #      . .  .  \---------
256 #           ^     ^    L1
257 #           2     3
258 #
259 # Arc / swing / center
260 #      a1 / 270 - 0   / (a1,  y + a)
261 #      a2 /  90 - 180 / (a3,  y + a)
262 #      a3 /   0 - 90  / (p3,  y + a)
263 #      a4 / 180 - 270 / (a4p, y)
264 #
265 #      a5 / 270 - 90  / (p3, y-a)
266 #      a6 /  90 - 270 / (a1, y-a)
267 #
268 #      L1 (a3, y+2a) (a3p, y+2a)
269 #############################################
```

Hacking the Script

Again, this is a table-driven script. As new elements are needed, new drawing functions can be added easily.

#47 Regular Expression Grapher

Finally, we have the re_graph.pl program. This does the actual work of graphing the regular expression.

The Code

```
1 #
2 # re_graph.pl -- Graph a regular expression
```

```perl
 3 #
 4 use strict;
 5 use warnings;
 6
 7 use IO::Handle;
 8 use English;
 9 use GD;
10 use GD::Arrow;
11
12 use parse;
13 use size;
14 use draw;
15
16 # Label location
17 use constant LABEL_LOC_X => 50;
18 use constant LABEL_LOC_Y => 50;
19
20 # Location of progress msg
21 use constant PROGRESS_X => 50;
22 use constant PROGRESS_Y => 70;
23
24 # Length of the yellow arrow
25 use constant YELLOW_ARROW_SIZE => 25;
26 use constant YELLOW_ARROW_WIDTH => 5;
27
28 use Getopt::Std;
29
30 use vars qw/$opt_d $opt_o $opt_x $opt_y/;
31
32 STDOUT->autoflush(1);
33
34 # Configuration items
35 my $x_margin = 16;        # Space between items
36 my $y_margin = 16;        # Space between items
37
38 #
39 # Fields
40 #       node    -- Node number
41 #       type    -- Node type (from re debug)
42 #       arg     -- Argument (optional)
43 #       next    -- Next node
44 #
45
46 #
47 # Fields
48 #       x_size   - Size of the node in X
49 #       y_size   - Size of the node in Y
50 #       x_loc    - X Location of the node
51 #       y_loc    - Y Location of the node
52 #       node     - Reference to the
```

```
53 #                        node in @re_debug
54 #     child    - Array of child
55 #                        nodes for this node
56 #
57
58 # Re we are displaying now
59 my $current_re;
60
61 my $re_to_add = "";      # Re we are adding
62
63
64 ###############################################
65 # usage -- Tell the user how to use us
66 ###############################################
67 sub usage()
68 {
69     print STDERR <<EOF;
70 Usage is $0 [options] [-o <file>] <re> [<str>]
71 Options:
72   -d -- Debug
73   -x <size> -- Minimum size in X
74   -y <size> -- Minimum size in Y
75 EOF
76     exit (8);
77 }
78
79
80 ###############################################
81 # find_node($state, $node_array) -- Find a node
82 #       the parsed node tree
83 #
84 # Returns the location of the node
85 ###############################################
86 sub find_node($$);
87 sub find_node($$)
88 {
89     # State (node number) to find
90     my $state = shift;
91
92     my $array = shift;  # The array to search
93
94     foreach my $cur_node (@$array) {
95         if ($cur_node->{node}->{node} ==
96                 $state) {
97
98             return ($cur_node->{x_loc},
99                     $cur_node->{y_loc});
100
101         }
```

```perl
102         if (defined($cur_node->{children})) {
103             # Get the x,y to return from
104             #   the children
105             my ($ret_x, $ret_y) =
106                 find_node(
107                     $state,
108                     $cur_node->{children});
109
110             if (defined($ret_x)) {
111                 return ($ret_x, $ret_y);
112             }
113         }
114         if (defined($cur_node->{choices})) {
115             my $choices = $cur_node->{choices};
116             foreach my $cur_choice (@$choices) {
117                 # Get the x,y to return from the
118                 #       choice list
119                 my ($ret_x, $ret_y) =
120                     find_node(
121                         $state, $cur_choice);
122
123                 if (defined($ret_x)) {
124                     return ($ret_x, $ret_y);
125                 }
126             }
127         }
128     }
129     return (undef, undef);
130 }
131 ##############################################
132 # draw_progress($cur_line, $page)
133 #
134 # Draw a progress page
135 #
136 # Returns true if the page was drawn
137 ##############################################
138 sub draw_progress($$$)
139 {
140     my $value = shift;    # Value to check
141     my $cur_line = shift;# Line we are processing
142     my $page = shift;    # Page number
143
144     # Check to see if this
145     # is one of the progress lines
146     if (substr($cur_line, 26, 1) ne '|') {
147         return (0);    # Not a good line
148     }
149     # Line containing the progress number
150     # from the debug output
```

```perl
151     my $progress_line = substr($cur_line, 0, 24);
152
153     # Location of the current state information
154     my $state_line = substr($cur_line, 27);
155
156     # Extract progress number
157     $progress_line =~ /^\s*(\d+)/;
158     my $progress = $1;
159
160     # Extract state number
161     $state_line =~ /^\s*(\d+)/;
162     my $state = $1;
163
164     # Find the location of this node
165     # on the graph
166     my ($x_location, $y_location) =
167         find_node($state, \@format_re);
168
169     if ($opt_d) {
170         if (defined($x_location)) {
171             print
172                 "node $state ".
173                 "($x_location, $y_location)\n";
174         } else {
175             print "node $state not found\n";
176         }
177     }
178     # If the node is not graphable,
179     # skip this step
180     if (not defined($x_location)) {
181         return (0);
182     }
183     # Create a new image with arrow
184     my $new_image =
185         GD::Image->newFromPngData(
186             $image->png(0));
187
188     # Create the arrow
189     my $arrow = GD::Arrow::Full->new(
190         -X1 => $x_location,
191         -Y1 => $y_location,
192         -X2 => $x_location - YELLOW_ARROW_SIZE,
193         -Y2 => $y_location - YELLOW_ARROW_SIZE,
194         -WIDTH => YELLOW_ARROW_WIDTH
195     );
196
197     $new_image->setThickness(1);
198
199     # Create some colors for
```

```perl
200     # the new image
201     my $new_color_yellow =
202         $new_image->colorAllocate(255, 255, 0);
203
204     my $new_color_black =
205         $new_image->colorAllocate(0,0,0);
206
207     # Make the arrow point
208     # to the current step
209     $new_image->filledPolygon(
210         $arrow, $new_color_yellow);
211
212     $new_image->polygon(
213         $arrow, $new_color_black);
214
215     # Get the size of the font we are using
216     my $char_width = gdGiantFont->width;
217     my $char_height = gdGiantFont->height;
218
219     $new_image->filledRectangle(
220         PROGRESS_X, PROGRESS_Y,
221         PROGRESS_X +
222         $progress * $char_width,
223         PROGRESS_Y + $char_height,
224         $new_color_yellow
225     );
226
227     $new_image->string(gdGiantFont,
228         PROGRESS_X, PROGRESS_Y,
229         $value, $new_color_black);
230
231     # Generate the output file name
232     my $out_file =
233     sprintf($opt_o, $page);
234
235     open OUT_FILE, ">$out_file" or
236     die("Could not open output".
237     "file: $out_file");
238
239     binmode OUT_FILE;
240     print OUT_FILE $new_image->png(0);
241     close OUT_FILE;
242     return (1);
243 }
244 ##############################################
245 # chart_progress -- Chart the progress of the
246 #       execution of the RE
247 ##############################################
248 sub chart_progress()
```

```
249 {
250    my $value = $ARGV[0];          # Value to check
251
252    # Value with ' quoted
253    my $quote_value = $value;
254    $quote_value =~ s/'/\\'/g;
255
256    # Regular expression
257    my $quote_re = $current_re;
258    $quote_re =~ s/\\/\\\\/g;
259
260    my $cmd = <<EOF ;
261 perl 2>&1 <<SHELL_EOF
262 use re 'debug';
263 '$quote_value' =~ /$quote_re/;
264 SHELL_EOF
265 EOF
266
267    # The raw debug output
268    my @raw_debug = `$cmd`;
269
270    # Discard junk before the "Matching" keyword
271    while (($#raw_debug > 0) and
272        ($raw_debug[0] !~ /^Matching/)) {
273        shift(@raw_debug);
274    }
275    shift(@raw_debug);
276
277    my $page = 1;        # Current output page
278
279    foreach my $cur_line (@raw_debug) {
280        # Skip other lines
281        if (length($cur_line) < 27) {
282            next;
283        }
284        if (draw_progress($value,
285                $cur_line, $page)) {
286            ++$page;
287        }
288    }
289 }
290
291
292 # -d    -- Print RE debug output and draw output
293 # -o file -- specify output file (template)
294 # -x <min-x>
295 # -y <min-y>
296 my $status = getopts("df:o:x:y:");
297 if ($status == 0)
298 {
```

```perl
299     usage();
300 }
301
302 if (not defined($opt_o)) {
303     $opt_o = "re_graph_%02d.png";
304 }
305
306 if ($#ARGV == -1) {
307     usage();
308 }
309 $current_re = shift(@ARGV);
310
311 # Compute the regular expression debug info.
312 my @re_debug = parse_re($current_re);
313
314 # Convert the data, get the size of the new node
315 my ($x_size, $y_size) = convert_re(\@re_debug);
316 $x_size += MARGIN;
317 $y_size += MARGIN;
318 if (defined($opt_x)) {
319     if ($opt_x > $x_size) {
320         $x_size = $opt_x;
321     }
322 }
323 if (defined($opt_y)) {
324     if ($opt_y > $y_size) {
325         $y_size = $opt_y;
326     }
327 }
328
329 $image = GD::Image->new($x_size, $y_size);
330
331 draw_re(\@format_re);
332
333 $image->string(gdGiantFont,
334     LABEL_LOC_X, LABEL_LOC_Y,
335     "Regular Expression: /$current_re/",
336     $color_black);
337
338 my $out_file = sprintf($opt_o, 0);
339 open OUT_FILE, ">$out_file" or
340     die("Could not open output file: $out_file");
341
342 binmode OUT_FILE;
343 print OUT_FILE $image->png(0);
344 close OUT_FILE;
345
346 if ($#ARGV != -1) {
347     chart_progress();
348 }
```

Running the Script

To graph a regular expression, run the program and give it the name of an output file (-o option) and a regular expression to graph. Here's an example:

```
$ perl re_graph.pl -o first.png '\s*test\s*'
```

If you want to graph the execution of the regular expression against a particular string, you'll need to specify an output file template and a string to match against the regular expression:

```
$ perl re_graph.pl -o re_%2d.png '\s*test\s*' 'testing'
```

The output file template is a `printf` style specification that will be used to generate a series of images showing the regular expression and its execution.

The Results

Let's start by taking a look at the result of graphing the regular expression:

```
/test/
```

The graph is shown in the following figure.

Regular Expression: test

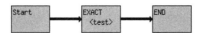

Perl's regular expression engine starts at the start node. The next node (EXACT) tells Perl that the string must match the text exactly. In this case, the text is test. If the match is successful, the regular expression goes to the next node, in this case it's END, indicating a successful match.

If a match is not successful (for example, if you were trying to match the beginning of "this is a test" against /test/), the engine moves forward in the string and tries the match again. In this case, it tries to match "his is a test" against /test/. Eventually it will match or run out of string.[1]

Now let's try a more complicated expression:

```
/^ *#/
```

---

[1] The regular expression engine has an optimizer that helps it guess where the best possible match of the string can be located. However, for the purposes of this chapter, we're going to assume the optimizer does not exist.

The graph of this expression can be seen in the following figure.

Regular Expression: /^.*#/

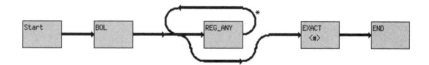

The first node after the start node is called BOL. This is Perl's way of saying, "match the 'beginning of line'."

Between the BOL node and the REG_ANY node you have a fork in the road. The regular expression engine will always attempt to take the upper branch of any fork. So if the next character is a space (matching EXACT< >), the upper branch will be taken and the expression will loop. If the next character is not a space, the lower branch will be taken. This takes you to an exact node that matches the # character. After this matches, the END node is reached and the match is successful.

There's one more major type of construct to consider: the branch. Take a look at this regular expression:

/a|b/

This regular expression matches a or b. Graphically this is illustrated by the following figure.

Regular Expression: /a|b/

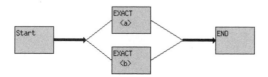

Remember that Perl always tries to take the top branch when it comes to a fork, so in this case, it will first try to match a and then try to match b. If neither one matches, it fails.

Finally let's look at what happens when you have a sub-expression specification, as in this example:

/\s*(\d+)/

The only thing new about this graph (see the following figure) is the big box around the middle expression. Anything inside that box gets assigned to the variable $1.

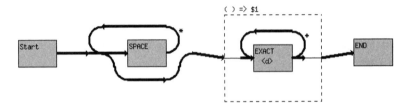

Regular Expression: /\s*(\d+)/

So far you've just graphed the expressions. Now let's see them in action. For this example, we'll use the following command:

```
$ perl re_graph.pl -o ex_%02d.png '^.*(a|b|c).+$' 'abc'
```

The command generates a series of images showing how Perl executes this statement:

```
'abc' =~ /^.*(a|b|c).+$/
```

The following figure shows the first attempt at matching. The letters abc are shaded, indicating that Perl has processed them. The arrow points to the graph of .*.

Regular Expression: /^.*(a|b|c).+$/
abc

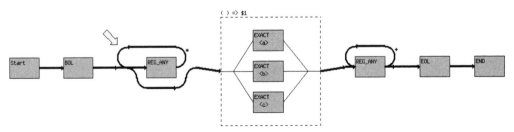

Perl will now try to match the rest of the string (consisting of the end of the string only) against the rest of the regular expression (/(a|b|c).+$/). The following figure shows the system trying to match the end of the string against b.

Regular Expression: /^.*(a|b|c).+$/
abc

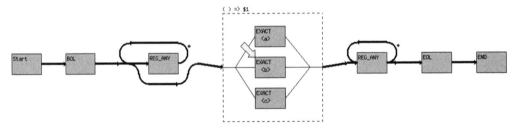

This isn't going to work, so Perl backs up a character and sees what happens when it matches ab against /^.*/. The following figure shows that Perl is trying to match the c of abc against the second item in the branch list. Notice that only the ab of abc is shaded.

Regular Expression: /^.*(a|b|c).+$/
abc

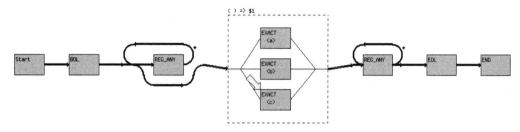

This step will fail, but the next one will succeed. Next Perl tries to match "end of string" against /.+/. This fails. So Perl backtracks and sees what happens if it matches a against /^.*/ and the rest of the string against /(a|b|c).+$/.

The b matches the middle element as we can see in the following figure.

Regular Expression: /^.*(a|b|c).+$/
abc

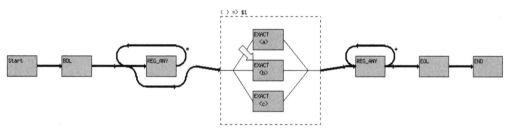

The c is checked against /.+/ as shown by the following figure. It succeeds.

Regular Expression: /^.*(a|b|c).+$/
abc

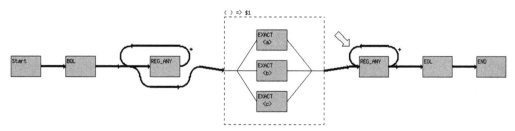

The result is a match. It took a while to get there, but you have a match.

The best way of fully understanding this script is to try it. By playing around with various expressions and values, you should get a pretty good idea of what goes on inside a regular expression.

How It Works

The system feeds the regular expression through the parsing module, places the nodes on the image with the layout module, and draws the basic regular expression with the drawing module.

Showing the Execution of the Graph

Once you have your graph, you can use it to show the regular expression engine in action. Let's take a look at the debug output produced by the following Perl code:

```
'abc' =~ /^.*(a|b|c).+/;
```

The debug code shows not only the compilation of the expression, but its execution:

```
Compiling REx `^.*(a|b|c).+'
size 19 Got 156 bytes for offset annotations.
first at 2
   1: BOL(2)
   2: STAR(4)
   3:    REG_ANY(0)
   4: OPEN1(6)
   6:    BRANCH(9)
   7:      EXACT <a>(15)
   9:    BRANCH(12)
  10:      EXACT <b>(15)
  12:    BRANCH(15)
  13:      EXACT <c>(15)
  15: CLOSE1(17)
  17: PLUS(19)
  18:    REG_ANY(0)
  19: END(0)
anchored(BOL) minlen 2
Offsets: [19]
      1[1] 3[1] 2[1] 4[1] 0[0] 4[1] 5[1] 0[0] 6[1] 7[1] 0[0] 8[1] 9[1] 0[0] 10
[1] 0[0] 12[1] 11[1] 13[0]
Matching REx `^.*(a|b|c).+' against `abc'
  Setting an EVAL scope, savestack=3
   0 <> <abc>           |   1:  BOL
   0 <> <abc>           |   2:  STAR
                            REG_ANY can match 3 times out of 2147483647...
  Setting an EVAL scope, savestack=3
   3 <abc> <>           |   4:    OPEN1
   3 <abc> <>           |   6:    BRANCH
  Setting an EVAL scope, savestack=13
   3 <abc> <>           |   7:      EXACT <a>
                                 failed...
```

```
  3 <abc> <>                  | 10:      EXACT <b>
                                  failed...
  3 <abc> <>                  | 13:      EXACT <c>
                                  failed...
Clearing an EVAL scope, savestack=3..13
  2 <ab> <c>                  |  4:      OPEN1
  2 <ab> <c>                  |  6:      BRANCH
Setting an EVAL scope, savestack=13
  2 <ab> <c>                  |  7:      EXACT <a>
        8                         failed...
  2 <ab> <c>                  | 10:      EXACT <b>
                                  failed...
  2 <ab> <c>                  | 13:      EXACT <c>
  3 <abc> <>                  | 15:      CLOSE1
  3 <abc> <>                  | 17:      PLUS
                              REG_ANY can match 0 times out of 2147483647...
Setting an EVAL scope, savestack=13
                                  failed...
setting an EVAL scope, savestack=13
  1 <a> <bc>                  |  7:      EXACT <a>
                                  failed...
  1 <a> <bc>                  | 10:      EXACT <b>
  2 <ab> <c>                  | 15:      CLOSE1
  2 <ab> <c>                  | 17:      PLUS
                              REG_ANY can match 1 times out of 2147483647...
Setting an EVAL scope, savestack=13
  3 <abc> <>                  | 19:      END
Match successful!
Freeing REx: `"^.*(a|b|c).+"'
```

Let's take a closer look at a typical debug line:

```
  0 <> <abc>                  |  1:  BOL
```

The first number (0) tells you that the regular expression engine has matched 0 characters of the string at this point. The next little bit of text shows a bit of the string matched so far (nothing, or <>) and a bit of the unmatched portion (<abc>). Then you have a vertical bar followed by the node that is currently being executed. In this case, it's node number 1, beginning of line (BOL).

We've gone through the execution of this regular expression before. Now let's see how the debug output relates to what you saw previously.

After matching the BOL, the engine tries to match abc against /.*/. Since /.*/ is greedy, it matches all three characters:

```
  3 <abc> <>                  |  4:  OPEN1
```

This line tells you that all three characters have been matched and the engine is now going to match the remainder (<>) against the expression starting at node 4 (the open parenthesis).

Next Perl tries to match the end of the string against the expression /(a|b|c)/. This fails:

3 <abc> <>	| 7:	EXACT <a>	
		failed...	
3 <abc> <>	| 10:	EXACT <b>	
		failed...	
3 <abc> <>	| 13:	EXACT <c>	
		failed...	

Perl goes back and decides to see if things will work better if it matches only 'ab' against /.*/:

2 <ab> <c>	| 4:	OPEN1

Things are better this time. When it checks c against /(a|b|c)/, it gets a match on the third try:

2 <ab> <c>	| 7:	EXACT <a>	
		failed...	
2 <ab> <c>	| 10:	EXACT <b>	
		failed...	
2 <ab> <c>	| 13:	EXACT <c>	
3 <abc> <>	| 15:	CLOSE1	

Next it tries matching the end of line to /.+/. This fails:

3 <abc> <>	| 17:	PLUS
	REG_ANY can match 0 times out of 2147483647...	
Setting an EVAL scope, savestack=13		
	failed...	

So the engine goes back again and sees if things will work better if only a is matched against the initial /.*/. This works. The b matches the middle, and the c matches the end. Success:

2 <ab> <c>	| 17:	PLUS
	REG_ANY can match 1 times out of 2147483647...	
Setting an EVAL scope, savestack=13		
3 <abc> <>	| 19:	END
Match successful!		

The execution of this regular expression took a bit of work and required the system to backtrack twice.

The regular expression graphing program illustrates the execution process graphically, as shown in the following figure.

1	abc	7	abc	13	abc
2	abc	8	abc	14	abc
3	abc	9	abc	15	abc
4	abc	10	abc	16	abc
5	abc	11	abc		
6	abc	12	abc		

Regular Expression: /^.*(a|b|c).+$/

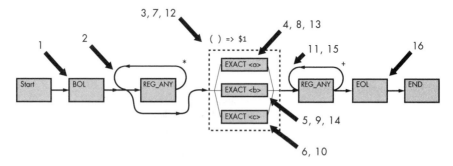

NOTE *The actual output of the script is a series of 20 images. However, they were consolidated to save space.*

Now how do you produce the images? It's actually quite easy. Let's take another look at a typical line from the debug output of the regular expression engine:

```
1 <a> <bc>           | 10:      EXACT <b>
```

The first number is the number of characters matched. On the other side of the vertical bar you have the node number of the parsed regular expression. These two numbers are the only pieces of information you need from this line.

To show the progress within the string, you draw the string and highlight the appropriate number of characters:

```
219   $new_image->filledRectangle(
220       PROGRESS_X, PROGRESS_Y,
221       PROGRESS_X +
222       $progress * $char_width,
223       PROGRESS_Y + $char_height,
224       $new_color_yellow
225   );
226
```

```
227    $new_image->string(gdGiantFont,
228        PROGRESS_X, PROGRESS_Y,
229        $value, $new_color_black);
230
```

To show which is the current node in the state machine, you draw a yellow arrow pointing to it. The only problem you've got is finding the location of the node. The location of each node is recorded with the node itself. All you have to do is find it.

Unfortunately, the complex data structure you created to make parsing and graphing easier makes searching harder. The find_node function, which performs the search, must not only search each node in the array, but also recursively search the children (if any) and the branches (if any) of the data:

```
80  ##############################################
81  # find_node($state, $node_array) -- Find a node
82  #       the parsed node tree
83  #
84  # Returns the location of the node
85  ##############################################
86  sub find_node($$);
87  sub find_node($$)
88  {
89      # State (node number) to find
90      my $state = shift;
91
92      my $array = shift;  # The array to search
93
94      foreach my $cur_node (@$array) {
95          if ($cur_node->{node}->{node} ==
96                  $state) {
97
98              return ($cur_node->{x_loc},
99                      $cur_node->{y_loc});
100
101         }
102         if (defined($cur_node->{children})) {
103             # Get the x,y to return from
104             #   the children
105             my ($ret_x, $ret_y) =
106                 find_node(
107                     $state,
108                     $cur_node->{children});
109
110             if (defined($ret_x)) {
111                 return ($ret_x, $ret_y);
112             }
```

```
113        }
114        if (defined($cur_node->{choices})) {
115            my $choices = $cur_node->{choices};
116            foreach my $cur_choice (@$choices) {
117                # Get the x,y to return from the
118                #     choice list
119                my ($ret_x, $ret_y) =
120                    find_node(
121                        $state, $cur_choice);
122
123                if (defined($ret_x)) {
124                    return ($ret_x, $ret_y);
125                }
126            }
127        }
128    }
129    return (undef, undef);
130 }
```

Once the node is found, you draw an arrow to it:

```
188    # Create the arrow
189    my $arrow = GD::Arrow::Full->new(
190        -X1 => $x_location,
191        -Y1 => $y_location,
192        -X2 => $x_location - YELLOW_ARROW_SIZE,
193        -Y2 => $y_location - YELLOW_ARROW_SIZE,
194        -WIDTH => YELLOW_ARROW_WIDTH
195    );
...
207    # Make the arrow point
208    # to the current step
209    $new_image->filledPolygon(
210        $arrow, $new_color_yellow);
211
212    $new_image->polygon(
213        $arrow, $new_color_black);
```

With the arrow in place, it's time to write out the image. The result is a series of image files showing the progress of the regular expression execution.

Hacking the Script

The script is in a state of almost constant evolution. As it currently stands, it parses and graphs all the regular expressions I've encountered. But it does not parse all possible regular expressions.

If you encounter a node that the script does not understand, it should be easy to hack it back into the script.

Also, I am not an artist. Although the graphs are technically accurate, they are not elegant. The whole thing has a functional look to it. I'm sure that through the use of colors and a smarter layout engine, the results can be made to look more beautiful.

But as it stands now the script is a really wicked and cool tool for understanding and learning regular expressions. It's amazing how something so complex and convoluted as an advanced regular expression can turn out simple and elegant when you graph it. Now that's cool.

INDEX

P

Parse_CGI function, CGI::Thin module, 52
Parse_Cookies function, CGI::Thin::Cookies
    module, 167
parse function, HTML::SimpleLinkExtor
    module, 28
parser, regular expression, 246
passwd command, 109
PATH (environment variable), 55
path function, URI module, 34
perldoc command, 2–3
Photo function, Tk::Photo module, 227
photograph gallery, 123
photographs, 117
Plain Old Documentation (POD), xvi, 2
Play-Doh, 181
PLUS node, regular expression, 298–300
PNG images, 142
POD (Plain Old Documentation), xvi, 2
POSIX module, 171
PostScript files, 142, 228
pray, hope, print, 55
Premature end of script header error, 48
print, hope, pray, 55
print, map control, 225
process, stuck, killing, 113
program
    add-user.pl, 104
    card.pl, 141, 143–144
    change.pl, 10
    dead.pl, 187
    del_user.pl, 112
    disk.pl, 100
    dis_user.pl, 108
    enum.pl, 184
    eol-change.pl, 194
    eol-type.pl, 191
    fix-names.pl, 92
    grace.pl, 176
    guess.pl, 153
    joke.pl, 58
    lang.pl, 155
    lock-out.pl, 41
    make_page.pl, 129
    mass-rename.pl, 96
    quote.pl, 79
    remind.pl, 14
    site-check.pl, 25
    site-orphan.pl, 32
    sym-check.pl, 98
    thumb.pl, 122
    who-hacked.pl, 36

protocol
    ed2k, 29
    FTP, 29–30
    HTTP, 29
    HTTPS, 30
    mailto, 29–30
    RST, 30
    telnet, 29–30
ps command, 115
ptkdb, 54
ptkdb (CGI programs), 53

Q

quiz
    CGI, 158
    vocabulary, 153
    web-based, 158
quote.pl program, 79

R

race condition, 169
random joke generator, 57
read function, 191
record separator ($\), 191
REG_ANY node, regular expression,
    295–297
regular expression
    /^ *#/, 294
    $1 $2, 244
    /a*b/, 246–247
    /a|b/, 295
    /^.*(a|b|c).+$/, 296–298
    BOL node, 295, 298–299
    BRANCH node, 267, 298
    debugger, 247
    END node, 247, 264, 267,
        294–297, 300
    EOL node, 296
    EXACT node, 247, 264–265, 267,
        294–297, 300–301
    grapher, 243, 286
    graph, layout, 248
    match progress, 301
    OPEN node, 298, 300
    parser, 246
    PLUS node, 298, 300
    REG_ANY node, 295–298
    /\s*(\d+)/, 295
    SPACE node, 296
    /\s*(\S+)(\d+)/, 243
    STAR node, 247, 264–266, 285, 298

user ID (UID), 104–105
USGS (United States Geological Survey),
    197, 207, 228
UTM (Universal Transverse Mercator)
    system, 207–210
UTM, Zone, Easting, Northing, 209

V

visitor counter, 60
vocabulary quiz, 153

W

waitpid function, 181
wall command, 101
web-based quiz, 158
web joke generator, 57
website, managing, 21
website link checker, 21
who command, 109
who-hacked.pl program, 36
widget, Tk Canvas, 179
wife, Chi, 69
wife, not, Karen, 69
Windows EOL type, 189
WINNT directory, 34
WINNT (hack), 37
word lists, 157
Write function, Image::Magick module, 228

X

X11 key names, 177
XE.com (currency conversion rates),
    16, 19
X server, 53

Y

Yahoo! exchange rates, 18–19
yelling at a user, 109

Z

Zone, UTM, 209
zoom level, map control, 225

 # Electronic Frontier Foundation
Defending Freedom in the Digital World

Free Speech. Privacy. Innovation. Fair Use. Reverse Engineering. If you care about these rights in the digital world, then you should join the Electronic Frontier Foundation (EFF). EFF was founded in 1990 to protect the rights of users and developers of technology. EFF is the first to identify threats to basic rights online and to advocate on behalf of free expression in the digital age.

The Electronic Frontier Foundation Defends Your Rights!
Become a Member Today!
http://www.eff.org/support/

Current EFF projects include:

Protecting your fundamental right to vote. Widely publicized security flaws in computerized voting machines show that, though filled with potential, this technology is far from perfect. EFF is defending the open discussion of e-voting problems and is coordinating a national litigation strategy addressing issues arising from use of poorly developed and tested computerized voting machines.

Ensuring that you are not traceable through your things. Libraries, schools, the government and private sector businesses are adopting radio frequency identification tags, or RFIDs – a technology capable of pinpointing the physical location of whatever item the tags are embedded in. While this may seem like a convenient way to track items, it's also a convenient way to do something less benign: track people and their activities through their belongings. EFF is working to ensure that embrace of this technology does not erode your right to privacy.

Stopping the FBI from creating surveillance backdoors on the Internet. EFF is part of a coalition opposing the FBI's expansion of the Communications Assistance for Law Enforcement Act (CALEA), which would require that the wiretap capabilities built into the phone system be extended to the Internet, forcing ISPs to build backdoors for law enforcement.

Providing you with a means by which you can contact key decision-makers on cyber-liberties issues. EFF maintains an action center that provides alerts on technology, civil liberties issues and pending legislation to more than 50,000 subscribers. EFF also generates a weekly online newsletter, EFFector, and a blog that provides up-to-the minute information and commentary.

Defending your right to listen to and copy digital music and movies. The entertainment industry has been overzealous in trying to protect its copyrights, often decimating fair use rights in the process. EFF is standing up to the movie and music industries on several fronts.

Check out all of the things we're working on at http://www.eff.org and join today or make a donation to support the fight to defend freedom online.

ELECTRONIC FRONTIER FOUNDATION · 454 SHOTWELL STREET · SAN FRANCISCO, CA 94110 · 415.436.9333

WRITE GREAT CODE, VOLUME 2
Thinking Low-Level, Writing High-Level

by RANDALL HYDE

Today's computer science students aren't always taught how to choose high-level language statements carefully to produce efficient code. In this follow-up to *Write Great Code, Volume 1: Understanding the Machine,* Randall Hyde shows software engineers what too many college and university courses don't: how compilers translate high-level language statements and data structures into machine code. Armed with this knowledge, readers will be better informed about choosing the high-level structures that will help the compiler produce superior machine code, all without having to give up the productivity and portability benefits of using a high-level language.

FEBRUARY 2006, 664 PP., $44.95 ($58.95 CDN)
ISBN 1-59327-065-8

THE BOOK OF™ PYTHON
From the Tip of the Tongue to the End of the Tale

by JOHN A. GOEBEL, ADIL HASAN, *and* FRANCESCO SAFAI TEHRANI

The Book of Python is a complete reference to the Python programming language. It begins with a discussion of Python's programming environment, then moves on to more advanced topics, including object-oriented programming, interacting with operating systems, creating GUIs and database interfaces, network programming, XML, web programming, and much more. To aid programmers in their day-to-day use of this book, functions and modules are cross-referenced throughout and multiple examples illustrate how to use Python.

JUNE 2006, 1000 PP., $49.95 ($64.95 CDN)
ISBN 1-59327-103-4

JUST SAY NO TO MICROSOFT®
How to Ditch Microsoft and Why It's Not as Hard as You Think

by TONY BOVE

Just Say No to Microsoft begins by tracing Microsoft's rise from tiny software startup to monopolistic juggernaut and explains how the company's practices over the years have discouraged innovation, stunted competition, and helped foster an environment ripe for viruses, bugs, and hackers. Readers learn how they can dump Microsoft products—even the Windows operating system—and continue to be productive.

NOVEMBER 2005, 264 PP., $24.95 ($33.95 CDN)
ISBN 1-59327-064-X

HOW LINUX WORKS
What Every Superuser Should Know

by BRIAN WARD

How Linux Works describes the inside of the Linux system for systems administrators, whether you maintain an extensive network in the office or one Linux box at home. Some books try to give you copy-and-paste instructions for how to deal with every single system issue that may arise, but *How Linux Works* actually shows you how the Linux system functions so that you can come up with your own solutions. After a guided tour of filesystems, the boot sequence, system management basics, and networking, author Brian Ward delves into topics such as development tools, custom kernels, and buying hardware. With a mixture of background theory and real-world examples, this book shows both *how* to administer Linux, and *why* each particular technique works, so that you will know how to make Linux work for you.

MAY 2004, 368 PP., $37.95 ($55.95 CDN)
ISBN 1-59327-035-6

HACKING
The Art of Exploitation

by JON ERICKSON

A comprehensive introduction to the techniques of exploitation and creative problem-solving methods commonly referred to as "hacking," *Hacking: The Art of Exploitation* is for both technical and non-technical people who are interested in computer security. It shows how hackers exploit programs and write exploits, instead of just how to run other people's exploits. Unlike many so-called hacking books, this book explains the technical aspects of hacking, including stack based overflows, heap based overflows, string exploits, return-into-libc, shellcode, and cryptographic attacks on 802.11b.

NOVEMBER 2003, 264 PP., $39.95 ($59.95 CAN)
ISBN 1-59327-007-0

PHONE:
800.420.7240 OR
415.863.9900
MONDAY THROUGH FRIDAY,
9 A.M. TO 5 P.M. (PST)

FAX:
415.863.9950
24 HOURS A DAY,
7 DAYS A WEEK

EMAIL:
SALES@NOSTARCH.COM

WEB:
HTTP://WWW.NOSTARCH.COM

MAIL:
NO STARCH PRESS
555 DE HARO ST, SUITE 250
SAN FRANCISCO, CA 94107
USA

COLOPHON

Wicked Cool Perl Scripts was laid out in Adobe FrameMaker. The font families used are New Baskerville for body text, Futura for headings and tables, and Dogma for titles.

The book was printed and bound at Malloy Incorporated in Ann Arbor, Michigan. The paper is Glatfelter Thor 60# Antique, which is made from 50 percent recycled materials, including 30 percent postconsumer content. The book uses a RepKover binding, which allows it to lay flat when open.

UPDATES

Visit **http://www.nostarch.com/wcps.htm** for updates, errata, and other information.